Bootlegging the Airwaves

Bootlegging the Airwaves

Alternative Histories of Radio and Television Distribution

ELEANOR PATTERSON

UNIVERSITY OF ILLINOIS PRESS
Urbana, Chicago, and Springfield

© 2024 by the Board of Trustees
of the University of Illinois
All rights reserved
1 2 3 4 5 C P 5 4 3 2 1
♾ This book is printed on acid-free paper.

Library of Congress Cataloging-in-Publication Data
Names: Patterson, Eleanor, 1983– author.
Title: Bootlegging the airwaves : alternative histories of
 radio and television distribution / Eleanor Patterson.
Description: Urbana : University of Illinois Press, 2024.
 | Includes index.
Identifiers: LCCN 2023023177 (print) | LCCN
 2023023178 (ebook) | ISBN 9780252045585
 (cloth) | ISBN 9780252087691 (paperback) | ISBN
 9780252055249 (ebook)
Subjects: LCSH: Video recordings—Pirated editions.
 | Sound recordings—Pirated editions. | Television
 viewers—Social aspects. | Radio audiences—Social
 aspects. | Fans (Persons)
Classification: LCC PN1992.5 .P285 2024 (print) |
 LCC PN1992.5 (ebook) | DDC 302.23/45—dc23/
 eng/20230710
LC record available at https://lccn.loc.gov/2023023177
LC ebook record available at https://lccn.loc.gov/2023023178

For Lorne and Andrew, who showed me how . . .

Contents

Acknowledgments ix

Introduction: Hacking Broadcast History 1

1. Homemade Entertainment: The Prehistory of Bootlegging Radio 23
2. Hello Again: The Informal Old-Time-Radio Economy 56
3. Freeze-Framing Queerness: Tape Trading in Buddy-Cop Fan Cultures 79
4. We Had to Do It the Hard Way: Bootlegging *Star Trek* in Australia 100
5. Enough of That Garbage: *Wrestling Observer* and the Intelligent Wrestling-Fan Community 123

Conclusion: Bootlegging after the Airwaves 147

Notes 161

Index 185

Acknowledgments

I think you will find this story amusing. Reading through my manuscript feedback, an anonymous reviewer noted that one of the chapters seemed to end abruptly, and they recommended adding a paragraph or two in order to better conclude the chapter. I went to the pages and thought to myself, yes, this does end abruptly, and as I brainstormed what to write, I began to get a strange sensation of déjà vu. I opened the file that had the most recent draft of chapter 4 prior to this review and realized that somehow, in the process of compiling chapters to send out as a single manuscript for review, I had accidently deleted the last page and a half of chapter 4. Shaking my head, my immediate thought was to call one of my writing group friends and amuse her with this blunder, and we carried on kvetching about the many missteps we have committed during the writing and publishing process. I share this story because it is a reminder that I did not write this book alone and have been the beneficiary of many gracious friends, colleagues, and anonymous reviewers whose support, feedback, and levity during moments of crisis made this book what it is.

I was incredibly fortunate to have Michele Hilmes, Jonathan Gray, Derek Johnson, Jeremy Morris, and Eric Hoyt as mentors at the University of Wisconsin–Madison. They pushed me to grapple with what it means to write cultural histories of broadcasting and taught me how to be a professor. I am so very grateful for their ongoing friendship and support as they have proved that being a mentor does not stop after the PhD is complete.

The idea for this book began to take form when I was a visiting professor at the University of Iowa. Tim Havens bought me lunch on many occasions while listening to me work out my plans for this book; thank you for your advice and friendship. I also thank my colleagues Jennifer Adams, Rob Agne, Sarah Aghazadeh, Justin Blakenship, Brigitta Brunner, Myoung-Gi Chon, Angie Chung, Brian Delaney, Nan Fairley, Victoria Ledford, Elizabeth Larson, Hollie Lavenstein, Mike Milford, George Plasketes, Gheni Platenburg, Kevin Smith, Sunny Stalter-Pace, Virginia Sánchez Sánchez, Michail Vafeiadis, Debra Worthington, and Ed Youngblood at Auburn University for your support and encouragement as I worked through the proposal and completion stage of this research. I was incredibly lucky to receive funding from the School of Communication and Journalism and the College of Liberal Arts and the Bronczek Fund for Excellence at Auburn; this money supported my research travel, archival scanning, and a semester course release, which gave me the resources and time to sort through the hundreds of documents I collected.

During my research adventures I fortuitously connected with Peter Balestrieri at the University of Iowa Special Collections, whose knowledge of UI's archival collection of science fiction and media fanzines was integral to my research efforts. I thank you, Peter, also, for connecting me with Jeremy Brett at the Texas A&M Cushing Memorial Library and Archives. Jeremy, thank you for your help navigating and finding materials in the Sandy Hereld Fanzine Collection. Many thanks to Mary Huelsbeck at the Wisconsin Center for Film and Theater for your assistance with the NBC collection. Carolyn Birdsall and Jennifer Vaughn with the Broadcast Archives Committee at the International Association of Sound and Audiovisual Archives connected me with a host of different contacts in the Australian film scene and at the National Library in Australia. You are magical, and I don't know if I deserved your pixie dust, but I am somewhat conflicted to thank you so publicly as I would rather selfishly keep you as a secret resource all for myself. I also thank Barbara Bishop, librarian for the School of Communication and Journalism at Auburn University, for getting me into several digital archives I did not have access to and helping me navigate the ones I did.

I am also very grateful to the collectors and fans who agreed to speak with me about their experience: Susan Batho, Steven Beverly, Jim Cox, Morgan Dawn, Sam Ford, Larry Gassman, John Gassman, Martin Grams, Sue Hamilton, Jay Hickerson, Walden Hughes, Brian Last, Laura Leff, Roy Lucier, John McAdam, Clare McDonald, Ian McLean, Joe Webb, Nikki White, and Craig Wichman. Thank you for responding to my email or phone call, for trusting me and for sharing your experiences. Your participation enriched this book far beyond what I could have hoped for. Jim Cox and Jay Hickerson sadly passed away during the course of working on this book; I am so grateful for the opportunity to know you and document your work preserving radio.

Writing groups provided the structure, sounding boards, and camaraderie to keep trudging forward even during the darkest days of inertia. Thank you to Pete Kunze, Autumn Lorimer Linford, Amanda McQueen, Adrien Sebro, and Nora Stone, who have been a part of the various writing groups I have belonged to while writing portions of this book. Thank you for making the time and showing up; these sessions helped me stay focused and honest with my commitment to writing and were fun as well. Research can be invigorating as a team sport. Somehow I ended up in a community of generous media-studies scholars that includes Elizabeth Affuso, Miranda Banks, Aniko Bodroghkozy, Andrew Bottomley, Chris Cwynar, Abigail De Kosnik, Evan Elkins, Liz Ellcessor, Hollis Griffin, Mary Beth Haralovitch, Charlotte Howell, Kit Hughes, Kyra Hunting, Deb Jaramillo, Amanda Keeler, Amanda Ann Klein, Bill Kirkpatrick, Kayti Lausch, Elena Levine, Jason Loviglio, Wan-Jun Lu, Catherine Martin, Maureen Mauk, Myles McNutt, Cynthia Meyers, Sarah Murray, Andy Owens, Alex Russo, Suzanne Scott, Josh Shepperd, Matt Sienkiewicz, Jennifer Smith, Tony Tran, Shawn VanCour, Neil Verma, Alyx Vesey, and Kristen Warner. I always leave our conversations feeling better about my life choices and smarter.

Kathy Battles, Kathy Fuller-Seeley, Joy Hayes, Andrea Kelley, Ramon Lobato, Al Martin, and Taylor Cole Miller read portions of this book and took the time to give detailed feedback. Thank you for wading through my scribbles. Your friendship and insight have been critically important to my development as a writer. I cannot give you an authorship credit, though you probably deserve it, but I can promise to buy you a drink at the next conference we attend together.

I pitched this project to University of Illinois media-studies acquisitions editor Danny Nasset at the 2019 Society for Cinema and Media Studies conference in Seattle, and he has been unwavering in his positive support through the crazy process of shepherding this book through the review process during the pandemic. My experience at Illinois with you has been everything an author could ask for and more. You have been the bedrock holding up this book, and I am so glad to get to work with you.

My parents, Lorne Albert and Andrew Patterson, sacrificed a great deal so that I could have the life I have today. They showed me how to chase after my passions while also remaining grounded and remembering where I came from. I am the first in my family to go to college, and I loved it so much I decided to do it for the rest of my life. I wouldn't have it any other way, and I would not have gotten here without you and the village you brought me up in. My father once told me that my writing was incomprehensible and brilliant at the same time, and, well, I do not think much has changed. If anything, I'm probably more practiced at being incomprehensible. I miss you and wish you were here to tell me if this book makes any sense. My mother is the hardest-working person I know. I don't think I will ever overtake your speed, energy, work ethic, or generosity of spirit. The older you get the faster you are, and sometimes I wonder if you have a motor in your belly. Thank you, Mom, for all the jobs you work, all the sleepless nights, and for showing me what a determined, tenacious woman looks like.

Lastly, I thank my husband, John, and my daughter, Madeleine, for putting up with all the academic folly that goes into living with one of us and loving me anyway. You are both so solid and kind, and your steadfast support made this book possible. I love you to the moon and back, and I only want to bootleg television so I can watch it with you.

Bootlegging the Airwaves

INTRODUCTION

Hacking Broadcast History

In December 1951 Joe Floyd, director of the Welworth Theatre Company of Sioux Falls, South Dakota, traveled to New York and New Jersey and met with engineers at RCA and NBC to propose a plan for what he was calling Exhibivision.[1] Floyd's plan envisioned broadcasting a schedule of films made especially for his company, a theater television service, that would transmit content simultaneously to local movie houses and homes as a subscription service similar to the early pay-television experiments of the 1950s like Skiatron or Telometer.[2] Stanton Osgood, NBC's assistant director of TV operations at the time, expressed his misgivings about Exhibivision in a letter to NBC president Pat Weaver:

> Mr. Floyd's basic idea is to enable a small-town theatre operator to enter the home television field as well as theatre television. I feel that this basically represents non-compatibility of interests. The ultimate goal for theatre television is to maintain exclusive programming of attractions which will draw money to the theatre exhibitors box office. Home television is designed as an advertising medium to stimulate the sale of clients' products. There is further cross-rough in Mr. Floyd's idea which represents home television program service on a metered basis. This type of program would obviously in the long-run have to be without advertising.[3]

Osgood rejected Floyd's proposal because he saw it as a basic violation of broadcasting's commercial model selling audiences to advertising clients, what Dallas Smythe termed "television's audience commodity."[4] People working in the television industries understood the nature of their business as one that created artificial scarcity for advertising-supported programming that audiences could only access in domestic spaces on the broadcasters' fixed-point schedule. Exhibivision would have allowed subscribers to get films showing in their local theater at home, a prototype pay-per-view service similar to the same-day-and-date-release model that several streaming platforms continue to experiment with. There is no reply letter from Weaver to Osgood or Floyd in the National Broadcasting Co. records at the Wisconsin Center for Film and Theatre Research (NBC Records); however, it can be assumed Weaver agreed with Osgood, as Exhibivision never materialized. Weaver began his career managing the radio production unit for the advertising agency Young and Rubicon, where he had been a vice president in 1949 before leaving to work as an executive at NBC's fledgling television network.[5] Thus, he was already well versed in the revenue models that had been established to fund American radio broadcasting and were now guiding television's development. Indeed, Weaver was a key architect of network television's transition from sponsored programming to magazine advertising during the 1950s, and it is telling that his television engineers, like Osgood, were already well versed by 1951 in the radio model that used programming as a lure to gather, measure, and sell the audience's attention.[6] For NBC executives in 1951, an ad-free film subscription service was incompatible with commercial network broadcasting.

We could imagine a different scenario in 1951, one where NBC might have signed on to experiment with a service to broadcast content into movie theaters and homes with a subscription. Both Weaver and Osgood oversaw the distribution of recorded television to nonconnected affiliates and stations via what was referred to as "quick kines." This was the term at NBC for the kinescope method of recording TV by filming a video monitor while a program aired. Talent agents, ad agencies, military departments, and schools all requested recordings of quick kines during this period of early television, and NBC considered creating a recording library to process and track these loans.[7] At the same time, RCA was already experimenting with closed-circuit cable distribution of broadcast content in Pennsylvania with what was known internally as the Antennaplex project.[8] The technological ability to invest in pay-per-view film broadcasting, like Exhibivision, or a television-recording rental program were feasible in the early 1950s. However, NBC did not pursue Exhibivision, and a commercial library of NBC's broadcast content was never realized due to concerns about copyright, unions, and sponsorship agreements.[9] In a memo about loaning out television program prints,

Theodore Kupferman, an attorney in NBC's legal department, commented in 1951,

> Because we do not register our programs for copyright under the Federal Statute, we cannot call in the FBI to assist in retrieving bootleg prints the way the motion picture people do, and with the limited output they are still faced with this problem all the time. I am quite sure one of your stars would not be happy to find that a kinescope of his show was being shown in Mexico in a local theatre or in Brazil on a new TV station or event at a summer hotel in the Borscht Circuit.[10]

These concerns reflect the commercial and legal dynamics of the broadcast networks, not technical limitations or lack of consumer interest, and, indeed, radio and television recordings were already circulating as bootlegs at the time Kupferman wrote this memo.

Bootlegging the Airwaves: Alternative Histories of Radio and Television Distribution offers an account of the overlooked technological practices and informal networks developed by audiences to overcome the ways companies, like NBC, functioned as gatekeepers that restricted access to program content. Bootlegging created an informal economy for programming outside of the industries' bottleneck distributing content via scheduled flow over the airwaves. Histories of bootlegging radio and television push us to grapple with several dominant paradigms that have framed the way broadcasting cultures, both past and present, are understood. My research in this book redefines the historical understanding of broadcasting's materiality, reconceptualizing the idea of a broadcast commodity and the significance of replay culture and circulation to interpretation. This history also highlights the distributive labor fans have done moving content to audiences. To understand how bootlegging histories teach about how people engaged with broadcasting in the past, it is first necessary to understand what bootlegging is and how it was shaped by the specificities of broadcasting's techno-industrial assemblages.

Bootlegging the Airwaves

"Bootlegging" became a household term in the United States during Prohibition, describing the unlawful distribution of alcohol. Media cultures adopted the term to describe media objects produced and circulated in ways unsanctioned by the companies that produced them. Here, then, bootlegging can refer to the productive act of making a recording, as well as to its movement via specific actors and processes. Although bootlegging can involve the work of making physical media, it falls within the arena of media distribution because it is distinct from the labor involved in what John Caldwell terms "production cultures," that is, the labor involved in creating media content. Distribution, in contrast, for Amanda Lotz, broadly encompasses circulation after production and the vast range of "processes involved in completed media reaching audiences."[11] Ramon Lobato advocates for inclusion of informal media work circulating content outside the official industries in his research on piracy and other nontheatrical cinema, foregrounding "the agency of informal operators" whose work at the margins of the media industries, nevertheless, play a significant role in distribution.[12] Media distribution equates to media power, as "decisions made about distribution . . . are—in the barest terms—attempts to control who has access to information and culture, and under what conditions."[13] Historically, then, those in the broadcast industries—the networks, sponsors, affiliates, and independent local stations—have held the levels of power in determining how people access radio and television content. To bootleg radio and television shows was to hack the airwaves, to use technological expertise in order to upend distributive hierarchies and make culture accessible. Bootlegging practices emerged as the result of audience struggle over control and access to broadcast content, and these hackers developed technosocial informal networks to obtain, circulate, and consume broadcast recordings and, in so doing, transformed the experience of engaging with radio and television.

Bootlegging media is different from bootlegging other commodities because it involves reproducing aesthetic texts. Lucas Hilderbrand refers to the "aesthetics of access," the way that the processes of duplicating analog media on tape can create an "altered look and sound of a text through its reduced resolution . . . a trade-off for our ability to engage with it and indexical evidence of its circulation and use."[14] These bootleg aesthetics of access are usually unintentional, although they can, for some fans, became a cherished part of a user's material experience to the extent that they prefer the altered imperfections of a bootlegged copy when professional duplicated recordings become commercially available.[15] Kim Bjarkman describes, "Unlike movie collectors for whom video is merely a packaging, or a vehicle transporting the text from the big screen to the small, for the television collector video recordings are themselves objects of historical interest that seem to seal in traces of the televised 'event.'"[16] Nevertheless, the production here is iterative, not derivative, and done primarily to make a recording for the purpose of capturing and storing media. Recording is, as Joshua Braun would say, part of the sociotechnical processes done to move products as part of a distribution system.[17]

Bootlegging involves the unauthorized movement of content, and the processes involved, whether strategically coordinated or haphazardly uneven. In this sense, like piracy, bootlegging comprises what Lobato and Julian Thomas term "an informal economy," in which practices of media duplication and exchange take place amid the "flow of communication, information and entertainment in unregulated spaces."[18] Hilderbrand explains that while piracy is the profit-oriented duplication of commercially available media content without copyright permission, bootlegs "fill in the gaps of market failure (when something has not been commercially distributed)."[19]

Historically, bootlegging has mainly been examined through the study of media that have consistently been understood as tangible goods, such as music and film.[20] This book is specifically about the processes, practices, and people who filled in the distribution gaps in radio and television access by bootlegging the airwaves, taking a form of media that was not, historically, commercially available as a concrete object and making it into a physical form that audiences could control, circulate, and collect. Recordings of radio and, later, television have been made by producers for syndication purposes since the 1920s; however, audience access was, through official channels, limited to the scarcity facilitated by broadcasting's model of one-to-many transmission of content via scheduled flow.[21] Broadcasting's one-to-many distribution model entails a power structure devised to limit audience access to content through fixed-point scheduling, that is, creating a predictable timetable that airs programs at a set, reoccurring time either daily or weekly. This structure forces audiences to sit through the sponsorship announcements. In this sense, broadcasters, local stations as well as regional or national networks, function as gatekeepers who controlled the conditions for audience engagement with broadcast content.

To consider the significance of dislodging content from the control of program schedules and recirculating it as physical objects, we must first consider what bootlegging is and what broadcasting has traditionally been understood to be historically. Broadcast content has often been defined by its distribution method. Jonathan Sterne notes that "the term 'broadcast' has a long history, as a general metaphor for dissemination, first for scattered seeds thrown in all directions (rather than planted in a line), then *like* scattered seeds."[22] During the 1920s and 1930s, broadcasting came to refer to the industrial formation of corporate one-to-many distribution of scheduled content. The conventions we associate with broadcast distribution, such as networked affiliation, dayparting, fixed-point scheduling, and serialized programs, were not predetermined but established through industrial practices pioneered during the 1920s.[23] These practices were motivated by the broadcasting industries' distinction as advertising-supported media, and this distinguished radio and, later, television from other forms of mass media by two central characteristics: scheduled flow and the commodity audience.

Bootlegging Broadcasting as Capturing Flow

Broadcasting's position as an ephemeral medium was, perhaps, cemented in the academia by Raymond Williams when in 1974 he defined broadcasting as planned flow: "In all developed broadcasting systems the characteristic organization, and therefore the characteristic experience, is one of sequence or flow. This phenomenon of planned flow is then perhaps the defining characteristic of broadcasting, simultaneously as a technology and as a cultural form."[24] In this statement, Williams reminds us that even though broadcasting as a technology afforded content producers the ability to distribute television in an ongoing, uninterrupted manner, this use of the medium was also planned, intentional, and shaped by cultural forces. Linear and ephemeral flow has, thus, been a controlling conceptualization of broadcasting throughout the study of its cultural history and a significant source of medium distinction in academia since the 1970s. Williams's characterization of broadcasting as planned flow is important because it is a reminder of the economic imperatives that continue to shape programming development and scheduling. Content flow is really about audience flow and maintaining audience attention for advertisements from program to program, day to day, week to week, and season to season. Even today, live reception is still the dominant mode of engagement with radio and television.[25] However, to define broadcasting historically solely through the model of scheduled flow is to suggest that broadcasting content ceased to circulate as a commodity after its initial broadcast in predigital eras.

The dominating power of scheduled flow as a historical paradigm for understanding broadcasting distribution has been reflected in academic histories of radio and television. As Derek Kompare has noted, "flow" was a term in the broadcast industries prior to Williams's usage of it;

however, "he introduced it to the academic study of television, and it has since been articulated with both Williams and television studies."[26] Home-recording technologies had long given users the affordance to record, circulate, and replay broadcast content when Williams wrote about broadcasting as flow in 1974. Yet, most broadcast history has maintained an overdetermined focus on the industrially sanctioned distribution of radio and television that operated in the service of networks and sponsors. This is evident in media scholars' arguments that television has been distinct from film by virtue of its ingoing flow of content in the home. Writing in the 1980s, Jane Feuer argued broadcasting content was defined by an ideology of liveness that presented content with a sense of immediacy and positioned spectators as continual viewers.[27] During the same period, Rick Altman argued that broadcasters structured flow in order to manage viewers' distracted viewing through the soundtrack: "It must be possible to follow the plot of a soap opera from the kitchen—or the score of a football game from the bathroom."[28] These analyses and others defined television content and spectatorship as inherently determined by casual viewing and television ephemerality in the 1980s during the same period media studies began to formalize as an academic field.

Media histories regularly characterize broadcasting as inherently ephemeral, transient, and fleeting. Understanding broadcasting's past as one characterized by ephemerality in some ways defies logic, because, of course, we still hear and see recordings from early radio and television, either available because the industries did record the most popular programs for transcription and syndication or because bootleggers have uploaded content to digital platforms, such as YouTube and the Internet Archive. A great portion of broadcast content was not recorded, yet we need only see, in the documentary *Recorder*, the crates of videotape recordings made by infamous television enthusiast Marion Stokes as they are being shipped to the Internet Archive after her death to understand that just as the digital age has not made all radio and television content available, a great deal of historical broadcast content is available because it was captured on physical storage media.[29] Indeed, because the commercial imperative of the broadcast industries was often at odds with the preservation of broadcasting content, media historians, such as Michele Hilmes and Elana Levine, have noted in their work how they explicitly relied on the recordings in bootlegged collections as unofficial content archives for their research.[30] The clear evidence that we access recordings, official and unofficial, has not stemmed the ongoing conceptualization of broadcasting in the twentieth century as fleeting and impermanent.

The reliance on scheduled flow as a frame for broadcast histories has created a binary between the analog past as forced-choice viewing versus a digital present where viewers are empowered through their freedom from the dictates of network schedules. In 2002 Kompare argued that peer-to-peer digital exchange of television episodes over the internet, alongside the emergence of DVRs and DVDs, was "directly transforming television's flow into discrete, malleable, and even mobile digital files" and, thus, changing the audience's relationship with television.[31] Henry Jenkins, Sam Ford, and Joshua Green stated in 2013 that television programming had shifted since the mid-2000s from an "appointment-based model of television viewing toward an engagement-based paradigm."[32] Here, then, live viewing or "appointment-based" television becomes a partition between the television past of "nonengagement" and a utopian present in which the audiences are empowered and the broadcast industries have adapted to provide intricate content that elicits engagement. Michael Curtin, Jennifer Holt, and Kevin Sanson similarly propose that selling television via DVDs, digital-content libraries, or digital files is a new disruption to broadcasting's traditional linear distribution.[33]

We might also ask, for whom are these practices disruptive? And how? Widespread nonlinear viewing of broadcast content is, of course, most disruptive for the legacy broadcasting companies, which have been complaining since the late 1990s about on-demand viewing and later about mobile devices and internet television in the trade journals while investing in companies like TiVo, Hulu, and other streaming platforms.[34] Audiences, on the other hand, seem to have embraced digital time-shifting, perhaps because they have already been doing it for decades. Media-analytic firm Nielsen reported in August 2018 that streaming television had overtaken other television outlets for the first time: streaming accounted for 34.8 percent of TV usage in the United States, beating out cable (34.4 percent) and over-the-air broadcast (21.6 percent).[35] This figure is slightly misleading, because the combination of traditional linear television (cable and over-the-air) viewing exceeds streaming. The report that cable and broadcast make up 56 percent of television viewing suggests that linear viewing will likely coexist with on-demand viewing for the foreseeable future. We might remember that radio listening continued after television-network executives proclaimed that it would be superseded by television viewing, a publicity strategy to encourage sponsors to invest in network television and best exemplified by NBC president Niles Trammell's 1949 pronouncement, "Within three years the broadcast of sound or ear radio over giant networks will be wiped out."[36]

History does not work like this, and technological innovation and use do not march along toward progress in an evolutionary manner. Certainly, the ongoing convergence between digital technologies and broadcast industries has ushered in more opportunities for officially sanctioned and monetized options for viewing radio and television content on demand. However, much of the research on broadcasting, historical and contemporary, has maintained an overdetermined focus on the industrially sanctioned distribution of radio and television that operates in the service of powerful stakeholders, such as networks, studios, and advertisers. Industrial determinism has been bolstered by the fact that most scholars focus on the initial production and distribution of radio and television content in their work and not the residual circulation of content. Furthermore, most of the traces of radio's and television's pasts available to scholars come from industrial materials in archives or trade journals, which encourage us to take on the broadcast industries' economic and distribution framework that emphasizes broadcaster's role selling the audience commodity to advertisers. Cultural studies of radio and television are often critical of the powerful forces that shaped and defined what radio and television would be but also usually reinforced the singular-distribution mode designed by broadcasters. This is the way that the broadcast networks framed their audience to advertising agencies and sponsors; however, it erases viewer agency, not to mention the messy, muddied heterogeneous nature of over-the-air broadcasting in midcentury.

This book functions as a corrective to broadcast histories by accounting for some of the material ways broadcast content has been circulated as a physical media commodity through bootlegging practices and communities. Before DVDs, iTunes downloads, and DVR or streaming-video-on-demand platforms and apps, audiences used home-recording equipment or industry contacts to obtain, circulate, and replay recordings of radio and television content. These bootlegging practices redefined broadcast content as a physical commodity valued within an informal economy and fostered interpretative practices through the replay affordances made possible by physical storage media.

Bootlegged Recordings as a Broadcast Commodity

Much like Williams's model of broadcasting as scheduled flow, Smythe's framework of the "audience commodity" has similarly structured the understanding of broadcasting distribution and the relationship between content producers and audiences.[37] Smythe differentiated between culture industries that produced and distributed goods (music records, books) and those that drew revenue through advertising-based models. The "audience commodity" framework is predicated on the idea that programming is a "free lunch" broadcasters used to attract eyeballs to content. Meehan has built on Smythe's proposal that broadcasters did not make tangible goods for sale to the public to argue that the measured and packaged audience ratings were the central commodity bought and sold within the broadcast industry.[38] Deborah Jaramillo deftly summarizes the industrial specificity of broadcasting from other media businesses during the twentieth century: "As a culture industry in which advertising is the main source of immediate funding, broadcast television yields no traditional, tangible product that a producer exchanges with a consumer."[39] This book intervenes to provide an alternative story about the processes involved in distributing broadcasting content outside of traditional mechanisms for content delivery. In doing this, I propose a framework for reconceptualizing the commodity within radio and television bootlegging cultures during the network era as the physical recording of a program itself. Writing about material culture from an anthropological perspective, Igor Kopytoff outlines commodification as an ongoing process.[40] The industry's definition of the commodity valued and exchanged in broadcasting has always been contested, and bootleggers developed an alternative economy based upon the valuation and exchange of broadcast recordings.

Where did bootlegged recordings come from, and how were they constructed as commodities? Kopytoff poses a similar question, distinguishing commodities from things, "What, then, makes a thing a commodity? A commodity is a thing that has use value and that can be exchanged in a discrete transaction for a counterpart, the very fact of exchange indicating that the counterpart has, in the immediate context, an equivalent value."[41] Bootlegged recordings of radio and television accrued value through systems in what Bjarkman calls a "gray" liminal space between commercial and noncommercial transactions.[42] Those who bootlegged radio and television formed what John Fiske terms "shadow economies," loosely organized structures and protocols that parallel mainstream broadcast industries at the same time that they change and rearticulate the commodity valued and exchanged in broadcast culture.[43] The communities studied in this book primarily obtained physical recordings of radio and television content in two ways. One obvious way that radio and television audiences were able to obtain recordings before they were sold as commercial goods was directly from the source. Local stations would close or clear out unofficial archives for space and give away, sell off, or throw old recordings away. Workers within the industry would obtain and sell personal copies, sometimes, for example, as in the case of *Star Trek: The Original Series* (*TOS*), an Australian businessman was able to procure officially made syndication copies on the black market in South Africa, presumably several exchanges after someone in the industry had circulated them through transnational underground networks. Some fans would make and circulate copies from obtained professional recordings, and it was a common practice for bootleggers, when possible, to claim their recordings were a certain amount of duplication generations away from a master professional recording.

The second and more common mode of making content from airwaves into a physical good for circulation is to record it off air, called an "air check," and duplicate it to exchange a copy for money, a different recording, or blank tapes. This latter practice is known in bootlegging communities as "tape trading," the process of exchanging radio and TV recordings made either on reel-to-reel, cassette, or videotape, between at least two parties for a mutually agreed-upon barter. Bjarkman has documented the strong sentiment against monetary exchange for recordings in some tape-trading communities, where participants see the production of recordings as a creative hobby while also remaining cognizant of copyright laws.[44] This book is not focused on copyright law, yet it is important to note that selling homemade air-check recordings of radio and television programs violates copyright law. Home recording has been the subject of the landmark 1984 court case, *Universal Studios vs. Sony Corporation of America*, in which the US Supreme Court decided 5–4 that the use of videocassette-recorder (VCR) technology to tape television was a fair use. The US Congress followed this decision up with the Audio Home Recording Act of 1992, which, among other things, allows for the use of cassette recording, provided it is noncommercial and for personal use. These precedents have created an environment within radio and television tape trading that emphasizes the exchange of blank tapes for duplication instead of cash bartering. However, my research has shown that tape trading has manifested in myriad ways and is a term used to refer to a mutually agreed-upon exchange of recordings, money, or other tangible goods. The process of bootlegging broadcast content, then, entails obtaining a program recording, either through air checks or tape trading or from the master copies. The redistribution of broadcast content through bootlegging networks with their hierarchies of value pushes us to redefine what the broadcast commodity is understood to be in media history.

The physical materiality of radio and television content as a bootlegged commodity reformats ephemeral content in a way that facilitates both the collection of objects and the ability to rewatch content. The case studies in this book demonstrate how collecting bootlegged recordings became a thrill in and of itself for fans, giving them the ability to control, arrange, and manipulate content. Documenting the historical circulation of physical recordings also points to the ways bootlegs allowed audiences to self-schedule, rewatch, and binge-consume episodes rather than view them weekly as part of a varied programming block content, decades before the so-called digital revolution. Discussing film and home video, Barbara Klinger has argued that repeat viewing provides a range of rituals and pleasures for audiences, such as familiarity, nostalgia, and therapy, to name a few.[45] This applies equally to communities bootlegging radio and television, as this book outlines, repeat consumption of radio and television was primarily predicated on access to bootlegs during the twentieth century. However, in addition, accessing broadcast content through a storage medium makes it possible for fans to study content through replay, an activity that provides audiences with the pleasure of discursive debate and identity formation, which, as discussed throughout this book, shape and reshape the interpretation of meaning. Replay of radio or television is also crucial to creative production of fan fiction or art.

Bootlegging recordings also unhinged broadcast content from its temporal context, making it possible for programming to circulate long after the initial transmission and have a long and active afterlife as residual culture. Acland argues that residuality explains the "half-life of media forms. . . . The residual, by definition, has been effectively formed in the past, but it is still active in the cultural process, not only and often not at all as an element of the past, but as an effective element of the present."[46] The circulation of physical broadcast recordings within interpretive communities through space and time has meant that content produced and aired in the past was and is actively a constituent part of the contemporary media landscape. We need only look at the bidding wars for the second-run syndication license for content like *Seinfeld* to see evidence of residual television's significance in the current media industries.[47] However, repetition has not always been a media business strategy, nor has syndication guaranteed access. Reconceiving broadcast content historically as a commodity valued and exchanged within an informal bootleg economy and long after its initial transmission forces us to reconceptualize the way predigital broadcasting cultures have been understood within academia since the 1970s.

Bootlegging as Distributive Labor

Looking at bootlegging histories allows us to rethink what broadcasting is and has been by tracing out the specificities of an interconnected set of technosocial processes that create access to commercially unavailable material. I am not arguing that bootlegging is an inherent liberatory practice; it often can inadvertently (or intentionally) work to promote media properties and drive audience engagement. However, the distribution of broadcast programming as scheduled flow determines who can participate in radio and television cultures, the terms upon which participation is predicated, and barriers to entry in broadcast production cultures. I use the term "distributive labor" for the various forms of labor involved in the processes that move content *between* production and consumption.[48] The histories of bootlegging the airwaves as a physical commodity in this book are really stories about the work that fans and other audience members did circulating radio and television content outside industrially determined avenues. For this reason, we should consider the work fans have done circulating broadcast content through bootlegging practices a form of distributive labor. Bootlegging has encompassed a shifting assortment of informal tasks, processes, and conditions related to making the ephemeral content physical and moving it to audiences, including home recording and duplication, but also usually involved establishing connections with other bootleggers, collectors, and enthusiasts and sharing information, recording techniques, and research.

The broadcast industries did not invest in selling officially produced recordings of radio or television to the public due to industry reliance upon the audience-commodity construct for revenue. It was also technologically unfeasible given the serial design of most broadcast programs as continuous goods distributed either daily or weekly to gain audience loyalty. The result was that many popular radio and television shows made during the classic network era would be renewed for several years. Take, for instance, *Suspense*, which ran from 1942 to 1962 on the CBS radio network. During these two decades, creators produced approximately 942 hour-long episodes. Another example of the bountiful nature of broadcast programming is the original ABC horror soap opera *Dark Shadows*, which was on the air daily from 1966 to 1971 and produced

1,225 episodes. The sheer volume of shelf space necessary to sell complete recordings of these series prohibited the original producers from selling broadcast content as concrete commodities through retail.

The extensive nature of broadcast content has also made bootlegging radio and television historically distinct, and this led to a recognition among radio and TV hobbyists that they needed to collaborate and work together to obtain recordings. To this end, radio and television collectors formed clubs, conventions, and fanzines to connect, trade, and discuss bootleg recordings with each other. These informal systems were not standardized in the same way that commercial broadcasting distribution was standardized through schedules; technological specifications, such as AM/FM or UHF/VHF frequency designations; or delivery systems, such as telephone lines or satellite reception. Though uneven and unstandardized, informal networks, Lobato argues, are still governed by communal trade guidelines (albeit, at times uneven and unenforced) and comprise a significant venue to "understanding depth and breadth of cinema's social circulation and cultural function."[49] Similarly, the bootleggers studied for the current volume had explicit and implicit guidelines for obtaining recordings, tape trading, and communal viewing, the main forms of bootlegging I found in my research. These guidelines often appear in fanzines as editorials on tape-trading etiquette or how-to directives, which range from duplication techniques to announcements of local station schedules for taping, as well as venues for group viewing of rare or commercially unavailable content. Bootleggers and collectors would often attempt to establish standards by publishing requests for peers to categorize the quality of recordings in shared catalogs or by detailing their contempt for collectors they felt were not being discerning in their duplication procedures.

Of course, actually standardizing bootlegging was and continues to be impossible because of its informal nature as fan labor, and, indeed, it has been an invisible category of the work audiences have historically done circulating broadcast content. Much of the literature on fan labor has focused on production and the creative derivative work fans have done making fan fiction, art, and videos or vids, as they are referred to in fan communities.[50] Looking at the work that fans do making their content freely available in the digital economy, Abigail De Kosnik argues that fans perform a techno-volunteer form of free labor, not only in producing content but in building, monitoring, and maintaining web sites to host this content that are designed to be free from the commercial imperatives of the formal media industries.[51] De Kosnik and Mel Stanfill argue that this free labor in the digital economy has come to represent a valuable form of promotional work that is now sought after and exploited by the commercial media industries.[52] Personal computers and networked access to the internet have made this free fan labor creating access to user-generated content more widespread and visible. The stories about bootleg communities in this book historicizes fans' iterative work circulating radio and television programs as a form of distributive labor, because once audiences had access to physical recordings, this altered how they encountered broadcast content and made it possible to reproduce and share these physical recordings with others, as well as fostering new modes of interpretation and identity formation.

Accessing Traces of Radio and Television Bootlegging

Getting at histories of bootlegging radio and television is not an easy task. There is no centralized archive of historical materials related to the grassroots circulation of broadcast recordings. History is made from the traces of the past available to scholars in the present, and as Christopher Anderson and Michael Curtin note, grassroots processes point to the deficits outside institutional records, as "ordinary viewers do not leave traces of their presence on the historical record."[53] Because of this, most of the research for this book has come from systematically going through fanzines to find discussions of home recording, tape trading, or communal viewing. Fanzines are independent, alternative publications, usually produced individually or collectively outside commercial publishing, perhaps at home or at the local print and copy store, by fans, with a relatively small circulation.[54] Throughout this book, the terms "fanzine" and "fan newsletter" are used interchangeably, a reflection of how fans used these terms to refer to their publications. While working on this book, I looked at over a thousand fanzines in the archives at the University of Iowa Special Collections, the Texas A&M University Cushing Memorial Library and Archives Special Collections, the National Library of Australia, and the Internet Archive's digital Old Time Radio Researchers collection and *Wrestling Observer* collection.

What does it mean to rely, primarily, on audience-produced fanzines to map out the histories of radio and television bootlegging? It means that this book is not a comprehensive study of bootlegging in the twentieth century. Instead, I use focused case studies of four different fan communities, within whose records I found documented discussions of bootlegging and tape trading: classic radio, buddy-cop TV, *Star Trek*, and televised wrestling. Histories are always shaped by available traces of the past, and narratives of a unified or holistic historiography are, as Roland Barthes has noted, "developed within the cauldron of fiction."[55] This is especially true for a practice like bootlegging broadcast content because it was a decentered practice undocumented in government or industry archives. A comprehensive study of transnational bootlegging broadcasting is not possible, and the research here focuses on case studies determined by the fanzines and materials available in the official and unofficial archival sources I found. Case studies allow for greater specificity and an analysis of the nuances and intricacies in bootlegging radio and television. The case studies detailed in this book provide what Michel Foucault terms "localized histories," a genealogy focused on small, concrete examples of bootlegging radio and television that challenges dominant narratives of broadcast distribution in the twentieth century.[56] I have contextualized the fanzine sources found in the archives with research in trade and popular-press archival databases, the NBC corporate archives at the Wisconsin Center for Film and Theater Research, and twenty-two interviews with fans who participated in the various communities studied.

Archival fanzine collections and interviews are not traditional sources for studying distribution, but when it comes to informal economies, perhaps they should be. This is because, as Lee Marshall relates about music bootlegging, "It is *fans* rather than casual consumers who buy bootlegs."[57] Much like production and consumption, distribution is an ongoing social process, and focusing on the informal economies of bootlegging within fan communities brings the lived social and cultural aspects of distribution to the surface. In his discussion, Marshall notes that he almost exclusively interviewed and interacted with fans while also demonstrating how bootlegging processes and fan communities are mutually co-constituting. Indeed, this observation bears out in my own research of radio collectors, for instance, because the very need to connect through clubs, conventions, and fanzines was precipitated by the overwhelming tasks of researching, finding, and obtaining recordings of classic radio programs. Working collectively to find radio recordings and exchange them with other fans became a way to manage the vast expanse of radio broadcasting's output.

If bootleggers were hacking industrial television distribution methods, this book is perhaps hacking the way broadcast history is done using these nontraditional sources. Isn't that the goal of cultural histories? Examining the bootlegging of radio and television content through the lens of specific fan communities accomplishes the larger goal of seeking out "histories from below."[58] Anderson and Curtin outline the work of cultural history as one that acknowledges multiplicity and that there is not one dominant history of broadcasting but, rather, an almost infinite amount of histories, especially if we turn toward "bottom-up perspectives that examine the fabric of everyday life while seeking out voices neglected or silenced by traditional histories."[59] Looking at fan-centered bootlegging practices as bottom-up practices illustrates my concept of "embodied distribution." Embodied distribution entails the recognition that broadcast content was at one point in time distributed by an official source, such as a network or station, and at another point the same content can be recorded on a storage format, like a videotape cassette, replete with perhaps other episodes of the same or a different program and with local commercials or no commercials and exchanged between two fans within the same interpretive community. These processes could be separated by months or decades. To consider distribution as an embodied act is a recognition that all distribution is done by real people inhibiting lived experiences, in which distributive labor is a material practice, not a one-time fixed occurrence. Histories of bootlegging in fan communities bring distributive labor into focus by laying bare how content is captured, exchanged, transported, and reconfigured within contingent historical formations shaped by social practices. Whether we look at distribution within official industrial practices or informal fan networks, it is always already embodied and reflects the specific context in which media access is facilitated.

Bootlegging is a social practice that takes place within larger ideological territories, and I draw on what Hilmes describes as an "informed cultural studies approach," which is to consider how bootlegging practices emerge as social processes that reflect cultural power related to gender, race, sexuality, and national identity.[60] To study histories of bootlegging radio and television is to study a grassroots practice that happens on the margins of media culture and to offer alternative correctives to dominant historical narratives. In this sense, I approach historiographical research from a poststructuralist perspective that interrogates the very way we construct narratives about the past, acknowledging my role in representing these histories.[61] Warren Susman reminds us that "ideological tension is an important part of any cultural analysis" and also encourages us, as scholars, to be mindful of our own standpoint as we do historiography.[62] This book takes up specific questions of how everyday practices, discussions, and rituals reveal implicit information about power and cultural identity within each chapter to engage with the specific dynamics of each case study.

Chapter Breakdown

This book begins with an overview of the context and conditions in which radio bootlegging developed. To this end, chapter 1 historicizes the convergence of home-recording technologies and broadcasting. The use of home-recording technologies to capture ephemerality and circulate radio and television content has its roots in the late 1800s, as leisure came to be associated with mass culture while consumer technologies were created that domesticated this culture. I argue that the development of the phonograph, kinetoscope, and amateur film cameras brought mass media into the home as physical commodities while also normalizing home recording at the advent of radio. This chapter provides an overview of the rise of a domestic media environment predicated on commodity culture and control and how home-recording technologies fostered and encouraged radio bootlegging in the Progressive Era.

The story of radio bootlegging continues in chapter 2 with discussion of how the development of magnetic tape fostered small clusters of radio tape trading in the 1950s and 1960s. This chapter goes on to focus on the formation of a network of radio bootleggers in the late 1960s and 1970s who were invested in connecting with each other through local clubs, fanzines, and conventions. This chapter challenges the dominant understanding of what a distribution network looks like, reconceptualizing tape trading as a many-to-many social network distribution process. The chapter then considers how distribution impacts interpretation, ending with a focused analysis of the controversy that arose among radio collectors concerned about racism and collecting the radio program *Amos 'n' Andy*. Debates among fans about *Amos 'n' Andy*'s meaning provide an informative case study to consider how meaning changes when broadcast programs circulate long after their initial production.

Chapter 3 considers bootlegging television and how female pleasure became articulated with videotape trading and collecting in fan communities dedicated to US buddy-cop television shows in the late 1970s and 1980s. The overview of the emergence of tape trading in television fandoms provides a basis for the following chapters on *Star Trek* and televised wrestling. This is followed by an outline of the significance of videotape recording and trading to buddy-cop fan communities and the relationship of tape trading, rewatching, and making sense of a television show's meaning. This chapter concludes with a consideration of the ways informal distribution of *Starsky & Hutch* television episodes on videotape made debates about queer meaning possible.

The transnational dimensions of bootlegging television are taken up in chapter 4 with a study of the distribution of *Star Trek* in Australia. Television history and culture are specific to location and technological systems, and this chapter considers Australia's development of television and industrial broadcasting practices. Color television did not become a part of the Australian television system until 1975, and it was not until the late 1980s that commercial stations were interconnected by satellite or cable. Furthermore, Australia's position in the windowing distribution schedule of US broadcasting, that is, the industrial practice where television distributors stagger international syndication to maximize profit, has meant that television made in the United States and syndicated to Australia has historically been delayed usually long after a show debuted in the United States. The first run of *Star Trek: The Original Series* (*TOS*) aired in Australia in black-and-white a year after it aired in the United States, and was sporadically and inconsistently rerun by stations in Australia, which had to share the originally purchased syndication copies via bicycle distribution routes, wherein only one station at a time could use the physical recordings before they were transported to the next station. The second *Star Trek* television series, *Star Trek: The Next Generation* (*TNG*), aired in the United States in 1987, however, it did not officially became syndicated in Australia until 1991. These factors coalesced to motivate a culture of bootlegged communal viewing, a history I document in two sections, one focused on the theatrical screenings of *TOS* episodes in movie theaters in Sydney and Melbourne and a second section that looks at the history and significance of communal viewings at *Star Trek* club meetings. Bootlegged-facilitated communal viewing in Australia would play a role in the growth of a large *Star Trek* fan community down under while also instigating a crackdown on unsanctioned communal viewing in the 1990s by the production company, Paramount, which ultimately led to the demise of grassroots *Star Trek* clubs across the country.

With a focus on televised wrestling, the last chapter continues to examine bootlegging's ability to expand the geographic reach of broadcast content. Professional wrestling and television have a unique history shaped by the industrial structures of both industries. As a result of TV-executive-taste cultures and the logics of wrestling promoters, televised wrestling was a distinctly local form of broadcasting from 1955 until

1976. Even after this, most televised wrestling consisted of taped matches in local TV studios, produced by regional wrestling promoters. These conditions encouraged the development of a wrestling-fan network that relied on wrestling magazines and fanzines to connect and redistribute local content (from the United States, Canada, Mexico, and Japan) across transnational boundaries. This chapter considers the history of tape-trading televised wrestling and the way audiences used bootlegging to overcome the challenges of space and time and gain access to recordings of wrestling matches from the past, as well as from other locations. Moreover, the research in this chapter points to the ways tape-trading wrestling became integral to the development of a masculine-intelligent wrestling-fan subjectivity characterized by a raunchy, often aggressive verbal style and the demonstration of detailed wrestling knowledge. The formation of this subjectivity was dependent and co-constitutive of work fans did redistributing local wrestling matches to a national audience, thus demonstrating the national market for wrestling to the World Wide Wrestling Federation (WWWF), which would later be known as the World Wrestling Federation (WWF) and now the World Wrestling Entertainment (WWE). The book then concludes with a consideration of how the contemporary media landscape has adapted the logics of radio and television bootlegging.

As Anderson and Curtin comment, "Social and cultural histories of broadcasting ask us to look beyond the institutions and technologies that have populated traditional histories, they ask us to shift our attention from momentous media events to banal forms of radio and television experienced in everyday life."[63] Histories of bootlegging the airwaves show how people did the work of redistributing radio and television content from a grassroots perspective and sheds light both on the actual social practices that surrounded some audiences' relationship with broadcasting while also illuminating the current broadcasting environment. The broadcast industries continue to function as content gatekeepers, and this power dynamic animates a great deal of contemporary debate about digital television platforms and streaming content and how access to content is controlled and monetized.

Take, for instance, the recent outrage from both creators and audiences over HBO Max's decision in August 2022 to cut record numbers of programs from its streaming-service catalog as HBO Max prepares to merge with Discovery. These choices were made to claim tax write-offs, as well as refocus the HBO Max platform brand toward adult viewers. The cuts included unreleased films like *Batgirl* and unaired episodes of shows like *Summer Camp*, whose existing content was purged from the platform alongside other titles, such as *Aquaman: King of Atlantis*, and a large swath of reality and children's media that included two hundred episodes of *Sesame Street*.[64] Twitter user Daniel Mitchell, who posts as @GigaBoots, tweeted on August 18, 2022: "The HBO Max news has me infuriated. If this is the future of streaming platforms, destroying catalogs with no heads up for tax write offs, people will start pirating [bootlegging] this shit instead."[65] A discussion about the list of titles, critiques of HBO Max's greed and shortsightedness, questions about how tax write-offs and Hollywood math, and much more ensued on the @GigaBoots thread. These comments illustrate several continuities between classic network broadcasting and media in the digital age, namely, how economic strategies, such as branding or tax incentives, drive media-distribution decisions; the ongoing mutability and fluctuation of these distribution strategies; and audiences' feelings of ownership over media content and the belief that they, not media corporations, should determine how they access and control that content. *Bootlegging the Airwaves* shows how the struggles between media corporations as gatekeepers and audiences who desire access and control over their media experiences have activated audience engagement with media content since the birth of broadcasting. What broadcasting is and how it is accessed have never been fixed, rather, they are a complex and everchanging assemblage of technological apparatuses, industrial imperatives, and popular culture.

CHAPTER 1

Homemade Entertainment
The Prehistory of Bootlegging Radio

This book examines the informal networks that emerged to reproduce and recirculate radio and television recordings outside of the purview of the media industries that created them. It is a story about broadcasting *without* broadcasting, so to speak. But how did these practices first emerge and develop? What social and technological changes spurred the aspiration to obtain, collect, and share radio and television programs? To answer these questions, this chapter explores the history of home-recording technologies and the rise of mass-media commodity culture during the Progressive Era. Bootlegging radio programming did not emerge in a vacuum, and primary archival sources from trade journals and the popular press identify the cultural conditions that developed in the 1890s through the 1920s to make bootlegging radio both feasible and desirable.

The development of what is now called home entertainment can be traced back to the late nineteenth century and the social transformations spurred by the Industrial Revolution. Technological innovation, mass production, and the professionalization of the advertising business normalized the growth of consumer culture in the United States. The growth of the middle class and consumer culture reconfigured domestic life by the 1890s, changing the dynamics of popular culture, technological convergence, and domesticity. Mechanical devices, such as the phonograph and kinetoscope, converged with leisure culture and the nascent commercial entertainment industries to establish a new ideal of home entertainment at the same time radio broadcasting emerged. Indeed, inventors like Guglielmo Marconi, Reginald Fessenden, and Lee de Forest, as well as amateur operators, politicians, and journalists, participated in the process of redefining wireless telegraphy as broadcast radio during the same period that the Victorian parlor became reconceptualized as the center of domestic entertainment during the Progressive Era.[1]

An examination of the reconfiguration of mass-media industries, home entertainment, and audience engagement in the late nineteenth and early twentieth centuries provides a critical context for interpreting how audiences engaged with radio in their everyday lives and began bootlegging radio in the Progressive Era. Cultural practices, like bootlegging, are always negotiated through various economic, social, and political imperatives and the contextual social processes, imaginations, and desires that shape everyday life. In particular, four social transformations coevolved and encouraged radio bootlegging: the discursive construction of a preservation culture focused on ephemeral media and experiences, the ongoing commodification of public entertainment as domestic media objects, the domestic media production and distribution practices facilitated by a technologically converged electric parlor, and the widespread formation of social organization networks and media fan-club culture. These developments changed how media were made, promoted, and engaged with, arising as both an outcome and a constituent force within the industrial revolution's reconfiguration of social, geographic, and economic structures. Between 1890 and 1920 popular entertainment became something a person did not have to leave the house to experience directly, as new technologies made the fleeting vaudeville performance permanent and available through physical storage media that audiences could collect, playback, and control within their parlors. The practices outlined in this chapter emerged out of larger questions about whom leisure and popular entertainment were for, where leisure should take place, and what it meant to capture and commodify popular culture.

Ephemerality and Preservation Culture

The desire to capture the ephemeral became a significant force in popular culture during the late nineteenth century in response to the "subtle processes of industrialization, urbanization, and centralization which began accelerating in the 1870s."[2] Advances in printing technologies and press circulation led to the exponential growth of daily newspaper and magazine circulation.[3] Railroads and telegraph wires compressed space and time, hastening trade, tourism, migration, communication, and military campaigns. Amusement parks, baseball games, and vaudeville circuits provided public forms of leisure for the expanding middle class.

By the 1890s the United States had entered what Paul Starr has called the era of modern mass media.[4] And, anxious for control amidst the uncertainty of burgeoning modernity, people tried to grab hold of the transitory media and experiences that were redefining their social world. The desire to capture the fleeting ephemeral moments of modern life became a prominent fixation of transatlantic culture during the significant economic and social changes of the late nineteenth century. Susan Zieger defines ephemera of this era as "the trivial printed documents and objects of everyday life, from bus tickets, bookmarks, and business cards to more consumable, yet still disposable, items: newspaper, illustrated magazines, advertising tokens, and giveaways."[5]

We can look back and see the popularity of activities during this era of heightened mass media and consumerism that were directly concerned with storing up and keeping the ephemeral aspects of everyday life for posterity. For instance, art critic Charles Baudelaire popularized the use of ephemeral sketching to document trivial moments, such as prostitutes walking the street in Paris, arguing this art rendered the contingent fixed and, thus, also important.[6] The impetus to record and relive ephemeral moments in popular discourse is epitomized by George du Maurier's 1891 novel *Peter Ibbetson*, in which a central aspect of the narrative was the fantasy of using the mind as a palimpsest to store memories for later playback.[7] Capturing brief experiences was also the subject of Oscar Wilde's short 1894 poem "The Artist," concerned with the desire to create a permanent image of the momentary "Pleasure that Abideth for a Moment."[8] This yearning to capture and store fleeting aspects of modern life became more prominent as photography promised to freeze a single moment.[9] It is telling that Louis Daguerre referred to the image plates developed through his photographic system as "mirrors with a memory," positioning the invention as a repository device similar to the mind, a common narrative surrounding storage media, and also the fixing of the momentary refection in a mirror.[10] Like photography, the developments of sound recording and cinema were made sense of by their promise to give users the ability to fix and represent the ephemeral.[11] These activities varied from the growth of hobbies, such as scrapbooking newspaper clippings, to the business practice of developing phonetic notation systems for reporters and stenographers to record fleeting conversations accurately, to the tradition of using postmortem photography portraits to enshrine the deceased.[12]

Bootleggers' impulse to capture, control, and playback radio and television content followed from the same preservation logic concerned with making ephemeral content permanent and grew from the practices used by readers to clip recipes, articles, and poems from newspapers and preserve them in a scrapbook. In her study of nineteenth-century scrapbooking, Elizabeth Gruber Garvey argues that newspaper readers managed the flood of disposable print information by "finding, sifting, analyzing, and recirculating writing that mattered to them" through clipping and scrapbooking sections they found meaningful, an act that separated content from newspapers' otherwise ephemeral existence. Scrapbooking infused ephemeral information with new personalized value and meaning, whereby readers were "*performing archivalness*, acts and gestures of preservation, they [scrapbookers] expressed the will to save, organize, and transmit knowledge through a homemade archive."[13] Gruber Garvey's description of newspaper readers' scrapbooking practices could easily refer to radio bootleggers of the mid-twentieth century, listeners who sought to capture recordings from the ongoing ephemeral, scheduled flow of broadcast entertainment; circulate them among fellow radio enthusiasts; and in so doing, detached program content from radio's ephemeral transmission and refashioned it into a physical commodity that was special and valuable.

The desire to capture and fix ephemerality also motivated the development of mechanical technologies like the phonograph. Inventor Thomas Edison was inspired to develop the sound-recording technology because he sought to make the fleeting ephemerality of the spoken word more like transcribed print information. Edison, who had been a newspaper reporter, had long desired an invention that could "'bottle up' speech for posterity."[14] He brainstormed several possible uses for the phonograph, including education and music reproduction; however, he saw its potential to make companies more efficient as its most valuable use, and, thus, early marketing framed the phonograph as a dictation tool that used sound reproduction to assist professional businesses improve efficiency.[15] The phonograph's original intention as a technology for recording and playing back speech led to the moniker "talking machine," a reference that would become a catchall for the different competing machines that played back recorded sound, that is, the phonograph, the gramophone, the graphophone, and others.[16]

The phonograph's promotion as a professional tool technology for preserving ephemeral speech made it particularly appealing to White American ethnographers performing what Brian Hochman has termed "salvage ethnography." Academics who believed Native American culture was being extinguished by US military's genocide saw the phonograph as a modern technology that could preserve and study tribal cultures. Harvard scholar Jesse Walter Fewkes declares, "[Thomas] Edison has given us an instrument by which our fast-fading aboriginal languages can be rescued from oblivion, and . . . posterity will thank us if we use it." And while this proclamation overestimated the quality of phonograph recordings at the time, the sentiment that sound-recording technology could function as an antidote for the perceived ephemerality of Indigenous culture is evident.[17]

Salvage ethnography is but one example of how the talking machine designed for business dictation became appropriated by users for alternative means, a reminder of the malleability of sound-recording technologies outside of corporate plans.[18] The phonograph would go on to have numerous intended and actual uses, many of which were motivated by Edison Speaking Phonograph Co.'s early promotional strategies and public demonstrations of the phonograph in 1877 and 1878, almost twenty years before the phonograph was redesigned and sold for domestic use. The introduction of the phonograph into popular culture in 1877 made the practice of taking ephemeral aural events and fixing them as material objects that could be controlled, reproduced, and intelligible to people for the first time. Once the concept of the phonograph left the control of the inventor's laboratory, its social construction would be redefined by the circuit between industry, popular discourse, and fantasy.[19]

During the 1870s and 1880s, the phonograph was not a device for domestic entertainment. As with many cultural-technological formations, the *desire* to possess, playback, and share music recordings existed in the social imagination long before it was recognized as a viable commercial practice. This can be seen in a cartoon that artist George du Maurier drew for the magazine *Punch's Almanack for 1878*, the year after Edison first unveiled his phonograph invention to *Scientific American*.[20] Inspired by Edison's phonograph announcement, du Maurier presented readers with a fictional invention that could record and store live music concerts (see figure 1.1). The cartoon presents a man and woman in late nineteenth-century clothing, organizing on their cellar shelves what looks like wine bottles labeled with contemporary music by composers like Paolo Tosti and opera singers like Zélia Trebelli. These bottles function in the cartoon as music-storage containers, and one symphony is so large, it is contained in a beer barrel.[21] The caption reads,

> By the Telephone Sound is converted into electricity, and then, by completing the circuit, back into sound again, Jones converts all the pretty music he hears during the Season into Electricity, bottles it, and

BY THE TELEPHONE SOUND IS CONVERTED INTO ELECTRICITY, AND THEN, BY COMPLETING THE CIRCUIT, BACK INTO SOUND AGAIN. JONES CONVERTS ALL THE PRETTY MUSIC HE HEARS DURING THE SEASON INTO ELECTRICITY, BOTTLES IT, AND PUTS IT AWAY INTO BINS FOR HIS WINTER PARTIES. ALL HE HAS TO DO, WHEN HIS GUESTS ARRIVE, IS TO SELECT, UNCORK, AND THEN COMPLETE THE CIRCUIT; AND THERE YOU ARE!

Figure 1.1. George du Maurier's cartoon imagining the possibilities for storing sound using electrical machines and telephone technology. (George du Maurier, "The Telephone," *Punch's Almanack for 1878*, December 14, 1877, 2)

puts it away into Bins for his Winter Parties. All he has to do when his Guests arrive, is to select, uncork, and then complete the Circuit; and there you are![22]

Du Maurier's somewhat prophetic "Telephone Sound" cartoon presents readers with the fantastical ability to bottle up "all the pretty music" that would otherwise be an ephemeral, fleeting experience as sound recordings that they can "uncork" later, equivalent to alcoholic beverages, collected and stored in the cellar to amuse guests. This may be one of the earliest depictions of using electric technologies, albeit imagined technologies, as home entertainment. Thus, while Edison may have conceived the phonograph as a tool for industry, this cartoon tells us how du Maurier and others imagined sound recording as a form of domestic media entertainment that could be collected, controlled, played back, and displayed as a symbol of wealth, taste, and social-class distinction.[23]

Du Maurier's illustration is also significant because it tells us something about the hopes and desires accompanying the advent of electricity in affluent Progressive Era homes and the historical conditions that brought media recordings into the home as commodities. The uneven trajectory of the sound-recording technologies from business talking machines to popular music playback devices included several failures and false starts and restarts that have been so well documented by scholars, such as Jonathan Sterne and Lisa Gitelman, there is no need to detail this history here.[24] However, understanding technological adaptation within popular culture as a social process is significant to the history of bootlegging radio, as I see recording ephemeral radio entertainment with home-recording equipment as part of a longer social process that began during the Progressive Era of commodifying entertainment as both the making and playing back of audiovisual recordings.

During the early 1900s the use of the talking machine to capture ephemeral sound became reframed as an act of entertainment in and of itself. A 1903 catalog published by the National Phonograph Co. describes one of the machine's many attributes: "The privilege of recording you and your friends' voices for future use is a never-failing source of amusement."[25] This was listed alongside the phonograph's ability to play back speeches, songs, and music on the molded wax cylinders that were the phonograph's first recording medium. In this sense, this period of the late 1890s was significant not only in reconstructing the talking machine as a domestic entertainment technology but also as a technology specifically designed to give users access to the ephemeral. Talking machines defined domestic sound-recording devices as technologies that provided users with the tools to capture ephemerality on their own terms, as the same 1903 catalog published by the National Phonograph Co. declares the talking machine gives users the ability to "preserve what otherwise would have perished . . . making permanent the otherwise fleeting pleasure."[26] Here, we can see how talking machines were closely articulated with home recording when they were redesigned and imagined for domestic consumers.

The commodification of media technologies and recordings marketed for domestic use during the Progressive Era would come to include home movie cameras, projectors, and films. Indeed, the urge to make the ephemeral into a fixed record was also the guiding motivation for experiments in the development of moving-image technologies. Indeed, Edison's laboratory was working on sound-recording technologies concurrently as Eadweard Muybridge and others experimented with moving-image technologies in the 1860s and 1870s, an endeavor Edison Labs would also come to explore. Muybridge's experiments with his zoopraxiscope system in the 1880s were a continuation of his photography work and goals to capture ephemera in urban and natural settings.[27] The content from early film producers, such as Edison or the Lumière brothers, consists mainly of scenes from everyday life, such as factory workers leaving work, tourists at a beach, people walking down a street, a woman sneezing or performing a dance, boxing matches, and the like, revealing how moving-image systems were invested in "the drive to fix and make repeatable the ephemeral."[28]

Despite the fact that cinema was, at this time, silent, convergence with sound-recording technologies was desired and pursued after. In 1897 Edison spoke about recording an opera performance in London and replaying it on the stage in New York as an example of the moving image's promise to record, preserve, and reproduce ephemeral performances that were more theatrical: "I believe that, in coming years, by my own work and that of [William] Dickson, Muybridge, [Étienne-Jules] Marey, and others who will doubtless enter the field, that grand opera can be given at the Metropolitan Opera House at New York without any material change from the original, and with artists and musicians long dead."[29] A writer at the Edison Laboratories newsletter, *The Phonoscope*, took Edison's dream to use the "combined powers of the kinetoscope and phonograph" one step further. "Yet with this apparatus," the writer muses, "on a smaller scale, any citizen of New York may sit in his parlor and enjoy the whole performance of any play or opera his fancy may select."[30] It was only within the broader context of the 1890s growth of consumer culture and leisure activities that included the sheet music industry, vaudeville circuits, and the kinetoscope film parlors that fantasies of a converged parlor equipped with mechanical entertainment devices would come to be realized.

Technological convergence is the process of bringing together discrete devices to create a new functionality previously not afforded, blurring the boundaries between the different mediums. This term has almost been used exclusively in reference to digitization, as Gabriele Balbi relates, "Most historical approaches that have reconstructed the term media convergence have considered digitization as a key prerequisite or the starting point of convergence."[31] Convergence was popularized as a framework by Ithiel de Sola Pool during the 1980s to describe both the "blurring the lines between media" and the erosion of the "one-to-one relationship that used to exist between a medium and its use."[32] Building on de Sola Pool, Henry Jenkins broadly defines technological convergence as the "process or series of intersections between different media systems," although he approaches it solely within the digital context. However, cultural historians have already demonstrated a wide array of industrial and technological convergence processes occurring during the Progressive Era.[33] This includes but is not limited to Edison Laboratories' vertical integration of phonograph hardware and a recording studio that released commercial sound recordings; experiments delivering music and other content via phone lines; RCA's vertical integration of consumer electronics manufacturing, broadcasting, music recording, and film studios, which provided cross-ownership synergy and promotion among NBC, RKO Radio Pictures, and the Victor Talking Machine Co.[34] Throughout the 1890s Edison Laboratories was experimenting with creating technological modes for convergence between the phonograph and kinetoscope to achieve synchronized sound that would accompany recorded moving images. As discussed in the next section, Edison Labs and the French Compagnie Générale des Établissements Pathé Frères Phonographes and Cinématographes (Pathé) would market similar systems for the home. The process of introducing talking machines and moving-image technologies to the home in the 1890s redefined the relationship between ephemerality and home entertainment by making transitory popular culture and private home experiences available as consumer media recordings that could be bought, manipulated, and played back on demand. By the time that wireless radio emerged, the notion that these technologies could be combined and manipulated was common sense, as was the use of home-recording equipment to capture the sounds being transmitted over the ether a logical continuation of using domestic consumer electronics to arrest and fix ephemerality.

Making Media Commodities Domestic

Talking machines and mass-produced media did not just enter the home, they had to be invited in, and Progressive Era users had to be taught how recorded sound would bring the excitement of popular culture into the safety of the home. Between 1877 when the Edison phonograph was publicly announced and 1895 when talking machines designed for home use were first released, the US economy underwent a dramatic shift from production-driven culture to a consumption-driven culture that reshaped Western life in the wake of the industrial revolution. These developments furthered a gendered binary between public and private life, and much of the popular culture and entertainment that catered to the emerging middle class in the late nineteenth century took place outside of the home.[35] Vaudeville performances and motion-picture exhibitions in public halls and theaters became established sites of commercial leisure during the late 1800s at the same time that resorts devoted to public forms of amusement, such as Coney Island, were developed and promoted.[36] Sporting events, such as boxing matches and horse racing, became increasingly popular forms of entertainment, while baseball began its ascent between 1860 and 1900 as the national pastime, with two major leagues and teams in most major cities by the early 1900s.[37] These factors created the expectation that mass entertainment happened in public, and many of these activities possessed an association with the working class, commercialism, pleasure, and new ideas of modern femininity.

Public leisure activities, such as minstrel shows, circuses, and dance halls, were understood as the purview of men and fallen women within what Barbara Welter calls the Victorian "cult of domesticity."[38] In contrast, the codes of upper-middle-class morality encouraged women to engage in appropriate domestic leisure activities, such as collecting flowers and shells, playing piano, doing needlework, studying the Bible, or reading literature.[39] Scholars have noted the role of colonialism and racial politics in the formation of the idealized middle-class home, arguing that the increased social emphasis on home life in the middle and late nineteenth century was also a response to the rise of American imperialism. Representations of White civilized domestic bliss in literature and media did the cultural work of reinforcing the White man's burden to civilize the savages of the world, while also functioning as a symbol of nationhood, retreating to the home and patriarchal order to protect itself from the threat of otherness at home and abroad.[40] The Great Migration of southern Blacks to urban centers in the Midwest and Northeast following the Civil War and the influx of working-class immigrants from Europe further deepened the boundaries of the White middle-class and upper-class construct of the home as refuge from perceived encroaching otherness of public city life.

Within this context, the design of the mid-nineteenth-century ladies' manuals, books, and early magazines reflects the Victorian domestic ideal of the home as place for spiritual rejuvenation and separation from urban centers and public leisure activities.[41] The parlor was not a place for entertainment but, rather, a site for the "formal presentation and the maintenance of family identity, where family albums and artwork would be combined with various styles of furniture and art to convey a certain identity to visitors and to family members themselves."[42] By the 1890s, however, the Progressive Era parlor was being redefined by the emerging middle-class consumer culture, and social status was increasing tied to the display of modern consumer technologies and commodities.[43] Barbara Klinger has argued in her work on film cultures that "public objects are not simply appropriated into personal universes; their transition and translation into private space entail a reciprocal relationship between producing and consuming culture."[44] Beginning in the 1890s, social status, values, and activities would increasingly be articulated with the consumption of goods and services imbued with "magical" qualities through marketing campaigns.[45] Manufacturers relied on the codevelopment of the mass media and advertising industries to facilitate new relationships with commodities at the same time that storage media, such as the photograph, phonograph record, and, to a lesser extent, film, began to be mass produced for domestic use. We can look at the rise of Tin Pan Alley and the ensuing way that domestic media systems and commodities were framed in advertisements during this period to understand the changing status of the home as a place for entertainment.

The National Gramophone Co. advertisement in 1897 is indicative of how talking machines were being framed as home entertainment. The heading "For Evening Entertainments" sits above an image of a family gathered around a gramophone, looking at it in amusement; the ad copy reads, "These people are certainly enjoying themselves, they are listening to one of the most varied home entertainments ever given." This is one of the earliest uses of the term "home entertainment" I have observed, a reminder that this construct is deeply rooted in the transition to consumer media culture during the Progressive Era. The ad continues by providing a "programme" listing the eighteen recordings the family listened to that evening, which ranged from piano solos to poem recitations to popular songs. The ad copy then extolls the technological prowess of the gramophone machine, the prices of different models, and the address to write for a catalog.[46] This portrait of a family enthralled by the gramophone's mechanical playback of popular entertainment emphasizes both the function of the talking machine for consumers, home entertainment, and the necessity to amass a collection of recordings in order to reproduce a similar "programme." Only those with the means to invest in building collections of media recordings for the home could enjoy the leisure and pleasure afforded by domestic commodity culture.

The ascendence of Tin Pan Alley played a pivotal role in the reconfiguration of the home parlor into an entertainment center for mass-produced popular media commodities. A new generation of publishers focused on selling sheet music of popular songs from public entertainment venues, such as dance halls and minstrel shows, at a low cost in the 1880s.[47] Tin Pan Alley sheet music functioned as a commodity that connected the public leisure spaces of the vaudeville theater to the family parlor. By selling sheet music directly to consumers as a physical commodity, commercial music publishers taught audiences to think of popular culture as an object they could possess, collect, and control in the privacy of their own homes. At the same time, the efforts by the Music Publisher's Protective Association to prevent so-called unauthorized sheetleggers from copying and selling sheet music were some of the earliest media industry campaigns against copyright infringement.[48]

Advertisements from the early 1900s indicate how nascent recording companies built on Tin Pan Alley's construction of a home market for popular songs from vaudeville and minstrel shows. For example, in the 1905 ad shown in figure 1.2, the National Phonograph Co. explicitly framed the talking machine and prerecorded music as a conduit between the world of public entertainment and private domestic space, through the use of a photo with several vaudeville minstrel performers in blackface next to the headline, "Vaudeville at Home with the Edison Phonograph."[49] The advertisement proclaims, "You need not be a millionaire to entertain your guests or children with vaudeville at your home. *All you need is an Edison Phonograph*. Then you can hear just the kind of vaudeville you like best *when* and *where* you please."[50] This ad promotes the recordings by highlighting user control over entertainment as

Vaudeville at Home
WITH THE
Edison Phonograph

You need not be a millionaire to entertain your guests or children with vaudeville at your home. *All you need is an Edison Phonograph.* Then you can hear just the kind of vaudeville you like best, *when* and *where* you please.

The new list of Edison Gold Moulded Records includes the funniest songs, duets, impersonations, and musical specialties that are offered on the stage. You can't hear them too often and *they never fail to produce laughter and calls for "more"*.

The genuine improved Edison Phonograph does not *imitate* but faithfully *reproduces* the gems of vaudeville. To appreciate this great advantage of the Edison Phonograph over ordinary *talking machines* you should

HEAR THESE VAUDEVILLE RECORDS FREE

9046 Comic Song—Now What D'ye Think of That?	9020 Bell Solo—Tell Me With Your Eyes.
8984 Vaudeville Specialty—Professor and Musical Tramp.	9030 Rube Talking Specialty—Courtin' Malinda.
9007 Rube Duet—Hey! Mr. Joshua.	9003 Tenor Solo—Rose-Marie.
8999 Banjo Solo—Yankee Land March.	9044 Xylophone Medley—Down In Blossom Row.
9036 Shakespearean Travesty—Antony and Cleopatra.	9014 Mandolin and Guitar Duet—An Autumn Evening.
9033 Coon Song—Shame On You!	9019 Male Quartette—Good Night, Beloved, Good Night!

If you have no phonograph, you should learn the entertaining qualities of Edison Gold Moulded Records. Fill in and mail the coupon. We will then send you our New List of Gold Moulded Records, and a letter of introduction to our nearest dealer entitling you to hear any of our thousands of Records FREE. Edison Phonographs cost from $10.00 up; Records 35c. each. Write now, before you forget it.

NATIONAL PHONOGRAPH CO., ORANGE, N. J.
NEW YORK, CHICAGO, SAN FRANCISCO, LONDON
I. C. S. Language Courses Taught by Edison Phonograph.

Fill in and mail this coupon.
NATIONAL PHONOGRAPH CO., 25 Lakeside Ave., Orange, N. J.:
Please send me Phonograph Catalogue and New List of Edison Records.

Name_____

St. and No._____

City_____ State_____

If you have a Phonograph, please give its number_____

Figure 1.2. Advertisement for Edison phonograph recordings describing the ways these recordings brought vaudeville into the private space of the home. (National Phonograph Company, "Vaudeville at Home" advertisement, *Overland Monthly*, August 1905, i)

a central precept of the phonograph record while also linking the sound recordings of vaudeville stars with images of vaudeville performances on stage. The phonograph thus was rendered as a bridging technology that brought together public and private, the theatrical stage and the domestic parlor. This ad also visually signals the racial politics of vaudeville and the popularity of "coon songs" and minstrel performances. Implicit here is the ambivalence of minstrelsy's racial dynamics, as the ad communicates a desire both to inhabit and consume non-White otherness and to experience it from the safety of the imagined White, middle-class domestic setting.

Representing sound recordings as a bridge between public and private spaces is repeated in other ads that similarly framed the phonograph as a tool to bring the sounds of the stage into the home. Another National Phonograph Co. ad depicts the opera stage above the acoustic horn of the machine, so that it almost appeared as if the opera vignette were emerging out of the horn (figure 1.3). Next to this image, the copy reads, "The voice of all the people *on* the stage—The Choice of all the people *off* the stage. The Edison Phonograph *is* the theatre—the opera, the drama, the concert, the vaudeville—offering a greater and more varied program than any theatre in the land—and playing to the biggest audience in the world." The ad then goes into a list of performers signed with Edison's recording label, asking the reader to imagine them "right in your own home theatre, or wherever you go and whenever you want them. That's what it means to you to own the Edison Phonograph and it means 'keep the boys at home.' The Edison is the original antidote for 'breaking of home ties.'"[51] In this ad, the phonograph is not only a domestic bridge to mass entertainment through the music commodity, it is also being defined as an antidote to gendered familial discord caused by the "boys" absence from home to attend live theatrical performances. This ad also includes an early use of the term "home theater" that predates visual-media technologies, demonstrating how the phonograph was the first technology to be articulated with the domestic use of media as a way of bringing the theater or live stage into the home through mass-produced recordings.

The April cover of *Talking Machine World* in 1912 features the ornate Victor Victrola gramophone in the president's personal quarters at the White House, demonstrating the home entertainment system's new cultural function conveying domestic social status.[52] Indeed, by the 1910s the talking machine was no longer a novelty but an accepted piece of furniture in the layout of middle- and upper-class homes.[53] Furniture

Figure 1.3. Advertisement for Edison phonograph recordings depicting them as a bridge between public and private spaces. ("Edison Phonograph" advertisement, *Collier's: The National Weekly*, October 14, 1911, 40)

companies designed ornate cabinets for phonographs and records, and companies developing talking machines created a range of models that spanned from tabletop players to simple oak cabinets to rococo cabinets like Edison's Louis XVI model made of Circassian walnut.[54] By the 1910s talking machines functioned as both integral physical components of the upper-class Progressive Era home and as a source of domestic entertainment that was designed to encourage the sale and collection of physical commodities. One of the ironies of this period is that Edison's wax cylinder would lose the format war with Victor's disc gramophone, but the name "phonograph" would come to be a catchall phrase used to describe talking machines and disc records.[55] The phonograph industry, with Victor at the forefront, would continue to grow as a lucrative sector of the economy, and by 1929 (before the stock-market crash) it was selling approximately $100 million worth of records and phonograph machines in the United States.[56] An outgrowth of media cultures before it, such as sheet music collecting and parlor piano recitals, the phonograph domesticated the exhibition of media and created a new culture where sound recordings become a significant part of quotidian home life. This was not a precursor to radio or television but, rather, a form of media engagement in its own right.

The phonograph's integration of recorded sound into the domestic space was not far removed from the entrance of screen technologies or broadcasting devices into the home, as the phonograph's technologies were developed in tandem with talking-machine technologies, often sold in the same shops or even as combined home entertainment systems. While domestic technologies for the playback of sound recordings and film recordings are often discussed separately as distinct media, they were developed and marketed during the same historical moment and were often used together. The Edison Co. first released film playback machines for public use in entertainment halls and saloons, like the peephole Edison Kinetoscope in 1893 and the Vitascope Projector in 1896.[57] A *Phonoscope* article from 1897 details Edison's plans for a projection system that would combine the phonograph and kinetoscope for synchronized replay of filmed stage projections, a vision whose scope and scale was far above the Edison Co.'s filmmaking at the time.[58] Grand theatrical performances were a far cry from the 1890s popular avant-garde film style Tom Gunning describes as "cinema of attractions" designed to shock or astonish audiences, which characterized the Edison Co.'s short vignettes of scantily clad women dancing, boxing matches, or couples

Figure 1.4. Advertisement for the first Edison home projection system, one of the earlier ads to use the phrase "home entertainment." ("Edison Projecting Kinetoscope," advertisement, *The Phonogram*, April 1901, 224)

kissing that were featured in these peephole Kinetoscope machines.[59] The development of a home projection device for moving-image playback was almost instantaneously realized. Between 1896 and 1912 about a dozen technological apparatuses of various quality and operability were released that attempted to facilitate home projection of photographs, slides, or short film strips.[60]

Homemade Entertainment   39

The first commercial product designed to project and play back film reels in the home was the Edison Projecting Kinetoscope, released in 1897, and a redesigned model B was released in 1901.[61] The 1901 advertisement shown in figure 1.4 claims the Edison Projecting Kinetoscope was "unequalled for HOME ENTERTAINMENT. The improved machine is now so simple that an amateur can operate it." This ad features a group of men and women watching horses ride across the wall of their living room while one gentleman stands by the projector to crank it, presumably reading a script that accompanied one of the films available in the advertised catalog. The audience is enraptured, their faces lit only by the illumination of the projector's light.[62] The presence of women and at least one child in this depiction of viewers underscores the implicit cultural work of "home entertainment" during the Progressive Era to protect middle-class moral standards. Home entertainment as a cultural formation was not simply relocating popular culture into domestic space but, rather, a social practice that reflected and reshaped the gendered, classed, and racialized dialectic between public and domestic spaces, public and private lives, and the cult of decency that would guide the development of self-censorship in broadcasting, sound recording, and film.

The advertisement for the 1901 Edison Projecting Kinetoscope provides another example of the use of the term "home entertainment" during the rise of media-playback consumer electronics, a phrase used in the 1897 gramophone advertisement discussed earlier in this chapter. This Edison Projecting Kinetoscope was one of the earliest technologically converged domestic systems designed to play back audiovisual media in the home (musical sheets and recordings were often released to accompany the then silent film reels). It was one of the first technologies to offer a new conceptualization of cinema as something to be bought and played back as home entertainment, several decades prior to television and almost a century before home video would come to describe lucrative divisions of every major media conglomerate. The phonograph was crucial in establishing the domestic entertainment market, and Edison's home projectors were sold in the same shops as his talking machines. Media industry workers made sense of technologies for visual media storage and playback in the home through their experience with talking machines. One film distributor in Chicago said in 1907,

> The moving picture will eventually be as popularly used for entertainment in private homes as is the phonograph.... I think the day is not far distant when every home can be supplied with a moving picture

outfit so that company may be entertained in the parlor the same as it might within a moving picture theater. The expense, of course, will be high at first, but science will provide a way for cheaper service so that it may be within the reach of almost every family man.[63]

Edison himself in 1911 made sense of his company's home projector as a part of the developing domestic entertainment formation: "The motion picture is here to stay. In the parlor it will occupy a companion place with the piano and the phonograph. Guests as they now bring their newest phonographic records for an evening's enjoyment will bring their latest reels of film."[64] The above statements demonstrate how home entertainment was both made legible to industry players by the phonograph and subsequently integrated into a larger technologically converged ideal for home entertainment culture during the Progressive Era.

We can see the recognition of technological convergence by consumer electronic companies by looking at how the second generation of home projection systems released in the 1910s were sold with phonograph hookups and sound recordings intended to accompany the projected films.[65] The two most well-known home-movie-projector models from this period were expensive high-end systems, such as Edison's Home Projecting Kinetoscope, which sold for between $75 and $100 (approximately $2,270 and $3,000 in 2023, respectively, when adjusted for inflation), and Pathé's Cinématographe de Salon Kok, or as it was renamed for the English-speaking market, the Pathéscope, which was $150 for the hand-cranked model or $200 for the motorized version (approximately $4,500 and $6,000 in 2023, respectively, when adjusted for inflation).[66] These prices are reminders of whom these technologies were made for: affluent upper-class audiences.[67] The release of both Pathé's Pathéscope and the Edison Home Projecting Kinetoscope (HPK) in 1912 corresponded to each companies' development of nonflammable safety film, a key engineering breakthrough in domestication of cinema.

Pathé and Edison pioneered the home cinema market with film buying and exchange programs to provide content for owners of their home projection. Edison's Home Projecting Kinetoscope (HPK) system only projected premade films from the Kinetoscope film catalog, filmed on 22 mm and designed to be projected by using the machine's distinct three parallel columns of sequential frames.[68] The film catalog was first released with 50 titles, growing to approximately 116 by 1915.[69] Participants would order films from the library and return them there, a model used by radio and television clubs who created lending libraries for members before this distribution method was popularized by video-rental stores in the 1980s. This film exchange program only operated for three years, closing when the Edison Co. discontinued its Home Projecting Kinetoscope in 1915.[70] Even with the short-lived investment from Edison, the HPK became a significant aspect of home entertainment for its owners, with the division processing 8,324 film exchanges during the three years it operated.[71] Audience members were still invested in using their systems into the 1920s, as one Peter J. Prinz of Jamaica, New York, asked *Motion Picture World* in 1920: "Would you kindly advise me as to what became of the Edison Home Kinetoscope . . . ? Would I be able to still obtain films, or is there any film on the market which the projector named will take?"[72] The editors of *Motion Picture World* seemed to think that this was a lost cause but urged fellow readers to contact Prinz if they had any films for sale that were formatted for the now defunct Home Projecting Kinetoscope.

While the Edison Co.'s investment in home cinema was brief, Pathé's entre into visual home entertainment was a commercial success. Like the Edison Co., Pathé also designed the Pathéscope with a unique film gauge to control production and distribution of both the technology and the media content, and in contrast to Edison's 22 mm, Pathé's was 28 mm. However, several elements made the Pathéscope distinct from the Edison HPK. The Pathéscope was more expensive and marketed solely to an upper-class clientele, which may have increased the perceived value for audiences. And, while the Home Projecting Kinetoscope did not allow owners to project amateur movies, the Pathéscope was sold with the ability to project home movies made using a similarly expensive Pathéscope 28 mm camera. Pathé also offered a catalog of films made by the company's theatrical division and reformatted on reduction prints for home use. Pathé's film catalog also offered material produced specifically for the home market, such as films that offered viewers dance lessons and were meant to be used in conjunction with recorded music that came with the film print, provided the viewer had purchased the accompanying Pathé phonograph equipment.[73] The Pathéscope would wane in popularity after the Eastman Kodak Co. began offering a less-expensive Kodascope home-movie system and film stock in 1923.[74] This was followed by the development of the Kodascope film library, which offered subscribers a catalog of films available for home use after 1924.[75] The home film entertainment sector did not equal the theatrical film exhibition market in size between 1896 and 1922; however, Pathé's and Edison's home projectors made domestic exhibition of films a widespread phenomenon and pioneered film-rental services. In addition to Kodak, Universal Pictures and several other film distribution companies followed Edison's and Pathé's subscription models and offered film-exchange programs in major cities like Boston, Chicago, and New York by the end of the 1920s.[76]

The rise of Tin Pan Alley, talking machines, and home film projectors during the Progressive Era brought the burgeoning mass entertainment industry into the home. This rearticulated popular culture as a media commodity experience through a technologically converged home entertainment system. Popular ballads, live performances, and moving pictures were not only ephemeral experiences, they were also now objects one could own and collect, forever redefining the materiality of media cultures in modern society. Political economists often point to the industrial significance of media recordings as public good commodities that are not used up during consumption. Once sunk costs have been invested in production, storage media can be reproduced for very little expense and recycled through distribution windows for profit ad infinitum.[77] The same can be said from a user perspective, as the home phonograph and film playback systems introduced a culture of repetition through storage media to audiences. Phonograph and home film projection users could replay the recordings they owned on demand, bringing power, control, and repetition to the center of domestic media consumption logics. These objects not only informed the complex experiences available to audiences in the home but they were also social artifacts that became imbued with cultural meanings and influenced audience ideas of the self. For instance, actors such as Edward G. Robinson, Jean Harlow, and Eleanor Powell all mentioned collecting phonograph records in their attempt to self-represent taste and distinction in interviews with the popular press.[78] By the mid-1930s, media recordings mass-produced for home use were embedded in forms of display and décor from which people make sense of themselves and others.

The Progressive Era should, thus, be reconceptualized as a period when the home entertainment market for media commodities was developed and expanded. Moreover, the domestication of media exhibition using physical commodities brought media distribution into the parlor. The home was now a significant point of distribution via catalogs and door-to-door sales. Indeed, even in the early 1900s, talking-machine trade journals advised their sales force to track customer taste and visit customers at home to sell new recordings, with one advice column telling them, "Human vanity plays some part in the matter of record collecting. One phonograph owner does not like to feel that his collection is numerically far inferior to that of a friend, and the tactful dealer by recommending records that he knows to be good will often make large sales."[79] The home's place as a site of media exhibition and distribution would only grow once radio broadcasting became the dominant form of home entertainment in the 1930s. Many radio listeners of the 1920s and 1930s had grown up in a media culture where home entertainment technologies had become a staple of everyday life. User control over media had not only been habituated by the popularization of record and film collecting but also by the widespread adaptation of home-recording technologies during the Progressive Era.

Home-Recording Technologies and Domestic Media Production

The commercialization of media recordings during the Progressive Era only introduced and defined the home as a space for media entertainment and normalized repetition as a mode of private, controlled on-demand engagement. Talking machines, amateur filmmaking systems, and radio sets were also promoted to consumers in ways that encouraged audiences to see themselves as media producers. Between the late 1890s and the early 1920s, the American home came to be defined as a space of media production and distribution, alongside consumption, allowing audiences to both realize the utopian fantasies of preserving ephemerality through home recording and forge new fleeting forms of ephemeral media themselves as wireless radio operators.

Talking machines were understood in hybrid terms as technologies that could entertain both through their ability to play back music and their novelty as home-recording devices. The phonograph and subsequent sound recorders were promoted to consumers through the 1910s and 1920s, even as talking machines had come to be dominantly understood as machines for commercial music playback.[80] The articulation between home recording and domestic leisure is evident in a National Phonograph Co. full-page newspaper ad published January 29, 1911, in the *New York Tribune* (see figure 1.5). The top portrays a White, middle-class family gathered around the phonograph. This familial image would come to be used in different derivative forms to promote the phonograph until Edison stopped making wax-cylinder machines in 1929. The drawing shows a table with a phonograph centered and the large acoustic horn facing to the left, where two men stand with open mouths, presumably projecting their voices into the horn. On the other

Figure 1.5. Advertisement underscoring the home-recording capabilities of the phonograph as a leisure activity. ("Edison Phonograph," *New York Tribune*, January 29, 1911, 18)

side, two women and a young boy listen intently. The headline reads, "Did you ever make a Phonograph Record? Did you ever hear yourself talk, or sing, or play? Talk about entertainment—there is nothing that approaches the fun and fascination of making records at home on the EDISON PHONOGRAPH."

The ad copy explains the technological virtues of the phonograph, such as its fidelity and easy operation.[81] As the advertisement extolls the fun of producing sound recordings and articulates this with domesticity, it also reminds us that domestic media production was represented in gendered terms. The National Phonograph Co. ad shows this by the division between the right side and left side of the drawing. The men enjoy the fun of recording sound into the phonograph, while the women and children are passive participants, content just to be there and listen attentively.

The talking machine's function as a home-recording device may not have been as popular as using it to play back prerecorded content; it was, nonetheless, a significant mode of engagement that would come to be part of broader Progressive Era culture of making media at home. The phonograph was the first technology to turn the home into a recording studio, a practice that continues to shape private and public technological sound cultures. As discussed later, Victor and Pathé would develop their own home-recording technologies using recordable discs in the 1920s and 1930s. The desire and ability to bootleg radio grew out of the burgeoning convergence culture facilitated by home-recording technologies in the early 1900s.

The phonograph's model of domestic media production practices arose concurrently with and influenced amateur film production and home movies culture during the Progressive Era. Filmmaking in the home can be traced back to 1897, when the first amateur film cameras and projectors were sold to the general public.[82] Over the next thirty years, home movie making would become a popular hobby very much embedded in domestic family life and, like the phonograph, spurred by the growth of the middle class and the articulation of home life with leisure activities. An assortment of camera models with varying film gauges proliferated in the first two decades of the twentieth century, and inventors experimented with paper film and camera design to overcome the danger of professional-grade nitrate film that was easily flammable.[83] Pathé and Edison both developed a nonflammable safety film in 1912, followed by Kodak's introduction of 16 mm nonflammable reversal film in 1923, which allowed for easy film development into a positive image. Reversal film became the industry standard for amateur hobbyists through the twentieth century.[84] Eastman Kodak also released the Cine-Kodak system in 1923, entirely designed for the home, that included the 16 mm safety film, a camera, tripod, projector, and emulsion techniques.[85] An entire ecosystem related to amateur filmmakers had developed by the 1920s, including film-processing centers in most major cities, local amateur film clubs, home-movie how-to books, and more.[86] These how-to guides encouraged the amateur filmmaker to use all resources at their disposal and to map out photoplays that could make use of settings in their home, town, or local area, and in this context, the home became a soundstage.[87]

The development of amateur film culture in the United States, as other scholars have noted, drew on still photography and mainstream cinema in similarity and difference. Like photography, making and playing back film in the home built upon previous pastimes like using magic lanterns to project still images in the home. Also, like photography, amateur film was seen as a way to document and display family histories, and there was an emphasis on choosing pictorial subjects, such as home life, nature, and social events with friends, rather than work or industrial settings.[88] However, amateur film had just as much in common with the phonograph, as the wax cylinder's possibilities for preserving family history was central to its framing as a domestic technology in the late 1800s.[89] Patricia Rodden Zimmerman discusses how the construct of the amateur as a social figure developed in response to the industrialization and urbanization of the mid-1800s: "Amateur film became the domain where one mastered and controlled technology, in contradiction to work where technology and technocracy controlled the worker."[90] Amateurism connoted the social distinction of investing labor and money into a leisure endeavor, and one could easily amend this sentiment to include the phonograph. The amateur nature of home recording was considered a selling point for one phonograph salesman, who in a 1907 column, suggested the amateur home recording was a persuasive talking point for salesmen: "Dealers should never lose an opportunity for talking home records to customers. The fact that they cannot approach the professional record has nothing to do with it. The little affectations of voice, strange inflections, etc., which would never be found in the professional record would add to the value of the home record, for it would add to the naturalness and lifelike effect produced."[91] The faux pas of the ordinary, untrained media producer at home was not only expected but a valuable aesthetic understood to convey the authenticity of home recordings.

The figure of the amateur media maker became a Progressive Era archetype rendered as an aspirational modern, affluent, and creative individual. The noncommercial nature of home media production linked amateurism to masculine qualities described by Zimmerman as "initiative, enthusiasm, and adventurousness . . . the new pioneer of economic and technological frontiers." Zimmerman goes on to argue, "Amateurism functioned as a residual site for nineteenth-century American male economic prowess . . . [and] connected nostalgia for self-made man with a resistance to corporate and professional domination."[92] The noncommercial nature and self-propulsion involved in this arena of Progressive Era do-it-yourself media production imbued amateurism with an aura of innovation, thought to be a labor of love and more creative and pure because of its lack of economic incentive. Zimmerman's discussion of the amateur filmmaker in the early twentieth century as a paragon of masculine inventiveness, spontaneity, and technological prowess is strikingly similar to Douglas's depiction of the masculine radio culture during this period.

Indeed, radio developed as another form of domestic media production during the 1910s alongside the phonograph and home movie system. Before radio came to be a one-to-many form of broadcasting entertainment in the 1920s, wireless radio was a hobby dominated by amateurs who were often represented through implicitly and explicitly masculine terms in popular discourse. Similar to Zimmerman's argument that amateur filmmaking offered users an opportunity for control and mastery in the postindustrial context of the Progressive Era, Douglas argues that the hobby of constructing radios and communicating through wireless technology became a subculture of young men "who found in technical tinkering a way to cope with the pressures of modernization. . . . For certain upwardly mobile men, a sense of control came from mastering a particular technology rather than succumbing to the routinization and de-skilling of the factory system."[93] The parallels in Zimmerman's and Douglas's analyses of the cultural functions of home movies and radio in the early twentieth century point to the gendered aspects of domestic media and consumer culture during that period.

Like other Progressive Era domestic technologies, wireless radios of the 1910s were designed to be put together and used in the home. At this time, radio use was being taken up by a handful of groups, including engineers, businesses, and the military, and primarily used for Morse code communication between and to ships. However, as with most new technological developments, few regulations existed during wireless radiography's formative period, and it was (and still is) possible for anyone who could buy the patented materials and assemble them into a radio to listen and broadcast out to others via the electromagnetic spectrum. Beginning in 1906 America experienced its first radio boom, as investment in wireless companies increased, and the general public grew increasingly interested in the technology. Wireless radio came to be discursively constructed as a modern marvel accessible to anyone with the time, materials, and gumption to try their hand at constructing a radio set. Amateur radio became masculinized by press coverage featuring young "boy wonders" as radio amateurs and discussed the assembly and operation of radio sets in masculine terms that emphasized strength, control, and "triumph over nature."[94]

Wireless radio was accessible and exciting when it became a domestic technology, and newspaper and magazine articles detailed how readers could build their own sets with easily available household items, including cans, bottles, oatmeal cylinders, and more.[95] A license to operate a radio was not required, and amateurs used the same frequencies as the US Navy, businesses, and commercial stations. Wireless communication came to possess a magical aura during its early cultural adoption, and it figured as both the topic of newspaper coverage and the subject of poetry, short stories, and popular ballads. As Douglas notes, wireless radio was understood as a technology that could transport users to faraway, exotic locales and powerful situations. Wireless radio's fantastic qualities were, perhaps, more significant because its powers to transcend space, time, and social categories through the ether were possible in one's own home. And the practice of amateur radio turned the attic, basement, or bedroom into both a home laboratory and radio station.

Technological Convergence, Domestic Media, and Radio Bootlegging

The phonograph, film camera, and wireless radio normalized the production of media within the home and converged with each other in ways both intended and unintended by inventors and corporations. Home movie systems advised their users to record accompanying sound on a phonograph or purchase music recordings to sync up and playback when screening home movies. Radio and phonographs also converged, first through amateur experimentation and then through the design and sale of home entertainment sets designed as preassembled commercial technologies for the home. Within this historical context, we can see how bootlegging broadcasting content developed as an extension of the broader Progressive Era domestic media culture and its emphasis on media recordings, collecting, and user control.

The first radio recordings were made by amateur radio hobbyists in the home. One of the earliest examples is hobbyist Charles Apgar of Westfield, New Jersey, who built a radio set and connected it to a phonograph wax cylinder with a highly sensitive radio headphone in order to record transmitted signals in 1913.[96] Another record of early radio recording includes Frank Capps, an engineer who had worked for Bell Labs, Pathé, and Columbia Gramophone at different times and also built his own equipment to record radio broadcasts in the early 1920s, including Woodrow Wilson's speech commemorating the fifth anniversary of Armistice Day in 1923.[97] These early home experimentations combining the phonograph with radio receivers were followed by commercial products released for domestic use. Several disc-cutting home recorders were released in the early 1920s, including the Pathé Voicewriter, Echo-Disc, Rekordo, Rekord, Marvel, and Repeat-a-Voice, and recorded sound via an acoustic phonograph with either premade grooves or a stylus that could crease the grooves in the disc itself.[98]

The technological convergence between broadcasting and technologies that could store and play back sound media came to be a part of industrial practices in the 1920s. Prior to RCA's purchase of Victor in 1929, the two companies had worked together manufacturing Victrolas with Radiola receivers in them in 1925, and in that same year, Victor began sponsoring the music variety show *Victor Hour* on RCA's WJZ chain.[99] The convergence of radio with the phonograph and home-recording capabilities became even more solidified in 1931 when RCA Victor released its Victor home-recording system that combined a radio receiver with a phonograph in the console that could record directly off the radio using pregrooved, soft-plastic discs.[100] RCA's 1931 Model R57 home-recording system allowed users to record radio broadcasts off air onto these discs.[101] The increase of instantaneous-recording equipment within the professional sound-recording community through the 1930s led to an increased interest in amateur home recording as companies, such as RCA, Remco, and Universal Microphone, began to sell high-end radio-phonograph consoles for home use in the late 1930s.[102]

American broadcast industries are often thought of as institutions opposing the development and use of technologies that allow audiences to record content off the air. The infamous battles between the US television producers and videotape companies during the 1970s and 1980s have

Figure 1.6. David Sarnoff, RCA chairman of the board, demonstrating the company's magnetic-tape television recording technology on December 1, 1953, and discussing its possibilities, including making a library of one's favorite television-program recordings. (David Sarnoff, "Sarnoff Reports Stage Set for Color TV as Science of Electronics Makes New Advances," *Radio Age*, January 1954, 3, www.americanradiohistory.com)

animated our modern understanding of bootlegging. The legal battle over television and home recording resulted in the 1984 *Sony Corp. of America v. Universal City Studios Inc.*, the US Supreme Court decision that defined private, noncommercial recording for the purpose of time-shifting as legal.[103] This decision formed the foundation for how scholars have discussed bootlegging in the subsequent decades, and it positions content producers and distributors on one side of a battle inherently opposed to the machinations of consumer electronics companies and manufacturing of home-recording technologies designed to converge and interplay with broadcast receivers. However, if we go back to the ways in which home-recording technology was imagined during its early ascension in popular culture during the Progressive Era, we get a more complete genealogy of the cultural history of home recording's relationship with broadcasting.

To make this point, I will divert for a moment to the invention of videotape recording technology in the 1950s. When RCA board chairman David Sarnoff oversaw the development of early videotape recording technology for television, he embraced the idea that audiences would use this to create home libraries of television content. Figure 1.6 is of Sarnoff at RCA's Princeton, New Jersey, laboratory on December 1, 1953, demonstrating the new product: magnetic videotape. We might imagine that he was mostly likely overjoyed thinking of all the money magnetic tape would save NBC. The film kinescope method of relaying East Coast programming to the West Coast used prior to magnetic tape was costly and time consuming, and its quality was unreliable. RCA predicted that because of its potential for reuse, videotape would cost 5 percent of what kinescope retransmission cost. However, as Sarnoff smiled and extolled the value of videotape recording in Princeton that day, he spoke optimistically of his vision for this technology. He foresaw multiple uses for videotape recording (VTR), including within the defense, education, and home entertainment sectors and predicted that recording "equipment could be . . . connected to the television set to make a personal recording of a favorite television program."[104] Sarnoff's belief that VTRs could be used for domestic television engagement demonstrates how bootlegging content off air was not always imagined to be at odds with the broadcasting industries' revenue models.

Indeed, Sarnoff came into his leadership of RCA during the Progressive Era when home media came to be defined by the cultural and industrial processes this chapter outlines. RCA began as a company that made radio sets and then founded NBC, in part, to further create demand for their consumer electronics. Given this, it is not hard to understand why Sarnoff understood home recording as a complementary practice to broadcasting. He had overseen RCA's purchase of the Victor Talking Machine Co. in 1929, which was subsequently followed by the release of radio-phonograph combination sets with home-recording systems built into them for audiences to record radio programming onto pregrooved blank discs.[105] Early convergence between broadcasting receivers and home-recording equipment in the 1920s and 1930s is a reminder that technologies are historically contingent cultural configurations. Bootlegging radio did not naturally occur but, rather, was the result of a larger development and convergence of domesticated media commodities, such as records and films, and the consumer technologies that facilitated playback and home media production cultures, and the economic convergence strategies that inspired such companies as Edison, Victor, Pathé, and RCA to want to vertically integrate and own the means of content production, distribution, and exhibition technologies. Broadcasting's informal bootlegging economies have always, to some degree, been intertwined with the official broadcast industries.

The development of machines to record radio was also influenced by the symbolic work during the Progressive Era that articulated preservation culture and popular media with domestic entertainment and consumerism. Since the release of the phonograph and home movie devices as consumer goods in the late 1890s, Americans have come to understand media both as objects and processes embedded in domestic recreation, and these practices shaped how broadcasting was taken up and engaged with. Indeed, by the time that prominent early radio stations like WJZ in Newark, WGN in Chicago, or WEAF in New York began broadcasting content in the early 1920s, radio was already understood as a technology that could be tinkered with, manipulated, and experimented with at home. Even as broadcasting came to be dominantly understood as a one-to-many commercial flow of content, the design and release of consumer technologies that facilitated home recording of radio content show that bootlegging broadcast content has always been a way audiences engaged with radio.

This early period of radio bootlegging is not well documented and is a hard history to tease out. Research for this book entailed quite a bit of time looking for traces of radio bootleggers in the NBC collection of corporate papers from 1923 to 1970 at the Wisconsin Center for Film and Theatre Research, as well as searching through industry trade presses from the first half of the twentieth century. With the exception of lawsuits against so-called disk pirates bootlegging pop music with off-air recordings in 1957, the broadcast industry was fairly hands off and ostensibly unconcerned with audiences recording content off air until the Hollywood studio's lawsuit against Sony first began in the 1970s.[106]

Indeed, the development of radio sets equipped with home-recording apparatuses by Victor and RCA in the 1930s encouraged the practice of off-air content recording. Radio-equipped home-recording devices were widely available to audiences by the mid-1930s. The extent to which they were used is uncertain. However, radio collectors in the 1970s would report that several recordings of early *Amos 'n' Andy* broadcasts circulating at the time had been originally made at home using these early disc-cutting or pregrooved disc recording methods.[107] The only acknowledgment I have found from within the industry is a 1938 *Variety* article discussing radio collecting.[108] According to *Variety*, several radio bootleggers with suspected ties to the radio industries were stealing transcription discs from the radio networks and then selling copies of them, at quite a profit:

> [T]he platters are exceptionally high priced and difficult for the uninitiated to obtain. Reason is that the selling of such recordings is contrary to copyright law and might be liable to heavy penalty. In general, therefore, only small fly-by-night outfits are engaged in the business and they operate very much on the sneak. Only a limited number of persons well known to such operators can obtain the transcriptions, even at the steep prices.[109]

This system did not use home-recording technologies, as the bootleggers in question would obtain transcription discs and set up their own equipment to produce copies, selling them at the high price of $10 apiece for each transcription of fifteen-minute broadcasts. The most sought-after recordings in November 1938 were reported to be *The Mercury Theater of the Air*'s "War of the Worlds" episode, King Edward VIII's abdication, the *Hindenburg* zeppelin explosion, sports broadcasts, and music recordings, such as NBC's Arturo Toscanini series.[110] This article makes clear that by 1938 a subculture of radio bootleggers existed, circulating recordings through various and possibly ill-gotten means. However, the widespread growth of radio bootlegging did not really occur until the 1950s, after the introduction of reel-to-reel tape-recording technology in the late 1940s enabled the growth of a community devoted to collecting and sharing radio-program recordings.

Domestic entertainment systems were developed during a transition period in the United States when postindustrial consumer culture was redefining the relationship between home life, leisure, and popular culture. At the same time, the desire to capture and control ephemerality was a distinguishing characteristic of modern popular culture that motivated the technological development of storage media. These inventions were not conceived of nor adopted in a linear manner; rather, technologies such as the phonograph and the home projector were redesigned and experimented within an ongoing cycle of market failure and adaptation while also influencing each other in defining the home as a space for popular entertainment via mechanical devices made for the home. Home entertainment systems came to be articulated with their ability to bring public entertainment live vaudeville, spoken word, and classical music into the home through prerecorded commodities, such as discs and films, as well as the affordance for users to create their own recordings. This story of the development of technologies that capture ephemerality and of their transformation into home entertainment systems embedded within Progressive Era consumerism and White middle-class domesticity is significant to the history of bootlegging the airwaves. The very possibility to record, control, collect, and exchange popular culture recordings of previously fleeting content was realized in this era, realized and capitalized on by consumer electronic companies like RCA, who released radio sets coupled with home-recording capabilities. These sociotechnological configurations led early radio users to experiment with technologies to overcome broadcasters' control over content distribution. Chapter 2 continues this history with an overview of what would come to be known as the Old-Time Radio fan community and the formation of a coordinated alternate distribution network for bootlegging classic radio recordings.

CHAPTER 2

Hello Again

The Informal Old-Time-Radio Economy

Sal Trapani was a comic artist who got his start as an apprentice at National Periodical Publications, more commonly known as DC Comics, working under Bob Kane, the creator of Batman, before going on to work at Marvel and other comic companies.[1] Trapani's work in the comic industry led him to start attending New York comic-book conventions in the 1960s, and while there Trapani started to think that this sort of organized event would be useful for his hobby: collecting classic radio recordings. As he watched the community of radio collectors grow and expand through fanzines in the late 1960s and early 1970s, Trapani began to promote his idea to organize a convention for radio enthusiasts. In 1971 Trapani cross-published the article "Convention?" in the radio collector fanzines *Hello Again* and *Epilogue*, writing

> I should like to propose an idea that I have been toying with for several years now, and believe that this is the time and the year for it. . . . I propose "The First Annual Eastern Convention of Golden Radio Buffs" to be held in New Haven, Conn. Sometime during the month of July, consisting of a Friday—Sunday weekend, and held at one of the hotels or motor inns in the area. Rooms could be set up with antique radios for exhibition purposes, or for sale, depending on the owner. Collectors may bring recorders with them for copying. Also, blank tape would be on sale on the premises. . . . If we begin now, we will arrange for golden radio personalities to be on hand as guests and later to address us with some interesting talk on the good old days of radio. The first night would also be ideal for a cocktail hour where we may all meet and get acquainted with one another. The hotel would also be ideal for out-of-towners.[2]

Epilogue's editor George Jennings added a note under Trapani's piece: "We are reaching a stage of development in the collecting of old radio where there *should* be enough interested parties to support the convention theme."[3]

How did radio enthusiasts begin to connect through fanzines? Why did they want to organize and meet up? And what does it mean for radio to circulate in media culture as physical commodity long after its original airdate? This chapter uses the historical development of informal distribution networks for classic radio in order to reconceptualize what networked distribution is; it outlines how a many-to-many social network formed through shared interests and interpersonal dynamics, and demonstrates how social networks became informal distribution networks. Also considered here is how the desire to collect radio programs necessitated bootlegging radio programs. One of the through lines in this book is the conceit that distribution shapes interpretation, and this chapter demonstrates how the material history of circulating radio programming changed how people made sense of radio content, beginning with the story of the old-time-radio (OTR) fan community's formation with Trapani's appeal to start a convention because his appeal highlights the significance of the few radio-focused fanzines at this time and their role facilitating the expansion of an informal radio-bootlegging network. Note how Trapani suggests in his appeal that attendees could "bring recorders with them for copying" and how "blank tape would be on sale on the premises," alongside other attractions, such as stars from the golden era of radio. Radio collectors like Trapani and Jennings had good reason to organize a convention where fellow collectors could bring recording systems, blank tape would be plentiful, and a special hotel rate could encourage collectors from out of town to attend. The unmeasurable expanse of broadcast radio programming during the radio network era, considered to be with slight variance from 1926 to 1962 in the United States, led to the development of a bootlegging culture that came to rely on reciprocity. To facilitate this, radio bootleggers began to create an informal social network that grew in the late 1960s and expanded in the 1970s to foster the collaboration their hobby demanded. Radio collectors were the forerunner of the tape-trading protocols that would come to define much of television bootlegging in the 1980s.

In the 1930s, 1940s, and 1950s, people were obtaining radio program recordings; however, documentation or oral histories that provide this kind of grassroots audience research are few and far between. But after reading the wealth of radio fanzines from 1966 to the present and interviewing several collectors, my impression is that radio bootleggers and collectors were fairly isolated in the time prior to this. Radio collectors certainly connected with other audiophiles, and some formed small clubs or loose associations where they lived. However, it was not until the late 1960s that radio bootlegging became more systematically organized and structured through clubs, fanzines, and conventions. Indeed, sometimes looking through the OTR fanzine archives it seems as though almost every radio collector wrote their own article, series of articles, or handbook on how to get into the hobby, what kind of equipment and tape to use to make duplication recordings, and the proper etiquette for sharing the sound quality of their recordings or sending tapes through the mail. One example is Charles Seeley's 1978 self-published manual *The Old Time Radio Collector's Handbook*, which comprises ten chapters intended to introduce new collectors to the norms of the hobby.[4] Five of the ten chapters are explicitly about tape trading, and bootlegging and exchanging recordings are discussed in the other chapters, including the introduction, conclusion, and chapters on clubs, reference books, and publications. This guide, along with the numerous articles on sound quality, duplication practices, tape selection, or equipment troubleshooting that were published in OTR newsletters, points to the role of reciprocity in this community.[5] Due to the sheer amount of radio produced during the network era, obtaining recordings through exchange was a fundamental practice in radio bootlegging, and collectors concerned about sound quality used instructional materials to mitigate against poor sound quality in tape trading.

The archival research in this chapter is the result of reading through over nine hundred radio fanzines, along with interviews with ten radio collectors who were active during the 1970s and 1980s. I was able to access radio fanzines from the 1960s and after because a group of old-time-radio fans is still active and have done the work of preserving the history of their fan community. Table 2.1 provides an overview of the most prominent fanzines within this community published between 1966 and the present. This group calls themselves the old-time-radio researchers (OTRR), and for the most part, they are radio collectors in their fifties, sixties, and seventies who first connected at the conventions and clubs of the 1970s (discussed in the next section of this chapter). Some got into radio collecting as teenagers for a host of different reasons, including nostalgia, technical interest in audiophile culture, or just the thrill of collecting radio programs and watching their recordings stack up.[6] The OTRR, in its current configuration, grew out of a collective

Table 2.1. Old-Time-Radio Fanzines, 1967–2023

Fanzine	Years active	Publisher
Radio Dial	1967–76	Radio Historical Society of America
Hello Again	1970–2019	Jay Hickerson
Stay Tuned	1971–72	Sound Tapes of the Past
Epilogue	1971–74	George Jennings
North American Radio Archives News	1973–2003	North American Radio Archives
Radio Gram	1974–2023	Society to Preserve and Encourage Radio Drama, Variety, and Comedy
Nostalgia Digest & Radio Guide	1974–2023	Founded by Chuck Schaden, currently published by Steve Darnall
Return with US Now	1975–2015	Radio Historical Association ofColorado
Illustrated Press	1976–2023	Old Time Radio Club of Buffalo
Airwaves	1976–78	Jerry Chapman and Joe Webb
National Radio Trader	1977–79	Phil Cole
Collector's Corner	1978–82	Joe Webb and Bob Burnham

effort to use networked computing in the 1990s through Usenet, Yahoo Groups, and the Internet Archive to digitally preserve the history of their fan community. The OTRR uses these online venues, which now include Facebook, to coordinate the search for classic radio missing from popular circulation, as well as to digitize and historicize collections of classic radio recordings, radio scripts, and a variety of publications from the radio-network era. In addition to posting thousands of radio programs to the Internet Archive, this group has scanned and posted over two thousand publications ranging from the late 1960s to today.

As self-trained historians working outside the official archival institutions of broadcast history, the OTRR comprises what Abigail de Kosnik calls a "rogue archive," that is, the creation of digital platforms that have zero barriers for access and that communities use to preserve grassroots histories often neglected by traditional archives.[7] De Kosnik uses fanfiction archives as her primary case study, looking at platforms that fan authors, who may not think of themselves as archivists or historians, maintain and organize to preserve digitally born fan fiction outside of official culture industry outlets. In contrast, based on my interviews and research, members of the OTRR often do make sense of themselves as historians. The term "old-time radio" connotes pastness and history, and collecting old radio as a hobby often involves doing research to find out a program or episode's producers, cast, or airdate. However, there is a distinction between training oneself on doing historical research on the radio industries and preserving the history of the radio fan community.

Radio fans have done both, but it is the latter that most fits de Kosnik's model of a rogue archive, and it is the latter that is also least likely to be represented in the official institutions that preserve radio history. It takes labor to collect, scan, upload, and maintain all the files OTRR has digitized on their open and freely available online archive.[8]

The next section of this chapter traces out how radio collectors developed an informal network through clubs, conventions, and fanzines to collaborate with each other to obtain and exchange classic radio recordings. Following is a discussion of the controversy that arose among fans about racism and collecting the radio program *Amos 'n' Andy*, used here as a case study to consider broadcasting's shifting temporal significance once it circulates as a physical bootlegged artifact. First, however, is an outlining of how tape trading relied on a bootlegging social network that was parallel and yet was distinct from the traditional chain broadcasting of network radio distribution.

From Networked Broadcasting to Networked Bootlegging

This section redefines the term "network" as it is traditionally understood in discussions of radio-content distribution. Radio bootleggers and collectors fundamentally restructured how, when, and within what contexts broadcasting content was encountered. This relationship goes both ways, as the formation of a radio bootlegging network redefined how people accessed radio content, and bootlegging practices and networks were shaped by the uneven and various tastes, practices, and interpersonal relationships that developed within radio-collecting culture. For instance, as classic radio content was made available through OTR's informal networks, the sociopolitical context of the 1970s reshaped the meanings associated with programs like *Amos 'n' Andy* and *The Lone Ranger*. Collectors began to debate whether these programs were racist, and the transformation in the cultural meanings articulated with *Amos 'n' Andy* illustrates how the social afterlife of broadcast programming was only possible once it circulated as a bootlegged object through social networks.

In his essay "The Social Life of Things," Arjun Appadurai suggests that in order to understand the complexity of material culture and the relationship between people and the objects they value, we must trace out the social life of these objects through their "biographies" as they travel within different social "regimes of value."[9] In his discussion, Appadurai argues that studying the social life of material culture illuminates the role of taste, distinction, and the production of knowledge that "characterize the process of circulation and exchange itself."[10] The rearticulation of *Amos 'n' Andy* as a problematic racist object within old-time-radio collection culture demonstrates the social and cultural dimensions of circulation and exchange of a physical broadcast commodity.

The term "network" deserves some brief delineation here. This is because the controlling definition of this term in broadcast history has been the assemblage of technologies used in the industrial distribution practice of linking affiliate stations to a broadcaster like NBC through telephone lines. Indeed, even today, the term "radio network" in common parlance would most likely be interpreted as shorthand for a distributor such as Public Radio Exchange, National Public Radio, or iHeartRadio. In a more general sense, the word "network" is a nebulous term. It has roots in the terminology used to describe certain types of woven fabric in the eighteenth century and came to popular use with the development of railroads and telegraph lines in the nineteenth century.[11] "Network," as a topic and an idea, has been taken up across multiple disciplines and areas of research, from sociologists studying globalization to organizational communication scholars looking at interpersonal connections. At the core of most uses, the word "network" denotes the "material and symbolic flows that link people and objects both locally and globally."[12] In US broadcast history, the flow, circulation, and exchange of media programs is often associated with the one-to-many formal processes of industrial distribution referred to as "network broadcasting."

The use of "network" as a description for US radio and television broadcasters originates with what was originally called "chain broadcasting," the use of telephone wires to send radio programs from one point of origin to a set of interconnected stations across the country. AT&T was the first to experiment with chain broadcasting in 1923 and used its infrastructure of telephone and telegraph wires to distribute content from flagship station WEAF in New York to stations from Maine to Kansas. AT&T used a toll model of chain broadcasting, wherein revenue was generated from companies willing to pay for airtime in the WEAF studio.[13] RCA, General Electric, and Westinghouse quickly established a competing chain of broadcast stations in 1924, using station WJZ in Newark, New Jersey, as the flagship but found expansion limited by AT&T's unwillingness to lease the use of its wires to a competitor. In September 1926 RCA and its WJZ partners finalized an agreement to purchase WEAF and lease AT&T's telephone and telegraph wires, thereby consolidating the production of radio hardware, content, and distribution with the creation of the National Broadcasting Company (NBC). NBC went live with the WJZ and WEAF chains in November 1926, which were retitled NBC Blue and NBC Red, respectively.[14] Over the next few years, the word "network" would come to be commonly used in trade journals and the popular press to describe the commercial broadcasting company, which distributed scheduled programming to a decentralized affiliation of radio stations linked by telephone and telegraph wires.

This history demonstrates how the physical and industrial formation of radio networks in the 1920s has structured the distribution of broadcasting for almost a century. Today there is no physical linkage through phone lines; affiliate stations connect to their ownership group and their network via satellite and broadband internet providers. However, "network" is still used within the radio and television industries to reference over-the-air broadcasting free to audiences and to reference the companies that facilitate and provide this programming. The dominating power of the broadcast network is reflected in academic histories of radio and television. Almost all academic scholarship on radio and television history has exclusively focused on the initial distribution of radio and television from the perspective of the broadcast industries, dictated by scheduled flow. Henry Jenkins refers to the social network of organized fan culture as the venues audience members used to connect and create community, such as fanzines, clubs, and conventions.[15] Alessandro Jedlowski notes that informal networks are often highly organized structures, even as they fluctuate between marginal and legal.[16] Informal social networks would come to function as distribution channels for radio bootleggers.

The Development of the Informal Old-Time-Radio Network

It is difficult to pinpoint one event that inspired the development of an informal social network of radio-recording circulation. Reading through the OTRR archive of fanzines, there are a few reflections from early lone radio collectors who were bootlegging radio programming on their own, isolated from other hobbyists. Radio collectors in the 1970s described encountering *Amos 'n' Andy* recordings made with the home disc-recording machines in the late 1920s and 1930s.[17] The practice of making radio home recordings coexisted alongside the subculture of organized bootleggers who obtained transcription discs from radio workers.[18] Precisely when and how radio bootleggers began recording and sharing programs are impossible questions to answer; however, some people would later publish accounts of their entrée into radio collecting during the network era. In a letter to the editor of the OTR fanzine *NARA News*, one such collector named George Schatz reflected in 1982 on his early experiments in the 1930s making off-air recordings and notes that by the mid-1940s he had become more serious and methodical in his collecting.[19] Schatz shared his history in the OTR community as a preface to a request for help in obtaining recordings for his collection of radio programs featuring actor Ronald Colman.[20] Here was a man, Schatz, who had been recording and collecting radio for over forty years and was still trying to "fill in the gaps" of his Colman collection. Indeed, the main reason Schatz sent this letter was to ask for help finding recordings of radio programs from an extensive list he had compiled from his own research in historical radio magazines and newspapers.[21] Schatz's letter to *NARA News* reveals two significant aspects of the OTR community: its longevity and the challenges involved collecting radio content.

A few other examples of this first generation of radio bootleggers show that there were radio fans actively recording and collecting content during the network era. Jennings is another early radio bootlegger who discusses his experiences in the pages of fanzines from the 1970s. In the first issue of *Epilogue*, editor Jennings describes how, in 1959, he was introduced to the hobby of taping radio programs off the air and trading them with others by a Dallas friend active in the hobby since the early 1950s.[22] It is likely that other enthusiasts were recording radio off air, like Jennings and Schatz, using magnetic reel-to-reel tape and recording devices that became available in the mid-1940s.[23] Jay Hickerson was well-known in the OTR community because he published his fanzine *Hello Again* from 1971 to 2019. Hickerson also set about trying to document some of the early history of his hobby and in 1980 published his search for early radio traders by sharing a list of people whom he had met and who had been trading recordings since the 1950s. Hickerson struggled with the definitiveness of claiming anyone was the first, while still wrestling with his desire to create a timeline: "Who made the first mail trade? Who had the first catalog? In 1968, Hugh Carlson had [a] catalog with 700 reels. Don Brush, Ernie Hack, Ed Corcoran were some Conn.[Connecticut-based] Traders."[24] The practice of trading recordings with other radio collectors can, thus, be traced back at least to the mid-1950s, the same time that some of the earlier OTR clubs were founded.

The Radio Historical Society of America (RHSA) was founded in 1956 and was one of the first radio clubs specifically geared toward collecting recordings and treating radio programs as historical artifacts.[25] RHSA was formed as a regional group by radio enthusiasts in the Midwest who shared a love of network-era radio history and traded radio recordings with each other. The founder, Charles Ingersoll, lived in Cloquet, Minnesota; other members lived in Illinois and Wisconsin, and the membership steadily grew between 1956 and 1967 when Ingersoll began to self-publish a collaboratively authored club newsletter titled *Radio Dial*. I am reluctant to say that *Radio Dial* was the first radio collector's fanzine, but it is certainly one of the earliest and by 1970 had a membership list of over six hundred people.[26] Considering the geographically disparate nature of tape-trading enclaves in the 1960s, it is unlikely that this encompassed the entire population recording and circulating radio programs in 1970, which probably exceeded several thousand.

By 1971 there were local clubs devoted to collecting classic radio in Chicago, New York, Boston, San Francisco, Denver, and other cities around the United States. Amid this development, at least four fanzines circulating were dedicated to the hobby: *Radio Dial* (1967–76), *Hello Again* (1970–2019), *Epilogue* (1971–74), and *Stay Tuned* (1971–72). By the end of the decade, the number of fanzines would triple, and most major metropolitan areas would have at least one local OTR club and a radio show airing on a local station featuring a fan using their collection of classic radio.[27] Trapani would go on to organize the first daylong mini-conference for "golden radio buffs" on Saturday, December 4, 1971, at the Holiday Inn in downtown New Haven, Connecticut.[28] Originally called the Society of American Vintage Radio Enthusiasts or SAVE on flyers, the convention was renamed the Friends of Old Time Radio (FOTR) convention in 1976 and would be held in the tri-state area of New York, New Jersey, and Connecticut from 1971 until 2011.[29] Conventions like this are still held, for example, the Radio Enthusiasts of Puget Sound old-time-radio club just hosted their annual showcase convention from October 20 to 23, 2022, in Bellevue, Washington.[30] Their program featured live reproductions of classic-radio plays, celebrity guests from the classic radio—network era, discussion panels and interviews, the same activities proposed and organized by Trapani at the first old-time-radio enthusiasts convention in 1971.

Fanzines were an important node in the informal old-time-radio economy because they connected individual radio collectors and local clubs with classic radio fans across the country. By the mid-1980s at least nineteen fanzines focused on the hobby of collecting classic radio had been in print for some duration of time. The growth of fanzines mirrored the growth of local clubs like the Boston-based Radio Collectors of America founded in 1970, the Texas Radio Historical Society founded in 1973, the San Francisco—based North American Radio Archives and Los Angeles—based Society for the Preservation of Radio Drama, Variety, and Comedy (SPERDVAC) both formed in 1974, the Colorado Radio Historical Association in 1975, Milwaukee Area Radio Enthusiasts in 1975, and Old Time Radio Club of Buffalo (New York) in 1976. Several of these local clubs are still active today, and a few of them, like SPERD-VAC, sponsor a fanzine-like newsletter and annual convention.

Many of the local clubs, fanzines, and conventions created before 1975 were founded by people who lived through the radio-network era and were interested in this form of media because they experienced its heyday firsthand. Ingersoll, RHSA founder and publisher of *Radio Dial*, was a retired World War II veteran, and his fond nostalgic tone permeates through every page of the newsletter. Regular columns, such as "Radio Reminisces" and "Remember," were followed by articles that detailed short histories of a program or genre (like *Fibber McGee* or children's radio in the 1930s). One about the classic-radio program *One Man's Family* is in the 1970 autumn issue. Ingersoll solicited essays from members for *Radio Dial* and published classified ads for program requests, pen pals, or radio-related merchandise. Between articles and classifieds, he placed short introductions or personal announcements from members, info on other fanzines, and radio-history trivia. Some columns were specific to radio bootlegging, such as a "Creepers Corner," which warned readers about people who had a reputation for not sending agreed-upon tape trades; other columns announced newly discovered recordings of classic radio shows.

The creation of a fanzine like RHSA's *Radio Dial* in 1967 represents an important shift in the collection of broadcast recordings, as it would be a template for future OTR fanzines. Many of the fanzines that came after *Radio Dial* were collaboratively authored, and the editors often adopted a similar informal tone that addressed readers directly and published friendly updates about births, weddings, moves, and deaths within the OTR community. Some editors designed their fanzines to replicate more polished magazines, such as *Collector's Corner*, published by Joe Webb and Bob Burnham from 1978 to 1982. *Collector's Corner* always had a cover image and included photos and art through the layout. Conversely, the fanzine *Hello Again*, published by Jay Hickerson from 1970 to the present, was put together with a more openly do-it-yourself aesthetic using a typewriter and mimeograph machine until the early 1990s when he began using a word processor. The style and content varied, but most

OTR fanzines featured an opening letter from the editor(s), reader letters addressing material published in previous issues, articles submitted by subscribers on topics ranging from a review of reel-to-reel tape brands to the legality of collecting and trading radio recordings to short pieces recapping classic radio programs to sharing a specific story from radio network history. Almost all fanzines published short ads from participants looking for radio episodes or information to share their personal catalogue of programs in their collection, as well as flyers for upcoming conventions and tape-trading round-robins.

One group that used fanzines to connect and talk about collecting and bootlegging in real time was the ham-radio group the Old-Time Radio Collectors and Traders (ORCAT). The ORCATs were founded in the early 1970s, when two OTR fans who were also ham-radio enthusiasts began using ham radio to discuss old-time radio.[31] In 1973 the ORCATs included members across seven different states and met Sundays at 9 a.m. Eastern Standard Time over a ham-radio frequency.[32] By 1980 they were meeting on Sunday mornings and Thursday nights, nineteen participants across nine states and Canada, not including those listeners who may have been tuning into the meetings without participating. Ham-radio meetings created virtual meetings in real time where collectors could speak informally and immediately about how they were looking for uncirculated programs and discuss and troubleshoot technical issues, such as duplicate recording, double speeding, tape quality, and more issues related to the hobby. The ORCATs also organized a round-robin buying group, in which members would buy a recording from an OTR dealer, one not held in anyone's collection, make a copy for themselves, and then send it around to group participants to duplicate for themselves.

The ORCATs were not the only group to organize bootlegging daisy chains. RHSA offered members a round-robin trading group, as did the fanzine *Collectors Corner*, while other collectors formed lending libraries and buying groups within their local community or OTR club. These modes of tape trading emphasize the informal nature of the old-time-radio tape trading and collecting. Because commercial radio did not rely on selling program recordings during the classic network era, fans interested in collecting and listening to classic radio programs had to rely on the informal network of tape traders to obtain recordings. Fans' primary routes for collecting radio included taping programs off the air from rebroadcast programs; finding or buying transcription discs at local radio stations, secondhand shops, and other secondary markets;

Figure 2.1. Old-time-radio collectors socializing, showing off their homemade T-shirts, and buying merchandise in the dealer room at the Friends of Old Time Radio annual convention, Bridgeport, Connecticut, in October 1979. ("Busy Dealer's Room," *Collector's Corner*, February 1980, 11)

and tape trading or buying recordings from old-time-radio collectors who sold duplicates from their collection as amateur dealers.

Tape trading and amateur dealing were also facilitated by classic radio conventions like the Friends of Old Time Radio (FOTR) convention (see figure 2.1). Several other OTR conventions were organized in the 1980s, including the Cincinnati Old Time Radio Convention, held annually from 1987 through 2012, and the SPERDVAC Old Time Radio Convention, held annually in the greater Los Angeles area since 1984. These events use FOTR as their model, and OTR conventions are distinct in the way that they offer radio fans the opportunity to connect with other fans, dealers, and classic radio stars in person. While it was held, the FOTR convention typically included a room where vendors sold or traded memorabilia, zines, and recordings, as well as organized workshops on using technology or radio history, trivia games, and an evening recreation of live radio shows featuring several performers from the network era. These conventions not only functioned as significant sites for the physical circulation of radio recordings through in-person trading or networking but also for participants' identity formation as "old-radio fans" through the ability to mingle and perform their fandom in concert with others. We get a sense of this communal identity and comradery in figure 2.1 from the 1979 convention, one photograph shows an OTR fan wearing his homemade T-shirt saying, "Old Radio Lives," a tongue-in-cheek reference to the 1975 fan-authored book about the television show *Star Trek*'s fandom, *Star Trek Lives*.[33]

Radio bootleggers of the 1960s and 1970s sought out connections with other collectors because finding classic program recordings could be difficult and might also involve reformatting and fixing storage degradation.[34] Collecting classic radio recordings is distinct from other collection cultures because there was and is no official episode guide or discography to use in order to organize or assess collection efforts. Furthermore, classic network-radio era broadcasters produced thousands of programs, and there is no centralized register of existing recordings. Thus, the development of the OTR social network was driven by the mutual benefit of collaborating on researching episode guides, seeking out recordings, and trading tapes of these recordings with each other. The informal economy that arose out of OTR culture in the 1970s was uneven and fluctuating. Some participants were dismayed at what they believed were inconsistent sound-quality standards, and others reported sending their agreed-upon recordings or money and never hearing from the other person they had corresponded with about trading radio episodes.[35] However, OTR fans came to rely on this informal network both to acquire radio recordings and make sense of them.

Historical Consciousness, OTR, and Race

It is, perhaps, not a coincidence that more people became interested in bootlegging and collecting classic radio during the 1970s. This is a period in American culture that M. J. Rymsza-Pawlowska characterizes as being preoccupied with history.[36] Elizabeth Guffey notes that the word "retro" entered the popular lexicon in the 1970s to describe fashion, ideas, or objects from the past.[37] Television was full of nostalgic representations of the past, such as *Happy Days* (ABC, 1974–1984) and *Laverne & Shirley* (ABC, 1976–1983), while punk rockers and fashion designers alike incorporated elements of postwar style into their clothing. Daniel Marcus argues that the nostalgia culture of the 1970s looked back to midcentury television in order to recuperate and represent the past as an idyllic time of teenage innocence and family stability amid the shifting cultural landscape and active social movements.[38] Nostalgia for television like *Father Knows Best* and *Leave It to Beaver* in the 1970s did the cultural work of encouraging a return to romanticized America of the past, according to Marcus, before the mainstreaming of counterculture politics and the civil rights, women's liberation, and gay rights movements.[39] For Marcus, this televised nostalgia set the stage for the success of politicians like Ronald Reagan, who promised a return to this stable and morally superior time period.[40]

Building on Marcus's argument that media had come to function as a form of collective memory, I account here for broadcasting's role shaping our understanding of the past by considering how nostalgia for early and mid-twentieth-century popular culture included radio. Small-scale radio syndicators, such as Charles Michelson Inc., marketed second-run syndication programming as "old-time radio," and it generated high ratings for local stations. By 1974 Michelson's company owned the rights to twenty-six different classic radio dramas, such as *The Shadow* and *Fibber McGee*, and sold them in 385 markets.[41] Much like 1970s sitcoms *Happy Days* and *Laverne & Shirley* referenced classic 1950s sitcoms, broadcasters, such as CBS and the Mutual Broadcasting System invested in new scripted radio dramas that were imbued with pastiche based on classic radio and the cultural cache from creating a form of media no longer mainstream.[42] Mainstream-radio nostalgia was epitomized by the fact that the restaurant chain Cracker Barrel sold Cathedral radio replicas for $9.95 through the mid-1970s, perhaps the most recognizable antique-radio design from the 1930s.

Prior to this, early fanzines like *Radio Dial* rarely used the phrase "old-time radio." As the radio-collecting hobby grew in the early 1970s and incorporated more enthusiasts born in the postwar baby boom, clubs and fanzines incorporated the term "old-time radio," which syndicators like Michelson were using.[43] By the mid-1970s, OTR was the dominant term used in radio collecting, and those involved understood their hobby as one rooted in historical artifacts. For many, bootlegging and collecting radio recordings became sublimated into the larger nostalgia culture and historical consciousness of the 1970s as the programs became known not just as radio but as "old-time radio." It is no coincidence that radio entertainment came to be culturally distinguished as "old" by the 1970s, even though post–network radio was a robust part of the 1970s media landscape. Indeed, the network executives themselves had been proclaiming the "death of radio" in order to hype the emerging television industries, and this narrative came to be a part of public sentiment and academic discourse.[44] Most broadcast history textbooks cease to discuss radio after the ascendance of television. The rhetoric of technological transformation that often accompanies new media, such as television was in the 1950s, usually attempts to convey technological change as an inherent evolution that leaves old media in the past, "ignor[ing] the way the dynamics of culture bump along unevenly, dragging the familiar into novel contexts."[45] As radio collecting became the "old-time radio" community, the social biography of these recordings shifted, and they circulated as commodities with historical meaning transmitting information about the past to radio fans of the 1970s.

Acland's idea of media as residual cultural elements is useful in thinking about how bootlegging radio changed audiences' relationship and understanding of radio content. Residuality helps account for old-radio programs' continued presence in the media landscape long after their air dates, here through tape trading and collecting. Raymond Williams first introduced the idea that media engagement is a historically contingent process, wherein media go through stages of being emergent, dominant, and then residual at different points in their life cycle.[46] Building on Williams, Acland argues that residuality accounts for the way that media "effectively formed in the past . . . is still active in the cultural process, not only and often not at all as an element of the past, but as an effective element of the present."⁴⁷ The redistribution of old-radio programming through bootleg networks meant that people in the 1970s United States were listening to radio from the classic network era, cultural expressions that had, by this time, become residual media. Most broadcast histories discuss production and distribution solely at the time of a program's initial creation. Recirculating old radio through bootlegging meant that such programs such as *Amos 'n' Andy*, a minstrel radio sitcom set in Harlem and distributed by both NBC and later CBS between 1928 and 1955, whose popularity peaked in the 1930s and 1940s, would come to be listened to, understood, and debated by audiences in the post–civil rights climate of the 1970s.

OTR fans debated the cultural significance and meanings of these classic programs within the social context of 1970s American politics and historically conscious atmosphere. Listening to and collecting network-era radio in the 1970s dislodged these radio programs both from their initial conditions of production as well as their original context of reception. And, while scholars like Michele Hilmes and Melvin Patrick Ely have noted that programs like *Amos 'n' Andy* were always problematic in their representations of racial difference via minstrelsy, it is evident that OTR fans of the 1970s felt that their deliberations of OTR's racist or sexist attributes were situated in the social consciousness of this era.⁴⁸ This caused a schism within the OTR community between fans who did and fans who did not see classic programs like *The Lone Ranger*, *Amos 'n' Andy*, and *Charlie Chan* as problematic.

The discussions in the pages of OTR fanzines give us a sense of how some fans engaged in these debates. The American Indian Movement successfully lobbied local Minneapolis station KQRS to discontinue rebroadcasts of *The Lone Ranger* in 1972, arguing that its representation of the character Tonto was racist and insensitive to Native Americans. And in November 1972, *Hello Again* reprinted an editorial from OTR fan Kevin Hancer defending *The Lone Ranger*:

> The American Indian is far too sensitive about this. As a matter of fact it attacked a character who was a great exponent of racial equality. Indians were shabbily treated more often than not, especially in children's literature. The notable exception was *The Lone Ranger*. I have read over a dozen *Lone Ranger* novels, over 1,100 *Lone Ranger* comic books and all the *Lone Ranger* pulp magazines. I have seen most of *The Lone Ranger* movies and listened to over 50 shows. In all of these one fact bears out: the Lone Ranger was no racist. . . . The character of Tonto, according to the creator of the series, George Trendle, was

created despite the fact that all other Western radio heroes had white sidekicks, because he wanted to show that great men—truly great men—have no racial prejudice. . . . AIM, through ignorance and oversensitivity, has caused this harmless old show to go off the air, merely succeeding in ending the fun for those who enjoyed this nostalgic old radio program.[49]

Hancer drew on authorial intent and explicit representational readings to defend *The Lone Ranger* against racism, and his comments expose the ambivalence of negotiating racial meaning in classic radio. In his work on *Amos 'n' Andy*, Ely comments abouts its creators and performers, "If [Freeman] Gosden and [Charles] Correll's work was nothing more than a heap of racist cliches, it is hard to explain their show's unique popularity and influence among both black and white [audiences]."[50] Just as with programs in today's media landscape, problematic racial and ethnic representations are often inscribed in entertainment programs that also might be pleasurable and enjoyable to consume. *The Lone Ranger* is a media property that has continued to capture audiences' and producers' imaginations because of the way its premise builds narratives around the mythic Old West fantasy. The storytelling pleasure of old-radio shows like *The Lone Ranger* or *Amos 'n' Andy* is not a phenomenon that occurs in spite of racial othering; rather, these problematic configurations are a part of the familiarity, humor, and adventures portrayed.

Old-radio fans of the 1970s began to publicly grapple with the problematic racial representations most notably in debates about the show *Amos 'n' Andy*. OTR fan and collector David Reznick began mailing in his criticism of classic radio programs' racism in OTR fanzines in the late 1970s. Reading his work, it is clear he both was disturbed by the way fans continued to engage with shows such as *The Lone Ranger* and *Amos 'n' Andy* and felt the need to defend OTR by holding up programs he enjoyed and believed were not racist. For instance, in the June 1978 issue of *Collector's Corner*, he published a half-page column lauding *Lum 'n' Abner* as a hidden and ignored gem within the OTR canon.[51] Reznick contrasts the talent and artistry he saw in *Lum 'n' Abner* with other shows to encourage other OTR fans to see it as a replacement for programs he thought were problematic.[52] His main target in this essay and in additional critiques is *Amos 'n' Andy*. The original radio program was created, written, and voiced by White actors Gosden and Correll, who employed a sonic blackface that drew on the minstrel tradition. While employing Black caricatures that depicted laziness, simple-mindedness, and incompetence, *Amos 'n' Andy* storylines avoided explicit racial discrimination and couched these depictions in a folksy dialogue-driven mode of comedy.[53] In his 1978 essay Reznick suggests that *Amos 'n' Andy* may have been more excusable during its historical context, but even that was, in his mind, questionable:

> History has caught up with A & A [*Amos 'n' Andy*]. No matter what pleasure we derive from our associative memories, the inescapable fact is that the program is rooted in social injustice and ugliness. The nature of the show is such that Gosden and Correll, no matter what their intentions might have been, couldn't help but appear condescending and superior. A & A appeals to our baser natures. I suspect we've always known that, but in the more innocent thirties and forties, we were allowed to plead ignorance, an attitude we'd be hard pressed to sustain today.[54]

The subtext here is that while *Amos 'n' Andy* was always racist, it is harder to excuse in a historical moment when racial segregation is no longer legal, and the civil rights movement had brought the violence and torture of America's racial politics into audiences' living rooms and public consciousness.

Reznick's use of the first-person plural, "we," suggests he thought of himself as a spokesperson for the OTR community. However, his position was far from unanimous, and several fans wrote into *Collector's Corner* to defend *Amos 'n' Andy* because, they argue, it did not have overt racist intent.[55] These dynamics continued to spark discussion about *Amos 'n' Andy* among OTR fans for several years. A heated exchange occurred between Reznick and Gene Bradford when several *Amos 'n' Andy* films were shown at the 1980 FOTR convention, and the two would go onto publish passionate defenses of their position in fanzines, reminding us that fanzines were truly one of the earliest "social media" platforms for engaging in a semi-public debate within a fan community. Bradford wrote,

> I openly defy anyone to show in any way that this program [*Amos 'n' Andy*] even attempted to assume the superiority of any race or to assume the right of one race to dominate another. . . . [R]acism in itself is a very missed and misunderstood subject; taking its general use in today's society as a political ploy. The purveyors of social discourse always take license with the work "racism" to condemn anything that might be considered traditional in another time. The foolish antics of these characters [that] never attempted to show inferiority of any race of the superiority of another. This was purely "ethnic humor" and

nothing else.... The integrity of Old Time Radio is above reproach. We cannot judge yesterday's radio by today's standards or virtue or justice.... My examination of the many shows broadcast on Network Radio of the Golden Era fails to find any show that focused on race as an issue itself or assumed any superiority or dominance for any race or creed. I, therefore, find Old Time Radio not guilty of the charges of racism.[56]

This statement reveals just as much about how Bradford made sense of himself through his identity as an OTR fan as it reveals how some fans negotiated their own participation within the hobby and showed a disdain for the critical discussion of racial politics that had come to be a part of mainstream discourse by 1980. This argument is also contradictory: one cannot argue that something is "not guilty" of racism and simultaneously tell people to remember they were made in a different time. If these programs were not problematic, there would be no need to historically contextualize their representations.

A year and a half later, Reznick published a longer and more detailed essay, "Racism and OTR," to expand his criticism of racism in the OTR fan community writ large beyond *Amos 'n' Andy*. He extensively critiqued what he saw as problematic representations of race and ethnicity on programs that included *The Jack Benny Show*, *Duffy's Tavern*, *Charlie Chan*, and *Life with Luigi*, among others. Reznick also used this essay to pointedly criticize fans of these shows:

I'd have to question the intelligence or sincerity of anyone who claims they can't see the harm done by *A&A*. They should have known then, but there is no possible excuse for not knowing it now.... During a time when, it seems to me, we are entering a frightening new era of reaction and intolerance, it seems valuable to examine these records of the past with an eye how they might help us cope with the future.[57]

As one may imagine, Reznick's entreaty to fellow OTR fans here did not inspire everyone to reflexively rethink their engagement with *Amos 'n' Andy* or other programs that relied on humor that implicitly drew on racial othering.

Indeed, this essay received contentious and reactionary response from fellow fans, the most vitriolic from a fan named George Wagner. Wagner's reply was notably longer than Reznick's two-page article and was vehemently self-righteous. He begins,

It has taken me nearly a year since reading Dave Reznick's "Racism and OTR" to calm down enough to reply to it. It is not my intention

Figure 2.2. The debate over representation and racism in the Old Time Radio community taking center stage in the cover illustration of *Collector's Corner* fan newsletter in the summer of 1981. ("Racism and OTR," *Collector's Corner*, Summer 1981, cover)

to defend classic radio against any of the charges made by Mr. Reznick. Rather, I am going to champion OTR. Oh Lord, am I ever going to champion it! Radio programming of the 1930s, 1940s, and 1950s, probably more than any other media, worked almost ceaselessly to eliminate racism from the American social conscience. Millions of Americans who had never known human beings of another race, or even of another religion, came to both appreciate and respect them through radio. People who had never met either a Jew or a Black fell in love with Jack Benny and Rochester. We will never know how many potential "American" Nazis were drawn back into the human race because of the magic of *The Goldbergs*.[58]

Wagner goes on to argue that *The Jack Benny Show*, *Amos 'n' Andy*, and *The Goldbergs*, among others, brought non-White characters into mainstream American culture. He then responds defensively to Reznick's statement questioning the intelligence of anyone who failed to see the harm done by *Amos 'n' Andy*:

Well, golly gee, Mr. Reznick, by your standards I must be both helplessly mentally retarded and shamelessly dishonest, for I can only see the tremendous good done by Amos n Andy. What Mr. Reznick saw as harm I see as exquisite beauty and I treasure it as I treasure little else in this usually imperfect world. . . . Mr. Reznick opened a very ugly can of worms, that of reverse racism. There is a widely-held convention today—a view, largely limited to Whites, which I find fraught with danger for a free society—that states that while Blacks are free to play White roles, Whites are never permitted to play Black ones. . . . To rule, as Mr. Reznick seems to, that Whites cannot play Black or Chinese roles, is as offensive to me as ruling that James Earl Jones can no longer play Macbeth. . . . Such reasoning would also rob the theater of Sir Laurence Olivier's version of Othello.[59]

Wagner's response is significant for two reasons. First, it demonstrates the passionate affective relationship some fans had with the programs they collected and listened to, programs that at this time were almost sixty years old. Second, reading this letter makes it difficult to dismiss Wagner as simply an uncritical dupe in his regard for *Amos 'n' Andy* or *Charlie Chan*. His response demonstrates the polysemic nature of classic radio, even in its residual circulation during the 1970s and early 1980s. Fans like Bradford and Wagner made sense of their appreciation for *Amos 'n' Andy* in the 1970s by pointing to the lack of explicit racism in the show. Unmentioned in these debates is the fact that *Amos 'n' Andy* was one of the few radio shows to present any form of Blackness during the classic network era, and collectors like Bradford and Wagner interpreted their own collection and engagement with *Amos 'n' Andy* as a form of appreciation for Black culture and a tool in the fight against prejudice. It is also impossible to ignore the fact that these debates occurred, at least publicly, in a fan community that is very White and, for that matter, very male when looking at photos from FOTR and other conventions in the archives. It is impossible to say with certainty the racial and ethnic identities of these specific participants. And looking through the letters and photos published in OTR fanzines of the 1970s, it is clear that women participated in the OTR community. Nevertheless, the OTR fandom was a very White and implicitly masculine culture, and this certainly informed the discussion of race and programs like *Amos 'n' Andy* in the post–civil rights era.

These debates demonstrate the complicated relationship between some OTR fans and the shows they collected. The debates are not representative of all OTR fans during this time yet are examples of how some OTR fans created new meanings and modes of interpreting these programs during the time that they became designated as "old-time radio." While discussions of race occurred during the initial run of many of these programs, the interpretational work of classic collectors in the 1970s was distinct because, as residual media, fans made sense of old radio as historical artifacts. The desire by fans to critique or defend OTR programs was shaped by the postwar political movements, and I see Wagner's reactionary defense of racial representations in classic radio as one suffused with the White male grievance backlash discourse increasingly popularized by conservative media in the 1970s.[60] In this sense, then, we should understand OTR fans as temporal travelers who encountered the residual radio programs from the past historically from their standpoint in the 1970s.

This chapter has outlined how radio fans developed an informal bootleg economy through clubs, fanzines, and conferences. OTR fans' labor finding, reformatting, and circulating bootlegged recordings of classic network-era radio preserved these programs and made them accessible both to collectors in this network and to radio listeners who tuned into local classic radio shows that many collectors hosted in their hometowns using their personal library of recordings. During the 1970s radio collecting came to be defined as an endeavor connected to the past and understood as "old-time radio." OTR fans not only participated in the continued circulation of network-era radio but also redefined its cultural meanings as "old time radio" as they debated the social significance of classic radio in the 1970s and beyond. This history outlines how the informal circulation of broadcasting is always already embedded within cultural ideologies and how cultural understanding of radio programming's meaning is never fixed but, rather, is contingent upon the material, social, and temporal context of its distribution. The role of informal networks in the circulation of broadcast recordings and the way these practices shape and are shaped by technocultural and social context are further explored in chapter 3's case study of buddy-cop television and female fans in the 1980s.

CHAPTER 3

Freeze-Framing Queerness
Tape Trading in Buddy-Cop Fan Cultures

In the May 1980 issue of the letterzine *S and H*,[1] devoted to the television series *Starsky & Hutch* (ABC, 1975–79), regular contributor Cheryl Rice ended her letter with the following note, and the editors, Diana Barbour and Kendra Hunter responded:

> I've been wondering how often other people [who] have the shows on tape actually watch them. (*Ed. note: Well, to date, we have worn out SWEET REVENGE, STARSKY VS. HUTCH, and DAVID SOUL AND FRIENDS from 1977*). I would guess it depends on how many episodes a person has. Personally, I get almost a miser's delight in simply knowing they're over there on the shelf. Tho occasionally I go on binges—3 or 4 episodes at a time. How about other people? Once a day? Once a week? (*Ed note: We feel like we're being tested for some new sex survey or something?*)[2]

This excerpt exemplifies how female pleasure became articulated with videotape trading and collecting in fan communities dedicated to US buddy-cop television shows, like *Starsky & Hutch*, in the 1970s and 1980s. Rice describes her satisfaction in being able to use her videotapes to rewatch *Starsky & Hutch* episodes, as well as her "miser's delight" in the knowledge that she possesses these television recordings. This passage is also significant because it highlights the call-and-response dialogue between fanzine participants with each other and the zine editors. Zines were precursors to contemporary online discussion sites and functioned as forums for subscribers to converse back and forth with each other on discussion topics. The letter above with the editors' playful responses highlights the collaborative and participatory nature of television fan cultures in the 1980s. This exchange between Rice and the *S and H* editors about bingeing episodes and wearing out tapes also hints at the ways replay culture already existed in television fandoms by 1980.

S and H was a monthly letterzine that was founded in 1979, the last year *Starsky & Hutch* was produced by Spelling-Goldberg Productions and the end of its initial broadcast run on ABC. *S and H* would be published through 1983 and was the forerunner of a host of *Starsky & Hutch* letterzines, fan fic anthologies and zines, fan videos (vids), conventions, and online forums that persist through to today and are part of a larger community of fans invested in buddy-cop shows. Fandom surrounding *Starsky & Hutch* and other 1980s buddy-cop shows like *Simon & Simon* (CBS, 1981–89) and *Miami Vice* (NBC, 1984–90) have comprised a significant fan community since the late 1970s. Francesca Coppa has mentioned the female buddy-cop show *Cagney & Lacey* (1981–88) in passing as a television show that received fan attention in the 1980s, but the preponderance of buddy-cop materials found in the fanzine archives led me to focus this chapter on *Starsky & Hutch*, *Simon & Simon*, and *Miami Vice* for several reasons.[3] *Starsky & Hutch* was not the first television program to feature a crime-solving duo; however, it was important in that it forged a model of a successful police drama that focused on the relationship between two male detectives that would be copied in the 1980s by the producers of *Simon & Simon* and *Miami Vice*, among others. Michael Mann, *Miami Vice*'s showrunner, got his start in television writing episodes for *Starsky & Hutch*. And, while police dramas have been written about in media studies, most media fan scholarship has tended to examine science-fiction and fantasy media culture.[4] This chapter broadens understanding of fan cultures by charting out the role of informal tape trading in a female-centered interpretive community centered on male buddy-cop duos in television. The informal distribution of television recordings was central to the female-centered fan cultures that were formed in the late 1970s and grew throughout the 1980s. This chapter focuses on the history of that formative period, first by providing an overview of the emergence of tape trading in television fandoms. This is followed by an outline of the role of tape recording in buddy-cop fan communities and the relationship among tape trading, rewatching, and making sense of a television show's meaning. This chapter ends by considering how the informal distribution of *Starsky & Hutch* television episodes on videotape made debates about queer meaning possible.

Tape Trading and Television

By the late 1970s thousands of television viewers were experimenting with videotape-recording equipment to capture television programming for time-shifting and collecting, and for many participants in TV fan communities, recordings, especially high-quality, first-generation recordings, were integral. Prior to the dominance of the VCR, videotape recording was often abbreviated as VTR in the 1960s, 1970s, and early 1980s. In his book about the history of video stores, Joshua M. Greenberg describes a community of early video enthusiasts (who he acknowledges were almost exclusively male) and the way they developed a community of videophiles who used video recordings to trade and build television program collections.[5] This current chapter expands our understanding of video enthusiasts and tape-trading networks by offering an alternative story about the history of bootlegging television that is centered on women, demonstrating the longer historical formation of uneven and multivarious tape-trading networks that engaged with television content.

VTR technology offered a new means of engaging with broadcasting content that built on the longer practice of using storage technologies to capture, trade, and collect broadcast programs. Indeed, several members of the OTR community examined in chapter 2 were already engaged in television taping in the early 1970s. George Jennings, editor of the OTR fanzine *Epilogue*, wrote an essay in 1970 titled "VTR: A Glimpse of Things to Come." Jennings discusses his use of the Sony CV2000, Sony's first consumer videorecorder, released in 1965, and how he used it to tape one show while watching another and record footage for his burgeoning collection.[6] Jennings also discusses his connection with a few other OTR collectors who had shifted to focus on television tape trading, such as a friend named Jim, whom Jennings describes as having "more or less phased away from audio filing in the past year, putting almost his full attention in television. His home is one big video catalogue with reels stretching across various walls. If there ever will be a developed hobby surrounding TV, Jim is certainly at the forefront."[7] In the same article, Jennings muses, "Who's to say that a collection of *Star Trek* or *Mission Impossible*, carefully kept intact into the far future might not be just as validly worthy of reminiscence as our own files [radio recordings] are today?" He ends his essay by reporting that Sony and Panasonic were announcing the widespread release of color VTR consumer electronics by 1972.[8] While this would not come to pass precisely on Jennings's predicted schedule, his musing about the desire to collect *Star Trek* episodes seems especially prescient. He wrote this essay within a year of the 1970 cancellation of *Star Trek: The Original Series* and would likely have been aware of its following and cult popularity.

Star Trek fans were already using audio home-recording technology in the late 1960s to tape, share, and collect television episodes. Indeed, Dana L. Friese, editor of the early *Star Trek* fanzine, *Vulcanalia*, advised readers during the middle of the program's first season to contact the fanzine's treasurer, Elyse Pines, if they wanted taped episodes in 1967.[9] *Star Trek* fans used fanzines to crowdsource audiotapes of TV episodes the same way that OTR fans did in the late 1960s. In another early *Star Trek* fanzine, *Plak-Tow*, contributor Shirley Meech wrote:

> I tape record *Star Trek*. I lack some of last season's shows, and am also looking for tapes of some of the appearances of ST stars on other TV shows (particularly Leonard Nimoy's second Pat Boone Show in Nov., and the Joey Bishop Show in April). Anybody want to trade tapes for ST color pictures, or for other tapes? Also, I understand some ST fans are interested in corresponding by tape or in starting tape round robins. If you'd like to do this, let me know and I'll put you in touch with the others.[10]

It is evident that the use of home-recording equipment to create and circulate television predates the emergence of the VCR or even videotape and that television tape trading was a key part of media fandoms devoted to specific television programs and genres, like *Star Trek* or, later, *Miami Vice*. It is also telling that in these examples from early *Star Trek* fanzines, we see some of the same participatory activities that radio traders engaged in, such as crowdsourcing episodes and forging round-robins to circulate recordings. And, like OTR collectors, television fan communities used fanzines, conventions, and local clubs to create informal networks for circulating bootlegged television recordings throughout the 1970s. Most media fandoms, from science fiction to anime, classic television, soap operas, and wrestling, incorporated tape trading as a key practice within their communities. Tape trading was imperative to anyone who wanted to write fan fiction or stay up-to-date on serial narratives or wrestling-match details, not to mention access content from other regions or time periods.

The centrality of tape trading to media fandom is, perhaps, epitomized by the emergence of the video room as a mainstay of media-fan conventions. In studying fanzines and other fan publications and forums from the late 1960s through the 2000s, it is evident that media-convention dubbing parties in video rooms were a mainstay in media fandom and central in circulating television in the 1980s and after. The earliest record of the video room I have found is in the planning report for the 1981 World Science Fiction Convention in Denver.[11] The *Starsky & Hutch* fan convention Zebracon also had a video room set up that would screen program episodes and a bulletin board for those who brought a VTR machine with them to connect with one another in order to duplicate episodes from each other's collections.[12] The annual Media West Convention in Lansing, Michigan, not only published a schedule of film and television viewings in its 1986 program but also made video decks available for participants to use.[13] Video rooms were a staple of media conventions at least through the early 2000s, as evident in the program for the 2003 Media West Convention, which offered both a room for fanvids and a main room for video screening.[14] I begin the next section describing how letterzines and conventions became opportunities for duplicating and trading television show episodes to better situate the broader technosocial practices within which buddy-cop TV show fans participated.

Female Fans, Buddy-Cop Shows, and Tape-Trading Culture

In the summer of 1979 Diana Barbour began the bimonthly *Starsky & Hutch* letterzine *S and H*, just after the ABC show ended its fourth, and final, season. Barbour had been a member of science-fiction fan communities as a teenager, first collecting Edgar Rice Burroughs books and then getting into *Star Trek: The Original Series* (*TOS*) fandom at the San Francisco Bay Area science-fiction and fantasy convention Baycon in 1968.[15] *S and H* was founded during a period when *Starsky & Hutch* fan fiction and art began to be published and circulated in anthologies like *Me & Thee*, and Barbour used the letterzine model from science-fiction fan communities she participated in to create an opportunity for *Starsky & Hutch* fans to share "letters, reviews, columns, artwork and S&H related material available for sale or trade."[16] Barbour's good friend and *Starsky & Hutch* vid collaborator, Kendra Hunter, would come on board as a coeditor in issue 2. In founding *S and H*, Barbour and Hunter played a significant role in establishing one of the first television-focused fan communities devoted to buddy-cop television.

Letterzines were one important node in the informal circulation of buddy-cop television episodes. Between 1979 and 1991, at least ten letterzines related to buddy-cop TV were started. Table 3.1, while not

Table 3.1. Buddy-Cop Letterzines, 1980s and 1990s

Television series	Letterzine	Years published
Starsky & Hutch	S and H	1979–83
	APB (UK)	1981–85
	Hanky Panky	1982–86
	Between Friends	1984–85
	Frienz	1988–98
Miami Vice	Vice Line	1985
	This Guy I Gotta Wait For (UK)	1985–89
	Bernay's Café	Unknown
Simon & Simon	Details at 11	1983–87
	Simon & Simon Investigations	1986–91
	Brothers, Partners, and Friends	1991–95

comprehensive, highlights some of the most well-known and longer-running zines available in media fanzine archives at the University of Iowa Special Collections and Texas A&M Cushing Memorial Library and Archives. The bulk of most letterzines is devoted to contributors' letters discussing, debating, and posing questions about canonical meaning and fan practices; sharing news; and responding to letters in previous issues. Most of the material discussed in this chapter comes from these letters, as many regular contributors disclosed their use of videotapes and the significance of this circulation to their engagement with television. Additionally, most buddy-cop fan letterzines also reserved a section at the end of their issues for advertising available or sought-after memorabilia. For example, *S and H*'s inaugural issue established Wants and Warrants, where participants could share announcements for *Starsky & Hutch* related items, such as selling printed photographs of the main actors, David Soul (Hutch) and Paul Michael Glaser (Starsky), or request and offer videotapes of television episodes, facilitating specific and targeted videotape trading (see figures 3.1 and 3.2).

Conventions have been another central aspect within the buddy-cop fandom's informal bootlegging culture. *S and H*'s debut issue has an announcement about ZebraCon 1979, the first convention devoted to *Starsky & Hutch* fandom. Zebra 3 was the call sign for Starsky and Hutch's bright-red Ford Gran Torino with a white stripe, and the name ZebraCon was a nod to the convention's origins as a *Starsky & Hutch* event, although it would eventually include other cop, private-detective, and spy-partner media. ZebraCon was an annual convention from 1979 until 2007, held in Kalamazoo, Michigan, the first year and in Chicago from 1981 onward. ZebraCon functioned as a place for buddy-cop tele-

```
WANTED:
     Mint condition VHS, Pal Secam Video tapes
     of MV episodes--GLADES and HIT LIST. Let
     me know what payment you'll accept!
     Desperate!  Write to: Linda J.Merryweather.

SALE:
     Starsky & Hutch collection, at very
     reasonale prices. Send Large SAE for ten-
     page list or state specific wants.
     Write to: Linda J.Merryweather.
```

ads, part 1

Video Co-op: Ann Teitelbaum (as if she weren't busy enough) is organizing a video co-op. Fans will contribute and/or buy tapes of their favorite series' "greatest hits". Each series will have one tape in the co-op with 6 or 7 of the best or most well-known episodes. So far, I've done S&S and ST, and will be adding ST:TNG, AN, UNCLE, Perf. Strangers, S&H, and more. SASE for details on adding your favorite show, or requesting one of the above.

Figures 3.1 and 3.2. Classified posts in letterzines requesting and offering to trade video recordings of buddy-cop shows. ("Wanted, This Guy I Gotta Wait For," April 1986, box 1, Bea Schmidt Fanzine Collection; "Ads, Part 1," Simon & Simon Investigations, August 1990, 4, box 113, Ming Wathne Fanzine Collection, both University of Iowa Special Collections)

vision fans to meet up with tapes and recording technology and "clone" episodes with each other, the term these fans would come to use for duplicating recordings at the convention or other smaller local get-togethers. After the first ZebraCon, several fans wrote into *S and H* to describe small, local "mini-cons" they organized to watch and share episode videotapes, including a group of *Starsky & Hutch* fans in Australia.[17] Buddy-cop television shows also became a mainstay of larger media-fan conventions, like Media West. Fans often brought their own VCR equipment with them for the main purpose of tape trading. One fan in 1995 announced in the *Starsky & Hutch* letterzine *Frienz*, "I may or may not make MediaWest. . . . I still hope I can do it though. If I can't make it, that will redesign the S&H room party, as I was bringing the VCR. All I can do at this point is hope for the best."[18] Here, then, we see how letterzines were intertwined with conventions, as a site for fans to discuss and crowdsource television recordings, as well as a forum to discuss and plan large-scale in-person events that also made tape trading possible.

Circulating bootlegged television recordings was also instrumental to other fan practices, such as fan art, fan fiction, and fan video productions. "Vidding" is the fan practice of editing together scenes and images from the canonical source text, such as *Starsky & Hutch*, in tandem with music, often a well-known pop song, to fashion a video that intentionally uses a song to comment on or reconfigure a relationship or message from the source text within a fan's specific artistic and narrative storytelling goals. Longtime media fan Morgan Dawn has done a lot of work to preserve the history of fan communities from the 1970s to the present, and my research relied on some of the fanzines she donated to the University of Iowa Special Collections. In her essay "A History of Vidding," Dawn notes that "the creation of fanvids required two things: access to consumer-level audio-visual equipment and the average fan's ability to obtain TV/movie video source."[19] Being able to duplicate television episodes at conventions was significant for fans, not only to study for any art they might create or fan fiction they might write but also as the literal source material they used to make vids. Indeed, video recordings were integral to the pleasure fans got making and sharing vids, and high-quality, first-generation recordings were especially sought after by vidders. The fanzine *Rainbow Noise*, named after the discolored dead space often in between vids on VHS tapes, was a publication that included video tapes with a subscription and encouraged readers to add their own vids to the end of the compilation and continue circulating the tape in the fandom.[20] Because this zine was specifically focused on vidding, tape trading, VCR reviews, and dubbing techniques were discussed at length in its pages. Tape trading was such a fixture in television fandom that by the mid-1990s, when Dawn first became involved in active fandom, it was common practice for fans to bring their own VCRs, blank tapes, and episode collections to conventions, making hotels into fan sources for television redistribution.[21]

Barbour brought the techniques being used across media fandoms through the 1970s to create an informal network of *Starsky & Hutch* fans who could use conventions and letterzines to connect with each other; however, this would grow beyond *Starsky & Hutch* to other buddy-cop television shows. Undoubtedly, Barbour and others in the buddy-cop fan community were already *Star Trek* fans prior to helping form the *Starsky & Hutch* fan community. There are some parallels in the appeal of a narrative pairing of two Starfleet military officers like Capt. James T. Kirk

Figure 3.3. *Miami Vice—Starsky & Hutch* crossover fan art by Maureen Burns. (Maureen Burns, *Between Friends*, September 1985, 46, Sandy Hereld Fanzine Collection, Texas A&M Cushing Memorial Library and Archives)

and his second in command Spock and the premise of most buddy-cop shows like *Starsky & Hutch*. However, going through fanzines devoted to buddy-cop TV shows specifically, I observed crossover between fans of *Starsky & Hutch* and later buddy-cop shows of the 1980s like *Simon & Simon* and *Miami Vice*. For instance, fan art, such as figure 3.3, blended the worlds of *Starsky & Hutch* together with *Miami Vice*. The cartoon features the two main characters from *Miami Vice*, Crockett and Tubbs, drawn reading a newspaper article about Starsky and Hutch busting a cocaine drug ring with the dialogue bubble, "I thought those guys were retired?" demonstrating how fans themselves understood these programs as generically related. Indeed, the September 1985 *Starsky & Hutch* fanzine *Between Friends* carried a classified announcement from Sandra Ferriday soliciting participants and subscribers for her *Miami Vice* fanzine *This Guy I Gotta Wait For*, a British publication.[22] Attendees of a 1985 *Starsky & Hutch* convention reported screening the season 2 premiere episode of *Miami Vice*, "Prodigal Son," because it had been directed by

Freeze-Framing Queerness   87

Glaser.[23] Fan Regenia Marracino shared with the editors of *Between Friends* that their *Starsky & Hutch* letterzine "comes at a good time . . . at a time when I'm finding myself captivated by S&H's sibling MV . . . and I find I would rather pursue that and *Simon and Simon*."[24] After the fanzine *S and H* debuted in 1979, it created a place for a fan community invested in the pleasures of male crime-solving duos on television that would grow and connect across future similar television shows using a host of letterzines, clubs, and conventions.

Starsky & Hutch, *Simon & Simon*, and *Miami Vice* all had diegetic worlds built around the lives of male protagonists. The masculine configurations of these texts have been the focus of most of the television criticism written about *Starsky & Hutch*, *Simon & Simon*, and *Miami Vice*.[25] Studying the early development of buddy-cop fandom allows us to understand how these shows were a part of feminine popular culture. It was not uncommon for letter contributors to these letterzines to disclose biographical details in order to take advantage of them as forum to connect and get to know other fans personally beyond their identity as buddy-cop television fans. In one letter in the May 1980 *S and H*, contributor Signe Landon shared her thoughts about other participants' analyses of *Starsky & Hutch*, her love of the new detective show *Tenspeed & Brownshoe*, and her gratitude for her VCR. In the middle of her letter, Signe takes a paragraph to share personal information: "Let's see, biographical info: I'm 23, female (aren't we all?), 5' 7.5", 140 lbs." She goes on with other details about herself, but this aside, "aren't we all," is telling.[26] This information is not described to flatten this fan community into a one-dimensional category of "woman," and indeed, it is noteworthy that not all participants identified as women. For instance, one male-identifying fan offered this assistance in the *Simon & Simon Investigations* letterzine:

> S/S WRITERS: want to do research, but are too embarrassed to go into your local gay video store to rent a movie, or have no local outlet? I have three gay porno movies cloned on a single tape which I will clone for a flat fee of $10 (postage included). Titles include "Brothers Should Do It," "First Times" (be forewarned, this segment is in bad condition), and "Strange Places, Strange Things." XXX rated hard core gay porno films. Age statement required, domestic mailings only. (Complete confidentiality maintained.)[27]

While this advertisement demonstrates the participation of fans who presented themselves as male, it reinforces the discursive formation of a cisgender, straight, and implicitly female community in the way that this author addresses readers, acknowledging the assumption in the 1980s that most slash fan-fiction writers were straight women. Indeed, Henry Jenkins notes how female fans appropriated male-centered stories to fit their own desires by reworking narratives through slash fan fiction.[28] It is significant, then, that looking at fan cultures centered around these programs allows us to understand the role of women and feminine pleasure for audiences who traded shows whose narratives were centered around masculinity in the 1980s.

Buddy-cop fandom was articulated with female pleasure from the inception of letterzines like *S and H* and persisted as the community grew through the 1980s. One fan explained in 1989 the pleasure she derived from what she described as the "smarm" of the partner relationship in buddy-cop shows:

> Whoa! . . . I think I love you! A S&H letterzine is just what I need! . . . You get it, frienz, *Starsky & Hutch*! I remembered that I adored the show the first time it was on, but it wasn't until I got some copies of the episodes that I realized just how much! . . . Reading over the letters from issue #1 it looks like I've fallen into a batch of kindred souls. . . . Ohboyohboy [sic] do I love a good smarmy story. Let's face it, there has been a lot of "buddy series" on TV, and a lot of them had the potential for an enormous amount of smarm, am I right? *Simon & Simon*, for example, or even the perennial favorite, *Star Trek*. Sure, we see great relationships between the characters but how much of that openness—that wonderful caring—do we really see? Zilch. And after all, isn't that what zines are for? We've built the relationships we want for these people, oftentimes from scratch. . . . Not that we've ever let that stop us, right ladies? But now, finally, we can see the caring and love between the characters. And—my goodness!—the hurt/comfort too! I mean actually see it instead of having to fill in the blanks later. Watched *Miami Vice* lately? Those cheaters take us right up to the brink of a smarmy scene and go to a commercial. The finks. But *Starsky & Hutch* not only carried it through, they carried us through, bless 'em. And yes, I am looking for every zine and episode in existence on the show. I've hung all my other fandoms out to dry 'till then.[29]

"Smarmy" is a term in fandom that originated in the buddy-cop fan community to describe canon or fan fiction where two characters are emotionally expressive, warm, and caring with each other. Smarm became a way for fans to account for storylines not engaged with explicit sexual content but, rather, love between friends.[30] This participant reinforces the female-centric understandings of this fan community as she compares the pleasures of smarm across *Starsky & Hutch*, *Simon & Simon*, and *Miami Vice* with her callout, "right ladies?" However, the disclosure of female pleasure in this letter is also clearly tied to the circulation of television episodes via tape trading. As this letter writer describes, she took more pleasure in being able to "see" the smarm in the taped episodes rather than having to "fill in the blanks" through textual poaching.[31] Indeed, studying the fanzines from this period paints a picture of buddy-cop television fandom that not only depended on an informal economy of tape trading but also found pleasure in videotape culture itself.

Buddy-cop television fans often discussed their use of videotape recording technologies and participation in tape-trading culture through cartoons, poems, and letters celebrating videotape culture.[32] Hunter published her own comic panel featuring a drawing of the television replaying *Starsky & Hutch* hooked up to a VTR machine (see figure 3.4), with this dialogue exchange in the caption: "Hey Kendra, where's your furniture?" "Who cares, I've got Diana's VTR and ALL the tapes!!!!!!!" (original emphasis). This humorous exchange about the value of cloning *Starsky & Hutch* episodes over furniture highlights the centrality of tape trading to this fandom. And indeed, fans' affective relationship with the video recording technology is a reoccurring theme among the buddy-cop fanzines from the 1980s and 1990s. One *Simon & Simon* fan in the letterzine *Simon and Simon Investigations* shared her anguish about her VCR breaking down,

> Remember my niece, the one who just got Simonized? The one who sits up all night watching my tapes as I sleep, so that I was worried that she'd wear the machines and/or the tapes out? Well, I got home from work yesterday to find a tape stuck in my machine. Not just any tape mind you, but a tape of all the new S&S episodes I'd just cloned and hadn't watched that closely yet. GAH! Dead niece! Sick VCR! . . . AAAARGH! I'd put an ill VCR and a stuck tape right up there with a major death in the family." [*The editor interjects*] "A double tragedy, what with the untimely death of your niece, and all."[33]

The letter writer's relationship with her VCR is conveyed as an emotional bond, akin to the familial relationship with her niece, while also being the mode of inducting family and friends into the fan community through videotape viewing exchanges.

Reading letters from these women describing their attachment to their video recording machines betrays the subtext that these women felt con-

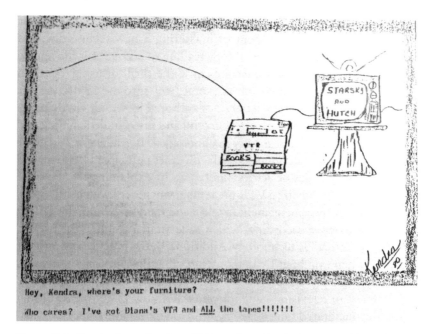

Figure 3.4. Comic drawn for S and H by editor Kendra Hunter self-mocking her obsession recording and rewatching Starsky & Hutch episodes. (Kendra Hunter, S and H, April 1980, 48, box 67, Morgan Dawn Fanzine Collection, University of Iowa Special Collections)

fident and possessive of this new form of technology. In her book *Video Playtime*, Ann Gray did interviews and ethnography with a sample of women and their families to understand how the VCR functioned as a domestic technology. Gray found that even though her study participants might have trained themselves on how to operate the VCR, she argued that this technology has a discursive masculine construct before ever entering the house, as "VCRs were marketed from the outset as hi-tech equipment which had to be mastered, thereby apparently addressing the male consumer."[34] In Gray's study, it was mainly the husbands who used the VCR for recording as hobbyists, as she observed the domestic nature of VCR use reflected the gendered division of labor in the home. For Gray the women she observed often felt a need to be working when in the home and reserve domestic technology for domestic chores while also possessing an internalized belief that the VCR technology was not for them.[35] Greenberg's depiction of the videophile community in his history of the VCR is of a community that was "overwhelmingly male"

Freeze-Framing Queerness   91

and one that, he argues, declined in the mid-1980s once the VCR was mainstream and the excitement of mastering a new technology was gone.[36] Broadening the history of tape trading to account for the female buddy-cop community demonstrates how the thrill of using VCRs to bootleg television continued, among some, well into the 1990s.

Indeed, close study of the letterzines authored by female participants of buddy-cop fanzines reveals a resourceful and savvy understanding and comfort with videotape recording technology. Kay Anderson, a regular contributor to *S and H*, commiserated with other participants who missed out on taping episodes or actors' interviews by explaining that "sort of thing has led me to having a VTR on, taping, whenever I watch TV."[37] For these women, active engagement in television fandom would, thus, often translate into active recording, which necessitated training themselves to deftly operate VTR technology. Additionally, the practice of constant recording when watching TV demonstrates that this fan community was intimately cognizant of television's ephemerality.

Awareness of television's ephemerality and how videotape recording technology facilitated fan engagement is evident in tape traders' discussions. One *Simon & Simon* fan commented in 1987,

> If you're wondering why a woman who is obviously such an, ahem, intelligent person has taken all this time to get into S&S fandom, blame it on the network! No, seriously, because of my work schedule, I was never able to watch the show BVCR (before VCR). I just got my VCR in September and so now, no matter how often CBS hopscotches S&S all over the schedule, I can keep up with the guys![38]

Indeed, 1980s television fans understood network scheduling and industrial practices like syndication. Ferriday actively wrote to BBC executives, demanding an explanation for their decision to stop syndicating *Miami Vice* in 1987. Ferriday would go on to publish her own poem of protest against their embargo of the show in her zine (see figure 3.5), a poem that would also pay tribute to her "video machine" because "it fills the gap" created by the BBC's blackout of new *Miami Vice* episodes.[39] Fans were invested in understanding how television-station scheduling and syndication worked because this was, for the most part, the most efficient way to record and collect program episodes. Transnational fans, particularly, depended on syndication to record television shows like *Miami Vice* for their own collections, and it is evident from *This Guy I Gotta Wait For* and other letterzines that fans in the United Kingdom

— Protest —

The BBC are a strange lot
who mess us about with Miami Vice
unlike NBC who haven't forgot
to give the Americans something nice!

The Brits have been told many times
different things like nursery rhymes
we've been without Vice since last July
a never-ending question
"why, oh why?"

The video machine, it's very useful
to see Sonny
Castillo and Rico
it fills the gap of that awful Lull
which gives us all
an everlasting glow!

by Sandra J. Ferriday, 1987 ©

Figure 3.5. Fan and zine editor Sandra Ferriday's poem protesting the BBC's suspension of *Miami Vice* episodes in 1987. (Sandra Ferriday, "Protest," *This Guy I Gotta Wait For*, May, 1987, 17, box 1, Bea Schmidt Fanzine Collection, University of Iowa Special Collections)

and Australia would circulate their tapes with friends and acquaintances and bring them into the buddy-cop genre fan community.

Tape trading and collecting were not practiced by all fans of the buddy-cop genre but were integral for the pleasure fans found in replaying episodes. Replaying recorded episodes was such a meaningful experience for fans, some would dupe their collection onto audiocassette so that they could listen to the episodes while traveling. One fan recommended this:

> Here's an idea to help make those long plane, train or automobile trips seem shorter: audio tape your favorite SH episode and listen to it on the car cassette player or on a Walkman. If you've never listened to just the audio portion of the show, you'll be amazed at how much of

the video your mind remembers when prompted only by the sound. I'll be taking "Coffin" and "Shootout" with me as I drive the New Jersey turnpike this summer.[40]

For some, audiocassettes had been the only medium available to capture television episodes, and relistening to these recordings was a gratifying experience in and of itself. In 1980 fan Dee E. Brendel shared, "I sure wish I had a VTR—Darn!!!" adding, "But then my tapes keep me company at home, at the office, and at play!" Here, specifically, Brendel appreciated how audiocassettes provided her the affordance of portability and almost constant companionship of her recordings.[41] Another fan would admit in 1990, "It's only in recent years that I've had a VCR and certainly know the enjoyment to be found in listening to audio-tapes of episodes, it's all I had for a long time."[42]

Being able to replay episodes was essential for fans who wanted to deconstruct, analyze, and discuss narrative and characterization of both canon storylines and fan fiction. This is evident when one fan complained of the disparities she observed between her recordings of *Simon & Simon* episodes and characterizations of main character AJ in fan fiction,

> I hate this tendency to make AJ weak too. . . . I've been watching a lot of episodes lately, mainly because my friend has got hooked on the show, and I've been cloning/showing her episodes. The AJ on the screen is almost a different person from the one I've been reading about lately. There's no way that such a weak, ineffectual detective as the fan fiction AJ would have survived as a detective. That's not to say that all the fan fiction is like that, of course, but rather too much of it has been lately. Come on, guys. How about a story where Rick is hurt and AJ has to be the protective one?[43]

Through these examples and others, the acts of accumulating and being able to replay episodes were practices that many fans found rewarding in and of themselves. However, replay culture was also an expectation of community membership, and it was a commonly shared belief that producers of fan fiction, fan art, or fan videos would be intensely familiar with the canonical diegesis of the television shows they sought to expand upon with their own creativity.

Fan debates and discussion about diegetic meaning were intertwined with replay culture and the ability to use the videotape recorder's technical affordance to pause, rewind, replay. One fan wrote about rewatching *Starsky & Hutch*,

> In freeze frame you have the leisure to admire expressions and actions as well as dialog and tone. Things like Hutch's poignant look of love and regret when Starsky stops him in the door and says don't let me talk us out of a nice quiet scrambled egg late supper next time. . . . Things like Hutch's kneeling over Starsky and hesitating until he sees him moving enough to assure his neck and back aren't broken, then lifting his head as if it were priceless. . . . While in freeze frame, you can admire Starsky not only unfocused but looking in two different directions simultaneously and not really contacting the outside world at all except for Hutch's voice and touch.[44]

Videotape recordings provided fans with a new way to watch television episodes in slow motion and use the pause button to freeze the moving image and analyze the romantic relationship between Starsky and Hutch. Buddy-cop shows are distinguished from other subgenres because their narrative focus is on a homosocial partnership between two main characters. However, not all fans of buddy-cop shows inferred the central relationship between these characters, such as Starsky and Hutch, Simon and Simon, and Crockett and Tubbs, as a romantic one.

Debates about queer interpretations and fan productivity have been an ongoing staple of this and other fan communities.[45] "Slash" is the term that describes fan-created texts that put characters in noncanonical gay pairings, and with television culture, slash has its origins in the *Star Trek* fandom communities that began producing fan-authored content that focused on a relationship between Kirk and Spock, or, as it was abbreviated, K/S.[46] Queerness as a conceptual framework, however, does not exclusively connote same-sex relationships. Eve Kosofsky Sedgwick defines "queerness" as "the open mesh of possibilities, gaps, overlaps, dissonances and resonances, lapses and excesses of meaning when the constituent elements of anyone's gender, of anyone's sexuality aren't made (or *can't be* made) to signify monolithically."[47] Writing fan fiction that placed Starsky and Hutch or Crockett and Tubbs in explicit sexual relationships was a popular fan practice by some members of these fan communities; however, the inherent homosociality and implicit homoeroticism at play in buddy-cop-television narratives also made close rewatching and pausing recordings a form of queering using the original episodes themselves. Alexander Doty's use of the term "queering," as a verb to refer to the act of interpreting and imbuing media with queer meanings, is useful to consider here because Doty argues that queerness can be present in a text whether or not these meanings were intended by the producers.[48] Texts can become queer through the adoption of "reception positions that can be considered 'queer' in some way, regardless of a person's declared sexual and gender allegiances."[49] Audience practices freeze-framing *Starsky & Hutch* in order to highlight the interpretation of these characters' emotional relationship queer this show through audiences' culturally positioned interpretation, regardless of their own sexuality or producers' intentions.

Rewatching and pausing television recordings and queer meaning figured prominently in discussion among 1980s *Starsky & Hutch* fans surrounding what is often referred to as "the kiss in the alley." This refers to a scene during the season 1 episode "The Fix," in which Hutch had been kidnapped by a mobster and given injections of heroin over the course of several days. Hutch escapes and is found by Starsky in an alley, and during this scene, Hutch falls off the alley wall and into Starsky's arms, and for a moment their faces come together in an embrace. This portion of the scene was shot at medium ratio from behind Hutch, so viewers are unable to see the space between the characters' faces. Fans would go on to use fan letterzines through the 1980s to debate whether the two cops kiss in this scene, and authority on this matter was often tied to possessing and rewatching the episode on videotape. British fan Janice Daniels wrote into *S and H* in February 1981 and, among other things, complained, "Penny Warren [another regular *S and H* contributor] seems to be obsessed with this homosexual theme. . . . I've seen 'The Fix' and they *don't* kiss."[50] Another fan, Connie Faddis, said in the following month that she had used her tapes to study the "suggestion of a kiss" in the alley scene and that, despite her desire to see this tender expression, she argued the kiss did not happen and drew a diagram of the scene using her VCR to support her argument (see figure 3.6). In the next issue of *S and H*, Penny Warren followed up with a rebuttal,

> Frame 3 of your schematic does not represent a kiss. To the best of my knowledge, no one has argued that it does. The frame that does show the kiss is substantially different. And since I don't draw, I'm going to describe it. Starsky is on the left, Hutch is on the right—Neither man is in profile. . . . Starsky's head is turned about 30° to his own right, so that, were his whole face visible, we would have something just less than a three-quarters view. . . . The portion of his face that we do see would be below and to the right (Starsky's right, viewer's left) of a line drawn from the left corner of his mouth to his right temple, at a point just beyond his right eye. We don't see the rest of his face because it's obscured by Hutch's hand. What does this mean? It means

Figure 3.6. Connie Faddis's diagram of the contested "kiss in the alley scene," drawn using the VCR pause button to prove that the characters Starsky and Hutch do not kiss in the episode "The Fix." (Connie Faddis, "Artwork," S and H, March 1981, 12, box 67, Morgan Dawn Fanzines and Fanvids Collection, University of Iowa Special Collections)

that Hutch is indeed closer to the camera. Point of agreement. It also means that Hutch's head is at a position intermediate between your frames 3 and 4. Point of disagreement. Now, Hutch's head is turned a few degrees to his own right. Not as much as Starsky's, maybe 10°. What does this mean? It means that Starsky's and Hutch's faces are turned toward each other. And their lips are touching. Just. What does all the above mean? It means that your frames 1–4 are not an accurate representation of what's on that film. And what does that mean? There are a couple of possibilities. I'm not going to speculate. You tell us.[51]

This debate would surface again on and off through the 1980s and 1990s in the letterzine pages of S and H, Between Friends, and Frienz. The use of these diagrams and detailed descriptions of camera angles was dependent on the labor fans invested in rewatching, pausing, rewinding, and studying their VTR recording of "The Fix" over and over again. A recent article in the magazine GQ argues that queer internet fans have taken over our interpretative reception to television by forcing mainstream attention to slash relationships.[52] Certainly, this is not new to digital culture, and these debates demonstrate how fans relied on their videotape collections and playback technology to queer the canonical text itself—the recordings of the television episodes.

These examples demonstrate how the informal circulation of buddy-cop television recordings was animated by deep analysis and embedded within situated debates over cultural meaning. Jason Mittell has argued that television of the 2000s and 2010s shifted in response to new technologies, narrowcasting, and transmedia storytelling conventions to create a new form of "complex television." For Mittell, this long-form, serialized storytelling presents "high-concept puzzles" and layers that encourage a mode of "forensic fandom" engagement in which fans drill down, "probing beneath the surface to understand the complexity of a story and its telling."[53] Mittell acknowledges that *Star Wars* fans and others have engaged in this sort of forensic fandom in the past with films they could rewatch ad infinitum. However, Mittell suggests that this drillable complexity has, in part, been made possible by contemporary digital platforms and the availability of television recordings on DVD, and he contrasts it with the ephemeral YouTube video, designed for instant and fleeting momentary engagement and circulation.[54] I find this comparison telling because until television production companies began offering DVD box sets in 1999, the industry did not imagine television viewers, for the most part, as "forensic" fans invested in rewatching television content over again. Indeed, television producers imagined their content as mainly ephemeral, and much of academic broadcast history has mirrored this understanding of predigital TV engagement. This is, perhaps, somewhat ironic, given the fact that the studios sued Sony over the release of video recording technology because of a fear that the VCR would be used to record television, although this was driven by the belief that audiences who engaged in time-shifting reused cassettes and recorded over content after viewing and that the VCR threatened commercial revenue.[55] The turn to the complex television narratives that Mittell describes is not an indication that new technologies, like wikis and DVDs, have created opportunities for the forensic study of television but, rather, the industrial recognition of this form of highly engaged viewer, and the potential to harness this engagement using digital technologies because of the ways narrowcasting and audience fragmentation have made the forensic fan more valuable to the television industries.

Looking through archives of television fanzines, it is very clear that television viewers have been engaging in TV rewatching and collective discussions about diegetic meaning since the 1960s. Tape trading of bootleg recordings was an integral form of circulating episodes of *Starsky & Hutch*, *Simon & Simon*, and *Miami Vice* at a time when the commercial release of program series on tape was not only commercially infeasible but also at odds with the television industries' lucrative second-run syndication model. Tape trading these television episodes gave fans the opportunity to study the canonical narrative in order to participate in their own forms of fan creativity, such as fan fiction or fan vidding. However, it also made possible deep engagement and debate over meaning possible, facilitating fans' affective relationships with the materiality of the physical television episodes themselves through recording, trading, and rewatching. This circuit of exchange worked to revalue television episodes of buddy-cop programs, not only through the cost of VTR technology and cassettes, letterzine subscriptions, mimeograph machines, or postage or any of the many connected technologies involved in the informal buddy-cop-TV tape-trading economy. The shift in materiality through tape trading allowed buddy-cop television fans to create new values for themselves and what these programs meant to their own identity and daily life. Chapter 4 continues to explore the ways that bootlegging changed audiences' relationship with television by providing a history of recirculating *Star Trek* television episodes in Australia.

CHAPTER 4

We Had to Do It the Hard Way

Bootlegging *Star Trek* in Australia

Let me set the scene. It is Sunday morning, August 17, 1975, and Aussiecon, the Thirty-Third World Science Fiction Convention, is taking place at the Southern Cross Hotel in Melbourne, Australia.[1] Australian *Star Trek* fan Diane Marchant is riding the elevator with a small group of people holding 16 mm prints of the *Star Trek: The Original Series* (*TOS*) episodes "City on the Edge of Forever" and "Naked Time," as well as a *Star Trek TOS* blooper reel. She is taking them to an 8:30 a.m. screening in one of the smaller hotel meeting rooms on the first floor, adjacent to the grand ballroom, where the main program events are taking place. The elevator doors open, and the area is thick with Aussiecon attendees who woke up early to join the impromptu *Star Trek* viewing, so crowded, in fact, that it was impossible to get out of the lift. Marchant and the others hold up the reel containers and yell, "WE'VE GOT THE FILMS!" The swell of bodies part like the red sea, and, like Moses leading the Israelites to the land of milk and honey, Marchant and her merry band of Trekkers lead the Aussiecon attendees into the first fan-organized, communal *Star Trek* viewing in Australia. Aussiecon's organizing committee had not originally planned any *Star Trek* events for the program until Marchant approached them at the last minute. Not anticipating much interest from the literary-focused World Science Fiction Convention, Aussiecon's committee offered the Sunday morning early timeslot of 8:30 a.m. to Marchant for a *Star Trek* episode screening. However, the prospect of viewing *Star Trek* is so popular, Marchant has to show the *TOS* reels in two successive sessions because the screening room they had been assigned is too small to fit everyone who wants to watch them.[2]

This was not the first *Star Trek* viewing at a Worldcon. Film and television producers have long used Worldcons as a venue to promote their work.[3] *Star Trek* creator Gene Roddenberry screened the *Star Trek* pilot and several other episodes at Tricon, the 1966 Worldcon in Cleveland, Ohio, as a publicity stunt to promote the show one week prior to its American broadcast debut on NBC on September 8, 1966.[4] However, the *Star Trek* screening at Aussiecon 1975 was significant for several reasons. First, it was fan organized, a practice that became a standardized component of Worldcon by 1981, as evidenced by the official video room on the program map of the Denvention II, the Thirty-Ninth Worldcon in Denver, Colorado.[5] Second, the aforementioned episodes screened at Aussiecon in 1975 were bootlegged copies supplied through questionable means. Third, while *Star Trek* fandom in Australia existed prior to 1975, the Aussiecon screening became a touch point for fans to connect, and active fan clubs emerged out of this meeting that would shape *Star Trek* fandom down under for the next twenty years. Indeed, the history of *Star Trek* fandom in Australia is a history of communal viewing of bootlegged episodes, a practice that led to the Australian fandom's growth and yet also its eventual decline in the mid-1990s when Paramount, newly acquired by Viacom, aggressively pursued cease-and-desist orders on unsanctioned club screenings.

This chapter focuses on the transnational aspect of unofficial distributional labor to consider how a globalized television property such as *Star Trek* circulated through an uneven hybrid constellation of official syndication and bootlegging practices. Why *Star Trek*? It is, after all, one of the most studied television properties in media and cultural studies, alongside other cult shows, such as *Buffy the Vampire Slayer*. However, very little has been written about how people have encountered and accessed these programs. As Roberta Pearson and Marie Messenger Davies have noted, scholars at first were invested in dissecting the significance of *Star Trek*'s representational meanings through textual analysis in the late 1970s and early 1980s.[6] In the early 1990s textual analysis of *Star Trek* was supplemented by studies of audience engagement and fan productivity.[7] Until Pearson and Davies's book on the history of *Star Trek*'s production, very little had been written about how *Star Trek* and its subsequent spin-offs (*The Next Generation*, *Deep Space 9*, *Voyager*, and *Enterprise*) had been made and how American television's economic imperatives and changing narrative formats have shaped the storytelling of these programs.[8] How audiences access *Star Trek* television content has been even less considered than its representations, production history, or fan activity. Yet, as consistently demonstrated in this book, the role of fan distributional labor circulating canonical content, here *Star Trek*'s television episodes, has always been the foundation for other fannish productivity, such as fanzines, fan art, fiction, and cosplay.

Fan letterzines show evidence of transnational participation in all of the communities discussed in this book. In letterzines I found evidence of OTR collectors in Canada and Mexico, *Starsky & Hutch* fans in the United Kingdom and Australia, and professional wrestling tape-trading networks that included participants in Canada and Japan. However, the existence of a large collection of English-language Australian fan letterzines in the Susan Smith-Clarke *Star Trek* collection at the National Library of Australia, alongside Australia's physical geography and industrial position in US-centered television windowing hierarchies, made the development of an informal economy of *Star Trek* television distribution in Australia an ideal case study to consider the role of transnational bootlegging opening up audience access to broadcast content.

Much has been written about the transnational syndication of television programming. Political economists such as Herbert I. Schiller put forth the economically deterministic cultural-imperialism framework that reasoned American culture was homogenizing Indigenous cultures around the world.[9] Other political economists, such as Armand Mattelart, used textual analysis to argue that products, such as Disney comic books, further demonstrate cultural imperialism because of their pro-capitalist content.[10] Pushing back on the use of textual interpretation or economic figures as evidence of cultural engagement or homogenization, scholars like Arjun Appadurai and John Tomlinson have demonstrated that even when US media products, like television programming, travel around the world, distribution and reception are uneven and shaped by the confluence of shifting technological infrastructures, political environments and regulatory policies, audience practices and local media ecosystems, and cultural configurations.[11] Tim Havens notes the role of international trade shows and local buyers in determining what gets distributed where, as well as the industrial practices that have given US television producers advantages in the global marketplace.[12] Havens illustrates the ongoing relationship between domestic television outlets and transnational television providers, noting that each local television industry is shaped through "their own internal political, economic and cultural logics."[13] As with syndication, the local Australian television industries and their interplay in the global television market shaped how *Star Trek* was bootlegged there. However, it is important to note that bootlegging is distinct from the official international syndication of television content, which Havens defines as the "process of global television exchange ... [influenced by] both the political-economic structures of global television and the culture worlds of the business people who operate within its constraints."[14] Transnational syndication is not the sale of recordings but, rather, the sale of the official licensing rights to broadcast a television program, sold market by market. In contrast, bootlegging television is very much about the circulation of physical recordings, and while it is an unofficial reproduction and circulation of television content, it is not disconnected from official transnational syndication.

In the case of *Star Trek*'s recirculation in Australia, most episodes of *Star Trek* viewed in cinema marathons or club meetings were obtained either by the sale of film prints initially created for official transnational syndication or were recorded off-air from syndicated broadcasts, or fans from other countries visiting friends or attending a convention transported them to Australia. Due to a number of reasons, including technological interoperability between NTSC (National Television System Committee) and PAL (Phase Alternating Line) format videotapes, as well as scarcity of viewing systems and episode copies, communal viewing became the primary mode for fans to view bootlegged copies of *Star Trek* episodes. This chapter, then, builds on Havens and a larger growing body of contemporary scholars who have outlined how the interplay between specific local and transnational factors determines how television moves between countries. The history of bootlegging *Star Trek* in Australia illustrates how audience access to *Star Trek* became predicated upon the interplay between official licensing efforts, Australian television culture in the 1970s and 1980s, and the distributive labor that facilitated *Star Trek* television episodes' availability. Indeed, *Star Trek* fandom in Australia, parallel to the United States, actually increased and continued to grow after NBC canceled the series from Desilu Productions in 1969. Indeed, *Star Trek*'s popularity and cult following in the United States were propelled by the profitable, widespread second-run syndication of *TOS*, most visibly culminating in the unexpected attendance of three thousand fans at the first New York *Star Trek* Convention in 1972, an event the organizers anticipated would attract only a few hundred participants.[15] It is, perhaps, even more compelling a figure when we consider that this was three years after the show was canceled in 1969, and no additional original episodes were produced. Indeed, it is likely that the continued growth of *Star Trek* fandom in the United States and abroad was sustained by a hybrid redistribution of the television episodes via both official second-run syndication and the circulation of bootlegged recordings during the ten-year interim between *TOS* and the feature-film franchise. In Australia, it was mainly the latter, as my research demonstrates that the official Australian television outlets gave little airtime to *Star Trek*, both *TOS* and later, *The Next Generation* (*TNG*), produced by Paramount Television Studios from 1987 to 1994. From 1971 to 1991, reruns of *TOS* episodes were only sporadically aired, and Paramount did not finalize its licensing of *Star Trek: TNG* in Australia until 1991, four seasons into its first-run syndication in the United States.[16] There is no way to conclusively prove this; however, it is very likely that if someone was viewing *Star Trek* television episodes in Australia between 1975 and 1991, they were doing so via bootlegged recordings in a communal setting. Indeed, because of the growth of a significant *Star Trek* fan community in the 1970s and the 1980s, the viewing of bootlegged *Star Trek* episodes flourished in Australia in stark contrast to the industrial indifference of Australian broadcasters, mainly due to the active growth of *Star Trek* fan clubs.

A *Star Trek* fan community has been present in Australia since 1968 when Melbourne native John Stepkowski founded the Australian *Star Trek* Club (ASTAC). ASTAC was defunct by 1970, but it was followed by the formation of several regional *Star Trek* fan clubs. One of these began when sixteen-year-old Susan Smith and eighteen-year-old Shayne McCormack organized an Australian component of Deluge Monday, a letter-writing campaign to NBC to renew *Star Trek* for a fourth season in July 1969.[17] NBC did not reverse its decision to cancel *Star Trek*; however, coverage in the Sydney edition of *TV Times* of Smith and McCormack's letter-writing campaign garnered a significance response from readers, with whom Smith and McCormack would go on to form the Sydney-based *Star Trek* club Down Under Space Kooks, later renamed the *Star Trek* Action Committee in 1973. Smith and McCormack merged their club with another group of Sydney *Star Trek* fans to become Astrex in 1976.[18] In the same year, a loosely connected group of *Star Trek* fans in Melbourne, Australia, launched the *Star Trek* club Austrek.[19] By 1979 there was an active *Star Trek* club in all six Australian states, with membership in the larger clubs in Sydney and Melbourne numbering over a thousand.[20] The growth of Australian *Star Trek* fandom in the late 1970s was also influenced by both the decentralized Australian television landscape, and these fan clubs' subsequent grassroots organization to redistribute *Star Trek* television episodes.

Communal Viewing of Bootlegged Episodes as Television Distribution

Marchant's organization of the communal screening of bootlegged *Star Trek* episodes at Aussiecon in 1975 was, in many ways, a catalyst for the fan-centered distribution of *TOS* episodes in Australia. Marchant was a significant figure in Australian science-fiction fan community. She was an early member of the *Star Trek* Welcommittee, a fan-run information center founded in 1972 to answer fan mail, connect fans with local clubs, or provide guides on how to start a fan club. The Welcommittee's strong relationship with Roddenberry engendered a symbiotic relationship wherein the committee positively promoted the show with fans, and Roddenberry and the studio would supply the committee with news and information.[21] Marchant's position on the Welcommittee placed her in contact with fan clubs around the world; for instance, she was an "Overseas Representative" in the British *Star Trek* Action Group fan club.[22] Marchant's active engagement in Australian science-fiction fan cultures serendipitously brought her into contact with Bob Johnson, owner of an educational-film company that distributed educational films for use in classrooms to schools across Australia.[23] Johnson's projectionist was working the Aussiecon convention, and when he learned of Marchant's interest in *Star Trek*, he informed her that his boss was a fan of *Star Trek* and had acquired several episode copies on 16 mm film. This meeting led Marchant to make the arrangements to borrow two episode prints from Johnson for the showing at Aussiecon described at the introduction to this chapter. Australian fan Valmai Rogers would reflect on the impact of this screening a year later:

> I've been a Science Fiction "nut" for over twenty years, and a *Star Trek* fan since it first came out. But it was only by pure chance that I found out about the Science Fiction World Con in Melbourne, Victoria, last August; So I was lucky I went down there, because I was introduced to the world of *Star Trek* fandom and found out there were others like me. All this time I thought I was alone, like a hermit living in a valley, when just over the next hill there was a *whole tribe* of people just like me.[24]

The viewing at Aussiecon became an opportunity for many isolated *Star Trek* enthusiasts to network and connect with other fans and demonstrated a market for communal viewings to Sydney-based businessman and film collector Johnson, one that he would foster and profit from when he began his *Star Trek* TV marathons at movie theaters in Sydney and Melbourne a year later in 1976.

Communal entertainment viewing has a long history, with obvious origins in the communal experiences of attending theater performances and later film screenings. It may be assumed that domestication of entertainment media with the advent of the phonograph, radio, and television made consumption of this form of content an individualized or solitary experience, but that has never been accurate. As discussed in chapter 1, the Edison Home Kinetoscope first released in 1896 and again in 1912, was marketed as an entertainment device for the family or for parties. Radio broadcasts were communal experiences from the days of early broadcasting, as the infamous Jack Dempsey—Georges Carpentier heavyweight boxing championship was organized in tandem with RCA as a publicity event, and many of the listeners heard the boxing match in communal spaces. Elks Lodges, bars, and theaters, such as Loew's New York Theatre, were set up with radios and speakers and advertised the broadcast at their establishment, with Loew's alone airing the Dempsey-Carpentier match to an audience of twelve hundred people.[25] Radio sets predated televisions as popular technologies integrated into public spaces, like bars, department stores, and airports, as well as being commonly used for entertainment or information in group activities that were already communal, such as civic or women's clubs.[26] This, of course, was extended and rearticulated in what Anna McCarthy has called "ambient television," which she defines as the "processes of adapting and integrating TV, and media power, into the social rhythms and material life of spaces outside the home."[27] McCarthy uses case studies to consider how television, as technological apparatus, production culture, and content flowing through television sets, is shaped by and also shapes institutional practices and public locations, such as taverns, airports, and malls.[28]

McCarthy's work is an important intervention in television history, as it pushes us to reconsider how audiences actually engage with television, beyond the private domestic experiences most often depicted in consumer electronic advertisements. The idealized image of the isolated, middle-class family watching television at home has been a mainstay of US broadcaster's industrial imagination since the widespread network adaptation of television in the postwar era. Spigel demonstrates how television sets were very much marketed in the United States as an electronic hearth that would bring families together through the consumption of broadcast entertainment. Spigel's analysis, however, focuses on the private nature of the domestic setting imagined in advertisements for television sets and, thus, understood television viewing as a ritual experienced within a familial group, with the imagined gendered dynamics of the patriarchal nuclear family that she saw idealized in 1950's US television culture.[29] As McCarthy has demonstrated, the imagined consumer of advertisements does not reflect actual audience behavior or social practices, and television has a long history within the communal viewing spaces of bars, restaurants, and transitory places, such as airports. Due to the uneven development of broadcasting infrastructures and other technocultural, political, and geographical variations in television adaptation, communal TV reception has been (and still is in some cases) a prevalent mode of intentional, rather than ambient, TV viewing for audiences both inside and outside of the United States.[30]

This chapter adds to this growing body of work on the way audiences experience television in their everyday lives with a focus on how a globalized television property such as *Star Trek* circulated through an uneven hybrid constellation of official syndication and bootlegging practices. Communal viewing of bootlegged *Star Trek* television episodes worked to facilitate transnational distribution in Australia, and while I mainly discuss *TOS*, *TNG* also comes up in this story. In Australia, communal viewing of *Star Trek* episode bootlegs emerged as a way to overcome the disinterest in rerunning *Star Trek* by the official television outlets that owned the Australian broadcast rights, namely, local stations, such as Television Corp. New South Wales (known and operated as TCN 9) in Sydney, which owned the *Star Trek: TOS* broadcast rights from 1969 to 1981, when Amalgamated Television New South Wales (known and operated as ATN 7) obtained the broadcast rights.[31] Officially distributed reruns of *TOS* were infrequent in Australia during the 1970s. Stations were loosely aligned in order to work together to license foreign programming, but due to a lack of technological infrastructure and government regulation, commercial Australian television was decentralized until the mid-1980s, when regulations were abolished.[32] Stations collaborated to buy programs like *Star Trek* and because they were not linked together by phone lines would share content via a "bicycle network," the term for distributing television by mail where program recordings are shared among a group of television stations, forming what Albert Moran and Chris Keating have called a "weak network" in Australian television.[33] Integrated national networks were not distributing content across all of the Australian markets until 1991. This meant that unlike the United States, where broadcast networks distributed the same slate of programmed flow to affiliates around the country, the Australian commercial television broadcasters operated as independent stations around the country from the 1960s to 1990s, with the most investment put into stations in the five capital cities: Sydney, Melbourne, Brisbane, Adelaide, and Perth.[34] Starting in 1963, commercial stations would make joint arrangements, such as producing or purchasing programming together; however, these were cooperative arrangements between independent stations.[35] For this reason, when *Star Trek: TOS* was first aired in Australia from 1967 to 1970, it was broadcast at different timeslots on different days, depending on a region's local station. Reruns were even more inconsistent, as, for instance, TCN 9, which had the rights to broadcast *Star Trek: TOS* in Sydney, chose approximately ten episodes to rerun after the debut of color TV in 1975 and scheduled these as a children's programming on Saturday afternoons.[36] These haphazard approaches to scheduling *Star Trek* were common, as one fan relates: "Sydney, Australia rejoiced in a 17-episode rerun of *Star Trek* in the last quarter of 1976—albeit out of sequence and only a fill-in, it was more than welcome in this deserted wasteland."[37] Australian *Star Trek* fan clubs regularly tried to overcome their "deserted wasteland" devoid of *Star Trek* programming by organizing letter-writing campaigns to local commercial stations that held the syndication rights. These campaigns reflected both the fans' lack of access to *TOS* episodes within Australian television's official distributive outlets and the role of fan collaborative labor in attempting to shape the distribution of television content in Australia.[38] In the absence of lasting results petitioning Australian TV channels, communal viewing of bootlegged episodes came to function as a central form of access to *TOS* episodes.

Archived fanzines, newspaper listings, and interviews reveal the history of two significant forms of communal viewing of *Star Trek* in Australia: fan-club viewings and Johnson's marathon screenings in Sydney and Melbourne theaters. Johnson's primary income reportedly came from his educational-film company, although he also was said to license out clips from his library of educational films for B-roll in film and television productions in Australia.[39] Australian schools did not have television sets until the mid-1980s, so educational-film-rental companies were an active part of the Australian media landscape through the 1980s.[40] Privately, Johnson was also well known in the Sydney film and independent-cinema community as a film-print collector.[41] It is within this latter capacity as a film collector that Johnson is said to have obtained bootlegged film prints of *Star Trek* episodes originally distributed as syndication prints from contacts in South Africa.[42] Transnational television-broadcast systems developed unevenly, and television did not debut in South Africa until

1975, a delay engineered for political reasons by the White minority government, rather than lack of technological ability.[43] In the absence of a television-broadcasting service, South Africa came to have a large black market of US film and television prints that were available in film libraries for home-viewing rental by members of the White upper class.[44] South Africa's film and television black market grew during the 1960s and early 1970s, and the country came to have numerous facilities that could duplicate film prints.[45] Johnson initially only brought a few episodes from contacts in South Africa, which fans remember being originally printed on 16 mm for syndication. Johnson lent these prints to his projectionist for Aussiecon 1975, an event that first showed him the extent of a niche market for *Star Trek* episode screenings after hearing about the crowds there. Johnson then began going back and forth to South Africa, obtaining the entire seventy-nine episodes of *Star Trek: TOS* piecemeal while programming monthly *TOS* episode marathons in Melbourne and Sydney in 1976.[46]

Johnson experimented with scheduling and available venues, first conceiving of his *Star Trek* episode marathons as midnight-movie equivalents. An early ad for Johnson's Melbourne marathons at the small independent Ritz Cinema lists the screening as "All-Night *Star Trek* Marathons" showing on Saturday nights at 7:45 p.m. "until Dawn."[47] These marathons were advertised alongside midnight viewings of a "Reefer Rock Party," which suggests Johnson considered *Star Trek* to be of interest to a younger, counterculture demographic. His ad told attendees to keep the "Easyrolls ready for Saturday night," presumably marijuana joints, for the scheduled *Star Trek* marathon. I have not found evidence that attendees to these *Star Trek* marathons were, indeed, passing joints around, but it would not seem out of place amid the festive descriptions found of these marathons and other communal-viewing events in Australian *Star Trek* fanzines. Indeed, many events featured an assortment of food and snacks, which, no doubt, would be welcomed by those partaking in the "easyrolls." The same copy in this early ad also boasts that the marathon will feature episodes that are "all color," a reminder that color television did not come to Australia until 1975.[48] Thus, Johnson's marathons provided the first opportunity for Australian viewers to see the episodes as they had been produced, seemingly engineered in 1966 to showcase the US color television system with their bombastic cosmic color scheme of clashing purples, reds, yellows, and pinks.

Johnson continued to experiment with schedule timing and location, and his marathons came to be a mainstay of *Star Trek* fan culture in the

1980s. By 1980 Johnson's *Star Trek* marathons settled into a standardized schedule, screening monthly on the first Saturday at 2 p.m. in Sydney, and in Melbourne at 6:30 p.m. at the National Mutual Theatrette or ANZAC House auditorium with an AUD$6.50 admission in 1983. The Sydney marathons moved to the Encore Theatre in 1987, and the Melbourne marathons were an evening mainstay at the National Theatrette until 1989. The location of these *Star Trek* marathons would change several more times during the 1990s.[49]

For fans new to *Star Trek*, the theater marathons became a way to catch up on canonical content from the television series as Paramount released the first six *Star Trek* films between 1979 and 1991. In a 2003 interview, fan Rachel Shave spoke about the role of Johnson's marathons as her only access to the *ST: TOS* content: "I went to Sydney and I came across a flier about the monthly Anzac House screenings of *Star Trek* episodes. This was even before the days of video, so it was the only way I could see episodes. It was through this avenue that I became an active member of fandom."[50] Shave was not the only fan who first accessed the *TOS* through the marathons, as Ian McLean also first watched *TOS* at the Sydney marathons and became interested in *TOS* after *Star Trek the Motion Picture* was released in Australia in 1979 and was hungry to catch up on the narrative canon of the *Star Trek* franchise. "We had probably about eight secondhand bookstores in the city, and I would spend every Saturday morning going to each one until I found all the [*Star Trek*] novelizations and everything I could find. It totally consumed me," McLean explained, his face lit up with energy as he reflected on his early entrance into the *Star Trek* fan community. Attendance at the marathons was motivated after reading an advertisement for a convention, McLean told me: "I was too scared to go, because I didn't know enough about *Star Trek* and I thought people would see that I was a phony, you know, yeah, so I think I talked myself out of going. Though, by August 1980, I had plucked up the courage to go to the *Star Trek* [television] marathons."[51] These experiences demonstrate the distributive significance of Johnson's movie marathons to the franchise and how bootlegging and official industrial releases work in tandem. Johnson's marathons and activities kept fans engaged while probably also attracting new audiences to *Star Trek* at a time when no new content was being produced. As Paramount released their series of *Star Trek* feature films, Johnson's movie marathons offered new fans one of the only routes in Australia to catch up on the original television series (see figure 4.1).

Figure 4.1. Sydney attendees (*left to right*) Ian McLean (as original character Therin of Andor), Karen Lewis, Jill Tanner, Mike McGann and Sakura Alison at a *Star Trek* marathon run by Bob Johnson in 1981 at the ANZAC House. (Ron Clarke, "Bob Johnson's Star Trek Marathons," *Fanlore*, https://fanlore.org/wiki/File:SydneyMarathon.png)

Johnson's *Star Trek* marathons exclusively used bootlegged syndication film prints of the television show, many scratched or damaged, that had been released during the first international syndication sale between 1966 and 1969 and bought on the black market in South Africa.[52] Austrek member Robert Jan wrote in his review of a marathon he attended in Melbourne in 1981 that the first episode played "Bread and Circuses," was "a thrice patched up, ruined mess. More butchery visited on this print than ever takes place in the Arena. All the good sequences, including Spock and McCoy in the cell, fall victim to the Gremlins of Time and splicing. A pity."[53] The prints were not all bad, as Jan commented in the same review that some prints were good. Print quality came up again in an interview with longtime Sydney-based McLean, who explained that the print Johnson had of the *TOS* episode "Journey to Babel" was so "cannibalized and in horrible condition that Bob never played it." However, Johnson took the time to screen it for McLean during an intermission at one of the marathons in the early 1980s because McLean had not seen it and loved Andorian characters, which feature prominently in the episode. "There were wide green lines, scratches in the print," McLean described. "So I had a running gag for quite a while that I was going to create a new Andorian character that had vertical green lines going down my blue face, like the print."[54] These stories embody Appadurai's proposal to consider the social lives of objects and consider how physical media become reconstituted as material things circulating through ongoing processes of exchange and revaluation.[55] Here, specifically, Johnson's *Star Trek* prints demonstrate the deterioration that occurs with regular screening of 16 mm television episodes prints.

In his discussion of videotape technology, Hilderbrand calls the deterioration of quality through bootlegged reproduction the "aesthetics of access," by which he means, the visual evidence of a bootlegged film or television show's circulation. The syndicated *TOS* prints Johnson obtained were not produced for longevity but, rather, a short-term, international syndication deal that anticipated a few playbacks over a short period of time, characteristics that would become visually evident in the deteriorated quality of several episodes. Fan reflections on the aesthetics and print quality of Johnson's *Star Trek* episodes point to the specificity of distribution as a temporal and localized phenomenon, dependent on an assemblage of technologies, such as a projector, screen, and the episode prints Johnson had acquired secondhand, several times removed from their original purpose. In repurposing syndication prints of *TOS* for communal viewing in Australian movie theaters, Johnson's bootlegging worked to reconstitute an object initially not understood as a public commodity and, thus, made for limited use. Syndication prints were created for the sale of a set amount of licensed broadcasts and exchanged between producers and broadcasters in order to sell advertisers an audience commodity. Within the Sydney and Melbourne marathons, these prints became objects shaped by their temporal trajectory from official syndication license to bootlegged commodities exchanged for ticket prices in movie theaters and evaluated for their unique materiality (damaged or clean film quality) and functioning as a mechanism for television distribution. The role of bootlegged aesthetics in Australian *Star Trek* fandom comes up again in the next section of this chapter in the discussion of fan clubs and communal viewing.

Johnson's *Star Trek* television marathons in movie theaters was one significant mode of communal viewing in Australia during the 1970s and 1980s. By the early 1980s it would coexist as one mode of communal viewing alongside convention video rooms and fan-club screenings. Incorporating *Star Trek* television screenings at clubs was not necessarily separate from the theater marathons. Indeed, the Austrek *Star Trek* Club in Melbourne coordinated its club meetings to line up with the local episode marathons, so that club members could go to eat and attend the marathons after their meetings.[56] Astrex, the Sydney-based club, listed the marathons in its monthly event calendars published and sent out in the club's letterzine *Data*, purposefully scheduling club meetings so members could attend the marathons together after the meeting. However, members of the Australian *Star Trek* community would come to have an ambivalent relationship with Johnson. They appreciated the access to *Star Trek* episodes his marathons provided and came to enjoy the social atmosphere that surrounded these screenings. Clubs would often have booths and sell fanzines and other *Star Trek* paraphernalia, and fans would dress up and cosplay for the events. However, these booths were meant as a service to their fans; most Australian *Star Trek* fan clubs were vehemently anticommercial and would even choose a local charity to donate any profits that exceeded the costs of their social events.[57] Thus, fans were also acutely aware that their volunteer work as hucksters, ushers, and promoters of Johnson's *Star Trek* marathons constituted free labor in the service of a commercial bootlegging operation and that Johnson was not one of them, that is, he was not a member of the fan community, and his revenue was not shared with the *Star Trek* fan clubs.

Yet, whatever their feelings about Johnson and his exploitation of fan labor, Australians had few options for viewing *Star Trek* in the mid-to-late 1970s. Videotape recorders were not widely adopted in Australia when Johnson first began hosting *Star Trek* episode marathons in 1976. Through the 1980s, communal viewing of television content in Australian *Star Trek* club meetings was shaped by technological conditions and can first be traced back to fan slide shows that functioned as proto–fan vids in the 1970s. Discussed briefly in chapter 3, vidding is a form of fan creativity that involves editing together scenes from the canonical TV show and adding in music in order to create a new narrative or meaning.[58] Before video-recording machines were widespread, *Star Trek* fans began to make slide shows using film clips from the television episodes that were being sold by fans in letterzines like *The Clipper Trade Ship* and by Lincoln Enterprises, the US-based mail-order company set up by *Star Trek* creator Gene Roddenberry and fan Bjo Trimble to sell merchandise related to the show.[59] Kandy Fong's "What Do You Do with a Drunken

Vulcan" is usually considered to be the earliest fan slide show set up to pair *Star Trek* film clips with a song.⁶⁰ Fong, perhaps, set the precedent for viewing fan vids in a communal environment, first presenting her "What Do You Do with a Drunken Vulcan" slide show in 1974 at the local club she belonged to, the United Federation of Phoenix, Arizona, before organizing repeat performances of her slide show at larger fan conventions in 1975.⁶¹ Like Fong's club the United Federation of Phoenix, Sydney-based club Astrex regularly incorporated slide-show nights into club meetings. However, during the 1970s, before the widespread adaptation of VCRs, Australian clubs, like Astrex, were unique in that their slide-show nights often included audio recordings of episodes cued up to play as someone changed slides with stills from a *TOS* episode. *Star Trek* fan Susan Batho explains this early form of communal engagement:

> I used to use a little handheld cassette recorder and yell at anyone who walked into the room while I was trying to record an episode [off the air].... And you'd have groups of people listening to them, sometimes we'd have scripts, we would follow the script, so you could see it more visually in your mind.... Also we had clips, which were basically cutting-room floor snips that were mounted into slides. And we could have a whole evening of putting up the slide in tune to the words in tune to the sound ... and doing that we almost recreated episodes.⁶²

These fans, then, were doing the work of collecting deconstructed parts of *Star Trek* episodes (the soundtrack, film clips, and scripts) to reproduce the television show within the communal setting of the fan club. This was a necessity shaped by the cooperative work needed to piece together this bricolage form of grassroots bootleg television redistribution.

These early experiments with slide shows and audio recordings made communal engagement with *Star Trek* episodes a common practice in Australian fan club meetings. It is clear from fanzine archives and interviews that Australian fan clubs were screening *Star Trek* episodes on video in club meetings by the early 1980s. The earliest evidence of this is an editorial in *Captain's Log*, the Austrek letterzine, in 1981 inviting members to a club meeting at 2 p.m. on February 7 with a video screening followed by discussion with snacks.⁶³ Jodi Williams, a member of Westrek, a Western Australia *Star Trek* club active from 1979 to 1995, describes the role of episode viewing at the first Westrek meeting in the late 1980s that she attended with a friend:

> We went in, and we got greeted at the door.... There must have been about thirty people that turned up, and there was the big TV, and

this huge big monstrous video recorder. It was about half the size of the TV cabinet, and we sat down and watched two episodes. And it was this realization that, "My God, there are other people out there who get together once a month." It was this really, really bizarre feeling, but it was like coming home. . . . Originally, that's all there was: watching episodes.[64]

Williams's point emphasizes how unofficial viewing functioned as a social event that brought people together, as a central part of Australian *Star Trek* fan club activities. However, communal viewing in clubs was also necessitated by limited access to episode recordings and the NTSC playback technologies needed to view them.

The discrepancy between access to *Star Trek* television programs in Australia and the United States was even more pronounced for the new television show Paramount created in 1987: *Star Trek: The Next Generation* (*TNG*). *TNG* did not officially begin airing on Australian television stations until 1991, and Australian fans began to use their contacts in the United States to obtain videotaped episodes. In a joint interview in 2003, Western Australian fans Fern Clarke and Jodi Williams reminisced about obtaining bootlegged *TNG* episodes:

JODI: [B]ecause we used to get episodes long long, well before channel 9 used to show them, so we were always getting the episodes from overseas sent to us, and we had to rely on one of the people in our group who had an NTSC converter.

FERN: Ah yes, the bum days of "I've got these episodes, but they're from America—I cannot play them! What do I do?"

. . .

JODI: Over here, to my knowledge, there were only two guys that had NTSC players and only one had a NTSC converter to convert them into PAL. It was also one of those unfortunate things that the quality sometimes. Sometimes, the episodes we'd get, by the time we got them through the converter.

FERN: Yeah—third generation at least. . . . bleached out. It was fairly shaky.

JODI: So that's how dedicated you were—you'd be watching an episode with no colour, the shakes, no detail—but you'd still watch it.[65]

Here then, we can see how communal viewing as a practice was further encouraged both by the industrial windowing strategies that Paramount used to stagger the release of *TNG* and by the noninteroperability of the PAL broadcast technologies developed in Europe and used in Australia and the NTSC analog broadcasting system developed and used in North America.

While not initially intended to function as a regional lockout system, the development of different broadcasting-system technologies in different parts of the world came to function as distributive control. The differentiation between NTSC video systems in the United States and PAL systems in Europe, Australia, and through the world supported the US media industries' windowing strategy of staggering releases between different geographical regions and economic markets.[66] Both officially released and unofficially recorded videotapes made on one system were incompatible with another, and this technological condition made communal viewing necessary for *Star Trek* fans who obtained *TNG* recordings from the United States. For most clubs, only one or two members of a fan club (such as Westrek, discussed by Clarke and Williams above) had a NTSC converter that would allow videotapes sent from the United States to play back on PAL machines in Australia. Technological interoperability here is then another factor that distinguished this form of television distribution. Playback through a converter would engender Hilderbrand's "aesthetics of access" differently, however, from the degradation of film quality on bootlegged copies, as a result of quality loss through use and storage. With system conversion playback, the quality loss is an aesthetic outcome of translation from NTSC television storage medium to the PAL system. Even so, fans like Clarke would sit through these screenings because this was one of the few options Australian fans had to access *TNG* episodes between 1987 and 1991.

The challenge of viewing US recordings in Australia is, perhaps, best epitomized by a story shared by Susan Batho, née Smith, and later Smith-Clarke, about her experiences getting and sharing US recordings of *Star Trek* episodes in the 1980s. "I was lucky. I had contacts.... Mama had contacts in those days," she told me, giggling a bit as she reminisced about the lengths she went through to provide access to *Star Trek*, particularly *TNG* in the late 1980s. Tape trading was just not feasible for many because of the noninteroperability of US TV systems. So, Batho was able to use her US fan contacts and involvement planning Australian *Star Trek* conventions to get fans visiting from the United States to bring her not only tapes but also, in one instance, an entire American television system. Batho explains,

> People would come to conventions and bring things with them....
> And in this one case was a very small television with a, a VHS, you

know, NTSC machine, plus a power source. They would give me that and then I would get tapes and those tapes then . . . were all incompatible with the Australian system. So, I would actually have to drive to different states to show them at other clubs. We'd have evenings watching fourteen different shows, mainly the newest one that had come out, *The Next Generation*. . . . And people would be desperate enough to set up a camera to record it off the screen, as it was playing in a different state because we had no way of copying it otherwise.

She explains how these road trips made her notorious in the Australian *Star Trek* community.

My friend Joanne and I got to be known because we would drive down Friday night or Saturday morning early. . . . It's a thirteen-hour drive to Melbourne, and we'd get there, and everyone would be so excited because we had the tapes with us. We'd sit down, they'd feed us, and while we were being fed, they'd start watching. And then they'd have a party at night, and the whole lot would come out again. And then in the morning, a different lot of people who come for breakfast and see them again. And then we have to drive home at lunch because we had to get ready for work on the Monday, so it was like a weekend down in Melbourne with at least twenty-six hours of driving.[67]

Hearing this story about Batho and her friend essentially creating a traveling television circuit that evoked a smaller scale of the traveling circus or vaudeville production is one of the moments researching this book that made me rethink how I approached the informal circulation of television in Australia. After finding some of the Australian *Star Trek* fanzines in the University of Iowa Special Collections, I had anticipated some sort of transnational tape-trading network, informal linkages between fans in the United States and fans in Australia, and packages being sent back and forth. After all, that was a dominant mode of bootlegging radio and television in the other fan communities I have researched. Batho's explanation of the technological incompatibility of American bootlegged tapes and her decision to travel across Australia, sometimes driving twenty-six hours in a weekend to physically bring television recordings along with the technological apparatuses (television set, VCR, and power-cord adaptor) to groups, was surprising. Her retelling of these clubs that would, in turn, feed and lodge her illuminates the communal nature of this form of bootlegged television distribution. Batho and other members of the Australian *Star Trek* fan community did this distributive work without monetary compensation. Their free distributive

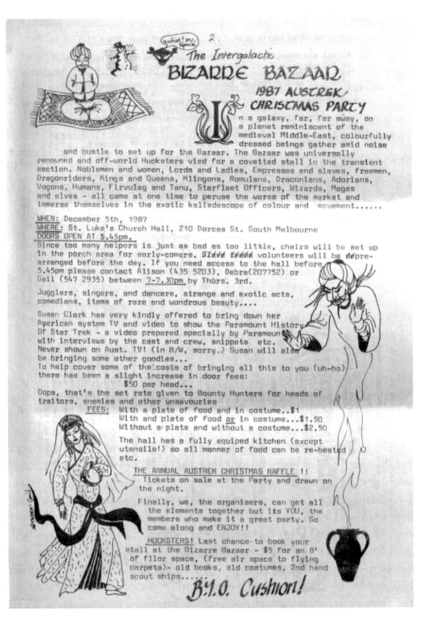

Figure 4.2. Flyer for the 1987 Austrek Christmas party, announcing a visit from Susan Batho, who would drive thirteen hours each way from Sydney to Melbourne for the event. ("Intergalactic Bizarre Bazaar 1987 Austrek Christmas Party Flyer," *Captain's Log*, December 1987, 2, Susan Smith-Clarke Star Trek Fanzine Collection, National Library of Australia)

labor facilitating communal screening of bootlegged episodes was one of the main ways that *TNG* was made accessible to Australian audiences between 1987 when it debuted in the United States and 1991 when *TNG* first began airing down under.

Reading through Australian *Star Trek* fanzine archives and fan interviews, it is clear that fans were cognizant of the legal implications of club television-show screenings. Announcements of video screenings were often intentionally vague in zines. For instance, figure 4.2, a 1987 Austrek Christmas party flyer, is an example of one such ambiguous announcement that Batho would be bringing her American system to share a Paramount-produced history of *Star Trek* and "other goodies." Members, maybe in costume, gathered at this event to eat, drink, and be merry as they celebrated the holiday watching *TNG* as a community. This was one of the twenty-six-hour sojourns Batho made from Sydney to visit Melbourne-based Austrek, and the undisclosed goodies were *TNG* episodes that would be screened amid the food and festivities of Austrek's Intergalactic Bizarre Bazaar Christmas Party on December 5, 1987.[68] Williams discussed the purposeful ambiguity fans used in the 1980s to publicize screenings and avoid getting in trouble for violating copyright law: "There was something learnt early on in the eighties: even then I was aware of how hush-hush we had to be about everything. We couldn't openly advertise when you were meeting, and you were going to show episodes. You could say *Trek* people are getting together for a social gathering. You never mentioned we were showing episodes. Just all hush-hush."[69] This approach to redistributing *Star Trek* television episodes through communal viewing at club events using nebulous wording was fairly effective through the 1980s and early 1990s, a time when Australian *Star Trek* clubs were not paid much attention by Paramount's legal team.

This changed after Viacom's acquisition of Paramount in 1994.[70] The Australian Film Commission had disrupted and stopped several instances of film and television screenings at a handful of *Star Trek* conventions in the early 1990s, and, thus, fans were familiar with the nature of copyright law and the prohibition of showing copyrighted media at public events with an entrance fee.[71] However, many of them did not anticipate that the struggle of copyright and club screenings would be central to the widespread dismantling of Australian fan-centered *Star Trek* clubs. When most of the Australian *Star Trek* clubs were founded in the 1970s and 1980s, they had contacted Roddenberry, often via Paramount's communication office, and asked his permission to start a *Star Trek* club.

Roddenberry had approved these requests and was usually given honorary membership and sent fan-club newsletters.[72] In 1993, as the deal to merge with Viacom was being ironed out and approved, Paramount decided to restructure international fan clubs so that Paramount could control global fan club activities. This led to efforts to establish locally sanctioned fan clubs and shut down unofficial clubs, and in Australia, Paramount contracted with the company Southern Star to handle local syndication, licensing, and merchandise for the *Star Trek* franchise.[73] Paramount executive Jonathan Zilli flew to Australia in March 1995 to meet with the leaders of local fan clubs from around the country and used his knowledge of their unsanctioned club television screenings to order them to shut down.[74] Clubs that continued to meet and show videos received cease-and-desist letters, and it came to be rumored that the leaders of Astrex were using their contacts and knowledge of the other Australian clubs to report other clubs to the Australian Film Commission.[75] These rumors became more widespread after it surfaced that the presidents of Astrex, at the time, made a backdoor deal with Paramount to run the officially licensed Paramount club out of Sydney.[76]

Prior to Viacom's takeover of Paramount in 1994, there were twelve active regional *Star Trek* clubs in Australia. By 2000 there were two.[77] No clubs were forced to shut down; copyright law in Australia places the onus on the prosecution to demonstrate copyright violations. However, after the establishment of an official Australian *Star Trek* club, more of the unofficial clubs experienced raids or received cease-and-desist letters from the Australian Television and Film Securities Office in an attempt to end bootlegged viewings at clubs. Batho studied the decline of unofficial clubs during the mid-to-late 1990s: "Many clubs simply folded rather than face legal prosecution," she concluded, while others decided it was not worth meeting if they could not freely screen television episodes.[78] The shift in strategy and approach to fan engagement by Paramount and the companies it was licensing *Star Trek* to in Australia created a rift among fans, and a significant portion of them felt betrayed by the conglomerate's actions against fan-run clubs. This conflict between Paramount and fans also occurred at a time when satellite- and cable-television operators expanded in Australia and with this the range of commercial channels and outlets showing episodes of both *TOS* and the newer series. Internet adaptation also increased during the mid-to-late 1990s, and so as fan clubs disbanded, active *Star Trek* enthusiasts turned to online outlets and developed digital *Star Trek* participatory cultures. As a result of these factors, only two fan-run unofficial clubs were active in Australia in 2000, and they had ceased publishing fan fiction or hosting video screenings in order to stave off legal challenges.[79]

It is a somewhat poetic tragedy that the decline of formal Australian *Star Trek* fan clubs would be prompted by a crackdown on the communal viewing of *Star Trek* episodes in clubs. Club viewings and support of Johnson's marathons were an integral force in the growth of Australian *Star Trek* fandom, providing most fans with their primary access to episodes of *ST: TOS*, and later, *TNG*. Johnson did not face the same legal challenges as the Australian fan clubs because he exploited the vague language of Desilu's international licensing agreements in the 1980s after channel 9 sent him a cease-and-desist letter and he won the case. The third season of *ST: TOS* was produced after Paramount purchased Desilu, and so this season had a structured and enforceable foreign-licensing agreement. Johnson agreed to only screen episodes from seasons 1 and 2; however, after his legal victory there was no oversight by the Australian Television and Film Securities Office, and he was said to eventually screen episodes from all three seasons of *ST: TOS* without consequence. Like the fan-club screenings, interest in Johnson's marathon screenings of *ST: TOS* tampered down during the 1990s. The marathons ceased being advertised in the theater sections of Sydney and Melbourne newspapers in 1990.[80] One fan-authored web page claims that the Melbourne marathons ended in the late 1980s although I found listings of the Melbourne marathons as late as 1993. However, by the mid-1990s, these marathons were no longer being held monthly but, rather, only a few times a year. Getting a precise history of these marathons is difficult. Johnson has been described to me by multiple fans as a "dodgy character," and not only are his business records not available in any official archive but one fan also explained to me that he would not be surprised if Johnson had shredded all his company's documents before he died. There is, however, some consensus that Johnson continued to organize several marathons a year in Sydney until his death in 2000.[81]

The difficulty dating the end of Johnson's marathons exemplifies the impossibility of precisely documenting the comprehensive history of bootlegging *Star Trek* in Australia. Writing histories of media bootlegging, in general, is challenging; this is the nature of doing cultural history where the only traces available are grassroot fanzines and oral histories, both of which can be incomplete and contradictory. Although it is impossible to account for all of the bootlegging activity and some of the exact timeline dates, this chapter demonstrates the significant role of *Star Trek* marathons and club screenings as television distribution during the 1970s and 1980s. The communal nature of these distributive events is a direct result of Australia's specific development of television technology, especially the lack of networked television distribution and the adaptation of the European PAL television systems, a result of Australia's position as a part of the United Kingdom's Commonwealth. Describing the lengths that he and other fans had to go to access *Star Trek* episodes in Australia, McLean explains, "America was so far along in the entertainment industry, the stuff that we had to do in order to see things was really hard. We had to do it the really hard way. And we didn't know at the time that it was the hard way."[82]

If nothing else, this account of fans' distributive labor making *Star Trek* episodes available to Australian viewers shows how much these audiences worked to gain access to television content. McLean's comments are illustrative, however, on a second level, because they demonstrate one way Australian fans came to make sense of their distributive labor as a necessary tool to overcome Australia's geographic and sociocultural position on the periphery of the global media industries, what Tama Leaver describes as the "tyranny of distance." Leaver built on the tyranny of distance political metaphor politicians used in 1960s Australia to "describe the fundamental role that the geographic distance from the United Kingdom—the cultural and economic centre of 'Empire'— played in forming the character and cultural identity of Australia's white population." In his article, Leaver discusses the ways in which global telecommunication developments have made it possible for Australian audiences to use digital peer-to-peer social networks to download American and British television content that would otherwise be delayed for broadcast in Australia by a windowing period of six months to two years.[83] Australians' desire to access content at the same time as other audiences is not a new phenomenon. Indeed, we should consider the digital collaborative practice of distributing current television through peer-to-peer social networks as a continuation of the bootlegging practices outlined here. However, in the digital model, the communal nature of bootlegged viewing necessitated by the technological and industrial nature of transnational television in the 1970s and 1980s is no longer experienced within the immediacy of the viewing experience but in the communal nature of uploading, transferring, and seeding copies together through digital platforms that comprise contemporary informal networks of television circulation.

CHAPTER 5

Enough of That Garbage
Wrestling Observer and the Intelligent Wrestling-Fan Community

On August 20, 1982, a young wrestling fan named Dave Meltzer wrote to Norman Kietzer, the editor of *Wrestling News* magazine, to announce the launch of his newsletter *Wrestling Observer*. Meltzer asked Kietzer to share the information in the magazine's fan-club section on how to contribute to and get *Wrestling Observer*: "You have my name and address on file for the trading of VHS videotapes and I am still most interested in that. The videotapes will make up (from my observations) a considerable portion of the copy material."[1] Four months later, Meltzer began publishing *Wrestling Observer*, using a typewriter in his apartment in San Jose, California, and the publication would come to be one of the most respected and long-running professional wrestling news outlets. In its current iteration, *Wrestling Observer* is no longer a fan newsletter—it has become a digital multimedia brand that distributes weekly newsletters, podcasts, articles, and merchandise online. *Wrestling Observer* became one of the most popular fanzines in the 1980s and 1990s because it offered subscribers and participants a forum to discuss regional match results and professional wrestling industrial news, topics which were not reported in newspapers or official wrestling magazines at the time. Most central to this book, however, is the function of the *Wrestling Observer* as a central node in tape-trading televised wrestling. According to a number of longtime wrestling fans, *Wrestling Observer* had a reputation during its formative years of the 1980s as *the* newsletter for wrestling tape trading.[2] *Wrestling Observer* came to have this reputation because its pages facilitated bootlegging processes in two ways: it provided fans with the schedules for wrestling programs on local television stations and cable operators, and, as with the other fanzines discussed in chapters 2 and 3, *Wrestling Observer* came to function as a clearinghouse for tape trading with short notices by editor Meltzer and other contributors requesting specific wrestling TV recordings or offering to share their personal recording catalogs.

Wrestling Observer's facilitation of tape trading was reciprocally connected to the open, in-depth discussion of the professional wrestling in its pages. *Wrestling Observer* was also unique for the way it honestly acknowledged kayfabe, the wrestling industry's term for the staging of predetermined events, outcomes, and storylines, which at the time was not openly discussed in official wrestling magazines published for fans. This candid engagement with professional wrestling is one reason *Wrestling Observer* played a significant role in the formation of an intelligent-wrestling-fan subculture that came to prominence in the 1980s. I use the term "intelligent" here to refer to wrestling fans' self-conscious presentation as knowing participants within the spectacle of professional wrestling's kayfabe. The term "kayfabe" originates in the wrestling industry's variant of pig Latin code used to conceal business secrets from audiences. When wrestling developed as a form of popular culture in the early twentieth century, promoters and wrestlers came to hold a perception of paying customers as "dupes to be financially swindled" and referred to ticket buyers as "marks."[3] Sharon Mazer introduced a "smarts" versus "marks" dichotomy in her 1998 ethnography of professional wrestling fans to account for fans who make sense of themselves as experts who are not only in on the con but are also invested in studying both the sport and industry and frequently display this knowledge within the various forums of the wrestling-fan community.[4] One fan referred to this category as "inside fans, people who know wrestling results are predetermined but don't care, who admire athletic brilliance for what it is in this particular arena."[5]

The formation of an intelligent, knowing fan in on the scam contrasts the female fans and feminized caricature of the "mark" that Chad Dell discusses in his history of televised wrestling in the 1950s.[6] Henry Jenkins has characterized professional wrestling as a masculine melodrama, an ambivalent cultural form defined by both a masculine subject matter, "the homosocial relations between men, the professional sphere rather the domestic, the focus on physical means to resolve conflicts" while also relying on feminine forms of address, notably, wrestling's serialized open-ended storytelling focused on an ensemble cast of characters, much like a melodramatic soap opera.[7] Mazer argues that the masculinity displayed in professional wrestling is so exaggerated and over-the-top that it becomes satirical parody of hegemonic masculinity, writing, "To some degree, a professional wrestler is always in drag, always enacting a parody of masculinity at the same time that he epitomizes it."[8] Both Jenkins and Mazer offer an ambivalent picture of professional wrestling's gendered dimensions, but these analyses are focused on the theatricality of the wrestling match.

Like wrestling itself, wrestling-fan communities are polysemic and influenced by specific sociohistorical contexts and cultural practices. This chapter looks at the process of tape trading wrestling TV as a form of distributive labor within an interpretive community that, as Cornel Sandvoss might say, invites the development of fan subjectivities through both self-reflection and presentation, as well as the ongoing reconstitution of one's self-images as a fan through group interactions and reflections.[9] Bootlegging wrestling television was and continues to be a process deeply connected to fans' identity formation. It is a ritual born from a desire to study matches through repeat viewing, much like *Starsky & Hutch* fans used episode recordings to study the homosocial scenes between the main characters, or *Star Trek* fans studied episodes to write fan fiction. Wrestling fans sought to study matches to gain broader knowledge of specific wrestler's techniques, interviews, and storylines and to create their own system for ranking wrestlers. *Wrestling Observer*'s publication of an annual yearbook with awards based on reader submissions has been an annual tradition of the publication since 1982 and established what was perceived as a more objective comparison of athletes beyond the contrived kayfabe that fans know determines official champions within the sport. These awards, as Jenkins might say, have been one of the ways intelligent fans rewrite the official melodrama that is professional wrestling.[10] As this chapter makes clear, the development of the "wrestling-fan-as-intelligent" modality became more mainstream in the wrestling-fan cultures of the early 1980s and was fostered by bootleg tape-trading networks and the in-depth analysis of professional wrestling, both of which were facilitated by Meltzer's *Wrestling Observer*.

Tape trading facilitated an intellectualization of professional wrestling for fans, and this functioned as an implicitly masculine recuperation of wrestling fandom from the feminized "marks" typically associated with wrestling. Tape trading is an inherently social act of bootlegging, emphasized by the second word here, *trading*. Wrestling fans also came to make sense of themselves as a community characterized by their studious dedication to wrestling via tape trading and debate, despite the perception that the owners and promoters of professional wrestlers did not respect them as rational, intelligent fans. The social practice of tape trading wrestling TV bootlegs gave fans the impetus and forum to perform the work of accumulating in-depth knowledge about wrestlers, promoters, and history, while fanzines gave them the platform to co-construct a technorational authority over a sport whose outcome was otherwise out of the fan's control.

Bootlegging televised wrestling is a set of technologically embedded processes contextualized by the broader history and specifics of professional wrestling in the United States. Communal tape trading between fans was driven by the unique regionalization of televised wrestling in the mid-twentieth century, as well as the profession's use of TV to promote in-person events with small-scale studio matches. Brian Last is a longtime fan and wrestling historian whose company Arcadian Vanguard produces several podcasts devoted to classic wrestling, and he explained,

> The difference between something like wrestling and something like *Star Trek*, is that the same *Star Trek* reruns were airing all around the country. With wrestling, tape trading was the only way of knowing what was happening in other parts of the country. And in a lot of places, like Los Angeles, the TV stations didn't keep anything, they just taped right over the local wrestling, and it became a lost history. If there are any recordings out there, it's because of the fans.[11]

From the late 1950s through the 1980s, televised wrestling corresponded to the decentralized nature of professional wrestling, as regional territories operated through a loose association of promoters. Early broadcasters, such as NBC and DuMont Television Network, experimented with nationally broadcasting wrestling programs in the 1940s and 1950s; however, after DuMont canceled its wrestling program in 1955, most televised wrestling was produced and broadcast within professional wrestling's industrial logics and decentralized regional structure. The history of bootlegging wrestling recordings is indicative of professional wrestling's distinct relationship with television in the United States. Thus, this chapter begins by mapping out the relationship between professional wrestling's regionalized structure and its relationship with television to situate the distinct distributive labor performed by wrestling fans who recorded matches and shared them with each other. Then the chapter charts out the ways wrestling fans used magazines and newsletters to connect and trade match tapes, specifically focusing on the history of *Wrestling Observer* as one of the more prominent fanzines for tape trading. Drawing on archival copies of *Wrestling Observer*, interviews, and articles from the mainstream press, this chapter demonstrates how fans facilitated the circulation of wrestling matches over time and space, sharing TV listings and home recordings. Fans used wrestling TV bootlegs to study and rank wrestlers and matches, which further heightened the broader desire to obtain and view recordings within the wrestling-fan community. Lastly, this chapter describes the ways tape-trading networks encouraged the development of an intelligent-wrestling-fan persona, as fans sought communal recognition and took pleasure in accumulating in-depth expertise about professional wrestling.

Televised Wrestling's Regionalized Structure

Wrestling as a sport can be traced back to the Greek empire, and it was popularized as a serious and legitimate sport in the United States by soldiers in Civil War training camps. Wrestling's heightened recognition occurred during a time when rugged masculinity was being valued within mainstream US culture as an antidote to the feminized consumer culture associated with the urban middle-class life of the Progressive Era discussed in chapter 1. President Theodore Roosevelt famously held matches in the White House to promote wrestling as a form of strenuous physical exercise during his administration. As wrestling became a prevalent sport during the gilded age, increased promotion and touring occurred during the same time that carnival and vaudeville circuits emerged, and wrestling was heavily influenced by these other forms of popular entertainment. During the 1890s and 1900s professional wrestling came to rely on "championship games, named stars, imported foreign competitors," and by 1905 most matches were already fixed to plan out theatrical performances that ended with an unexpected sensational outcome and were promoted using publicized ongoing feuds and storylines.[12]

Kayfabe's predetermined outcomes and theatricality made wrestling an attractive programming form for early television programmers. Field games like baseball and football were hard to film using early television equipment, while, in contrast, wrestling's arena setting and prearranged chorography made wrestling an ideal sport for early television technology. Chad Dell notes that "a first-round knockout in boxing would leave broadcasters with unfulfilled advertising commitments and unfilled airtime; likewise, extra innings in a baseball game could run up costly additional wire expenses"; in contrast, wrestling's kayfabe made matches more predictable and easier to produce for a set schedule with sponsorship spots.[13] However, NBC executives canceled the network's wrestling programming in 1950, despite high ratings and a sponsor, in order to align the network brand with the perceived prestige of expensive dramatic anthologies like *Philco Playhouse*.[14] Until the network's collapse in 1955, DuMont, on the other hand, aired wrestling programming because the matches consistently generated high ratings and were comparatively less expensive to produce than scripted drama.[15] Once wrestling matches ceased to be aired on national network television schedules, content shifted dramatically.

Professional wrestling in the United States has been tenuously structured by associations and affiliated regional promoters since 1904 when the National Wrestling Association was formed to encourage promoters to collaborate on coordinating tours, matches, and publicity.[16] This first association was designed as a "loosely united consortium" in order to evade anti-trust laws and government oversight and, thus, gave regional promoters independence to manage and control talent, matches, and regional championship titles in their area.[17] In 1948 the National Wrestling Association became part of a new, larger wrestling organization called the National Wrestling Alliance, a name whose acronym, NWA, gave professional wrestling continuity.[18] This new NWA further centralized how professional wrestling was managed and controlled by a small group of members and promoters, who eliminated competing championships, increased coordination between regional members, and created standardized guidelines for wrestler performance.[19] Following 1948 the NWA was essentially a monopoly comprising over thirty territories that cooperated with each other to blacklist promoters, bookers, and wrestlers who did not adhere to the organization's rules.[20]

Regional promoters had a somewhat ambivalent attitude toward television, especially as the technology came to be more widely adopted in US households by the early 1950s. Wrestling promoters were wary of televised wrestling matches in the 1940s and 1950s, even as NBC's and DuMont's programs were ratings successes that did not seem to impact ticket sales. Some believed that airing matches would decrease live-event ticket revenue, and several promoters instituted bans on broadcasting local matches in their territories.[21] In contrast, promoters, such as Toronto-based wrestling promoter Frank Tunney, credited his ability to sellout local arena matches with his use of televised studio matches in 1953.[22] Amid these debates, the NWA took a more reactionary stance and blacklisted wrestlers, promoters, and bookers who appeared in TV studio matches until an anti-trust lawsuit brought by the US Department of Justice in

1956.[23] As part of the consent order during this trial, the NWA agreed to cease discriminating against TV participants.[24] NWA's policy shift in 1956 ushered in a period of expansion by regional promoters that would last from the late 1950s through the early 1980s. During this time, television came to be defined within the wrestling industry as a promotional tool. Regional promoters started using taped studio matches, intercut with interviews, to hype up rivalries and publicize live events at large arenas. Thus, televised wrestling became a decentralized form of programming that varied from promoter to promoter and was shaped by the local TV station's technical equipment, signal range, and business practices.

The breakdown of professional wrestling into regional territories was well established by the time that Meltzer began to publish *Wrestling Observer* in 1982. However, it is difficult to trace out a comprehensive history of professional wrestling's promotional territories during the mid-twentieth century. Promoters would encroach into cities controlled by rivals, sell off sections to other promoters, change the name of their promotion companies, or go bankrupt and pull out of professional wrestling altogether, which would leave former territories defunct or dark. Let us consider a brief history of Pittsburgh, Pennsylvania, as part of a wrestling territory during the midcentury to understand the unstable nature of professional wrestling regional promotion companies.

Vince J. McMahon, the father of current World Wrestling Entertainment (WWE) owner Vince K. McMahon, owned the regional company Capitol Wrestling Corp., based in Washington, DC. The elder McMahon used TV studio matches and a joint-business agreement with New York promoter Toots Mondt to expand across the Northeast, covering territory in New York, New Jersey, Pennsylvania, and beyond, notably coming to control wrestling booking at Madison Square Garden.[25] Capitol Wrestling changed its name to World Wide Wrestling Federation (WWWF) and left the NWA in 1963 after a disagreement over the heavyweight championship outcome. Mondt moved to Pittsburgh to run the WWWF promotion office there and retired from the wrestling industry in 1969.[26] Pittsburgh was reportedly sold off to several different promotions and changed hands a number of times, making the history of this region arduous to fully study, especially after the dissolution of the local television program *Studio Wrestling*, which was broadcast on WIIC-TV from 1958 to 1974.[27]

Due to the shifting boundaries of regional wrestling promotional companies and the incomplete documentation of these changes, it is impossible to present a complete history of the wrestling territories during

Table 5.1. Promotions and territories covered in *Wrestling Observer*, July and August 1983

American Wrestling Association (Midwest)
Calgary, Canada
Central States (Kansas, Missouri, Nebraska)
Florida
Jarrett Promotions (Memphis, Tennessee)
Mid-Atlantic (Virginia, North Carolina, South Carolina)
New Japan Wrestling Association (nationwide in Japan)
Northwest (Oregon and Washington)
Nova Scotia, Canada
Polynesian Area (Hawaii, Hong Kong, the Philippines)
Quebec, Canada
Southeast (Alabama and Florida panhandle)
Southwest (San Antonio, Texas)
Toronto, Canada
World Championship Wrestling (Georgia)
World Class (Dallas, Texas)
World Wrestling Federation (Northeast and Los Angeles)

Note: This table is not a comprehensive list of all professional wrestling regions active in 1983, let alone ever, as territories and companies were constantly restructured. However, this list does provide an overview of the regionalized nature of professional wrestling that defined the sport from the mid-twentieth century through the 1980s. Some territories were listed by promotional company name, others by region. Area covered is in parentheses for clarification on regions where geography was unclear in listing. Considering that this is the list of promotions Dave Meltzer reported on, it also highlights the extensive coverage provided by *Wrestling Observer*.

Sources: Dave Meltzer, "Wrestling Notebook," *Wrestling Observer*, July 1983, 9–16, and August 1983, 8–15.

the 1970s and 1980s. Even through the pages of *Wrestling Observer* in the 1980s, the list of regions changed from issue to issue. Table 5.1 is a snapshot of the territories Meltzer reported on in the July and August 1983 issues of *Wrestling Observer* that demonstrates the regionalization of professional wrestling during this period. This regionalization was an obstacle for fans who wished to follow the sport because kayfabe had led most major newspapers to exclude reporting on pro wrestling in their sport or entertainment section. For these reasons, wrestling fans of the twentieth century had to forge their own communication networks to connect with fans in other parts of the United States and beyond in order to follow the ongoing narratives and outcomes of wrestling matches beyond their hometown.

Beginning in the 1970s, fans began to use these networks to trade tapes they recorded or obtained from territories in North America, as well as matches in Japan and Mexico. Fans began using audio cassettes, as Last describes:

> Wrestling was territorial, you had different areas of the country with wrestling shows, so if you were a wrestling fan in New York, and you saw a wrestler you started to really like, and then all of a sudden one day they're gone somewhere else, there was no way to follow what they did. There were no reports then, maybe you'd see something in a magazine, but it didn't have any of the specifics, so a lot of fans would start holding audio recorders to TV sets and taping the interviews and even some of the matches. Before the VHS tapes started getting traded around, wrestling fans traded audio tapes in the seventies.[28]

Many of the wrestling fans interviewed note that professional wrestling's territorialization was the motivating factor for their initial entrée into tape trading. Steven Beverly, a retired television producer and media scholar, as well as wrestling fan, explains tape trading in terms of a regional promotion's word-of-mouth buzz, using the Pacific Northwest territory as an example:

> There was a show in Portland, Oregon that was very popular. . . . You would only ever find out about it a month later in wrestling magazines. . . . But when VCRs became prevalent, then Don Owen's [the promoter for the Northwest wrestling region] matches were available, and there were a group of people up in the Pacific Northwest that were always glad to swap your lot with Don's shows. . . . Stampede promotion in Canada was another one that was very popular. If you found out that there was a really hot promotion that was doing well and had some extremely popular talent . . . you had to engage in trading to see it.[29]

These comments show how home recording facilitated access to televised wrestling across the disparate structure of professional wrestling. Beverly's last quote also highlights how popularity and fan differentiation of some territories as "hot" played a role in further encouraging fans to trade tapes. Beverly notes how he gained leverage within the wrestling tape trading circles because he received the signals from local stations that aired a combined twelve to thirteen different wrestling shows, including several that were extremely popular and hard to get.

During the late 1970s and early 1980s, two figures began the push to nationalize wrestling on television: Ted Turner and Vince K. McMahon. Turner began airing the Georgia Championship nationally through his

WTCG (later WTBS) superstation in 1976, while McMahon took over the WWWF from his father in 1983, changed the company name to World Wrestling Federation (WWF), and began buying out local television spots for WWF studio matches in competitors' territories.[30] McMahon also raided competitors territories for talent, stealing promising wrestlers from other regions.[31] These shifts toward greater exposure made TBS and WWF program recordings fairly common and less desirable in tape-trading circles, where promotions, such as Stampede, as well as many in the South, such as Mid-Atlantic, Mid-South, or Florida wrestling, were among the most highly sought after territories by wrestling tape traders.[32] Wrestling fans of the pre-internet era had to build their own video libraries to overcome the fractured and regionalized nature of US wrestling, and the fanzine *Wrestling Observer* was one of the primary places fans connected with each other to trade tapes, study the industry, and discuss wrestling from a knowing, reflexive standpoint.

Tape Trading and the Intelligent Wrestling Fan

Wrestling Observer was not the first wrestling fan–authored publication, as Dell has outlined how other wrestling-fan clubs and fan bulletins were being published earlier during the 1950s.[33] Mainstream newspapers did not report wrestling-match outcomes, and monthly wrestling magazines, such as *Pro-Wrestling Illustrated* or *Wrestling Eye*, were promotional tools used by the industry to publish glossy cover stories about high-profile wrestlers. The wrestling industry actively discouraged newspaper coverage and publication of results in official magazines because promoters changed characters from region to region and repeated match outcomes and storylines within their territories. For these reasons, they believed documented coverage of wrestling-match outcomes would hurt the revenue from event attendance.[34] In response to this, wrestling-fan clubs formed in the 1950s and were the first sources to publish and share pro wrestling—match results.[35] Often devoted to a specific wrestling star, like Gorgeous George, these early fan bulletins came to function as the only printed record of professional wrestling. By the 1970s a thriving, yet also uneven and ever-changing plethora of fan bulletins, newsletters, and fan associations, such as the Wrestling Fans International Association, connected wrestling fans in different parts of the country. Participants communicated and crowdsourced information through phone calls, written correspondence, and conventions, evincing a network of wrestling fans who had created a communal space to intimately discuss wrestling, their affective connections to the sport and its performers, and friendships across geographical barriers.

Meltzer was active in the wrestling-fan community before founding the *Wrestling Observer*, as his letter to *Wrestling News* quoted in the chapter opening makes clear. *Wrestling Observer* became distinct in the fandom because it consistently published comprehensive results for wrestling associations operating in the United States, Canada, Mexico, and Japan. *Wrestling Observer* issues published in the early 1980s generally followed this format: a cover story by Meltzer on a thought-provoking issue, such as "Should Pro-Wrestling Be Covered in Sports Pages," followed by the column Editor's Notes, topical articles, or regular columns written by participants in the wrestling community, followed by reader letters, newspaper clippings with stories about pro wrestling, in-depth reports on the regional promotions in the Wrestling Notebook section, classified ads from readers, and information on how to renew a subscription.[36] The regional reports often spanned seven to ten or more typed pages, with several black-and-white photos. Reports listed the outcomes of matches through each region, including venue, referees, feuds, moves, and notable business dealings and presented a far-reaching level of detail about professional wrestling hitherto unavailable in newspapers, wrestling magazines, or other fanzines. Meltzer's reporting was made possible by his connections within the wrestling industry and fan networks, but tape trading was instrumental to Meltzer's efforts publishing the broad scope of regional news featured in *Wrestling Observer*. Indeed, Meltzer regularly referred to studying VHS tapes in his coverage of specific wrestling territories. With regional reports, participant forums, letters, and topical think pieces, *Wrestling Observer* issues were often over thirty pages long and became popular among fans for its serious and upfront engagement with topics that ranged from promoters' practices and organizational politics to debates on aspects of wrestling performance.

Meltzer became one of the earliest avatars of the intelligent, masculine, authoritative wrestling fan, the "smart fan" distinct from the "marks." Sam Ford describes the "smart fan" in wrestling as someone who is on a "constant quest to learn as much as possible about the creative process and what is likely to happen in WWE, and potentially even use that knowledge to critique and oppose the company's creative decisions."[37] David Shoemaker calls this mode of fandom interchangeably "metafans" or "die-hard fans" a form of fan practice, and Nicholas Ware expands on this in his discussion of wrestling video games and what he calls the "dual consciousness" of wrestling fans, the acknowledgment and pleasure of kayfabe, alongside a desire to consume much behind-the-scenes information about the business of professional wrestling. Ware describes metafans as those who "are not just fans of the diegetic drama of professional wrestling but fans of the business itself, and follow the metanarrative of business deals, backstage politics, and real-world relationships that inevitably influence the pro wrestling product as presented on television."[38] These "smart" wrestling fans, then, distinguish themselves from more "casual" fans through their consumption, interrogation, and display of knowledge about the internal industrial machinations of professional wrestling. These different monikers, such as "smart," "meta," or "die hard" fan, all conjure the same contrast to the wrestling industry's assumed "mark" audience. The term "intelligent" is used here also to convey how the wrestling-fan culture that came to prominence in the 1980s was invested in studying wrestling through fanzines and taped recordings and performed their work studying professional wrestling at conventions and matches and in the pages of fanzines. These were not merely smart fans but critically engaged authorities who gained expertise through accumulating as much information as possible, then sharing and debating different aspects of wrestling from athleticism to promotional strategies and business practices. Mazer first broached this distinction between smarts and marks in 1998, and these other subsequent discussions of meta and die-hard fans have expanded on this dichotomy in an environment dominated by the WWE's transnational wrestling empire.

Meltzer and the history of the *Wrestling Observer* are significant because they demonstrate the early public debates about this internal hierarchy and awareness within fan communities in the 1980s. This history also highlights the role of fanzines and tape trading as important material processes that facilitated fans' identity as wrestling scholars who studied the sport and became wrestling experts. The *Wrestling Observer* offered its readers and participants a masculine, intelligent fan subjectivity, a tone masculine by virtue of the often blunt or at times slightly vulgar authoritative prose Meltzer and his fellow contributors used. We can get a sense of this distinct masculine tone from a few examples of the ire directed at the younger Vince McMahon after he took over his father's company during the mid-1980s, for what fans perceived as childish media gimmicks to make WWF a national company. Take, for instance, Meltzer's snark in this passage from a multipage story about Titan Sports, the parent company of WWF at the time: "Vince [McMahon] is really determined to bore the wrestling fans in KC.... I watched the tape at 1 a.m. with the express purpose of having it put me to sleep.

... Enough of that garbage and onto their garbage."[39] One contributor says in another issue, "My only comment on Vince McMahon is that I'm certain he's the biggest bastard of them all.... He reminds me of Caligula, someone who would destroy his own family to get more power."[40] Regular *Observer* contributor Mike McNulty comments, "If we're lucky, America will O.D. on WWF TV wrestling and puke up Jr. McMahon and his travelling vaudeville troup [sic]."[41] The juxtaposition of rough and sarcastic language like "garbage," "bastards," or "puke" with authoritative evaluation and highbrow references like Caligula exemplify the ways that participants' *Wrestling Observer* fan forum crafted a position at once masculine and also intelligent in their interrogations of the professional-wrestling industry. Fans' self-presentations in the pages of *Wrestling Observer* as aware analytical critics were diametrically opposed to the submissive, feminized, duped mark the wrestling industry imagined.

Meltzer's description of his motivation to create *Wrestling Observer* for mature college-educated readers also represents how he understood himself and the participants in his community as intelligent fans. Meltzer explains his motivation founding *Wrestling Observer* in a 1991 interview,

> I had this different idea for a newsletter.... It filled a niche that wasn't being filled at the time. I'll tell you what really prompted me. I was in college, and I used to always watch videotapes of wrestling during my lunch break with a lot of my friends in college. And they were all wrestling fans. The newspapers were never covering wrestling. The wrestling magazines would cover it, but they were writing for kids. And all these people who I went to college with, and my newspaper class, these people, they were interested ... in wrestling, and they wanted to know what was going on ... and I figured, "If all of these people are interested in reading about wrestling in this way, then obviously people around the country should be." So, I decided I wanted to start a newsletter for this kind of person, a person who goes to college. I mean, that was the age I was looking at, people who go to college, a little bit older, and what they would be interested in reading about wrestling, and what's going on.[42]

Here, Meltzer emphasizes his imagined audience of fellow college-educated wrestling fans, similarly invested in following the inner workings of the wrestling industry, as a reflection of his own identity as an intelligent, critical wrestling fan. It is also telling here that Meltzer foregrounds videotape viewing as a component of his fannish practice. The ability to access wrestling from multiple regions and countries and replay this content was a crucial component for the intelligent fan who wanted to study wrestling culture. Accessing and replaying matches and the interviews included in the flow of the studio wrestling matches allowed fans to obtain and display a comprehensive knowledge of wrestlers, wrestling moves, announcers, and storylines while also providing them with the resources to repeatedly rewatch matches, and to find and study "shoots," the term for wrestling matches that go off script.

The *Wrestling Observer* facilitated tape trading both by connecting fans with each other and by publishing television schedules and leads on how to access television content. Televised wrestling in the 1980s was a distinctly local configuration determined by professional wrestling's shifting regionalized territories, independent station programming, and ever-changing syndication deals, as well as the inconsistent availability of international content through multisystem operators. Fans would write in to the *Wrestling Observer* to share information on how to watch wrestling programs, with notices like this 1983 letter from Walt Wolansky telling other wrestling fans, "The Dallas TV show is syndicated and shown in Boston, Atlanta, Salt Lake City, St. Louis, Houston and now Memphis. . . . In retaliation to the Boston broadcast of the World Class show, the WWF switched one of its shows from noon to 11 a.m.—the same time as World Class."[43] Meltzer also regularly shared information on opportunities to watch various wrestling programs, such as this 1984 note to readers,

> One last note about some TV shows many of you could/should look out for. For those with satellite dishes, besides the shows on WOR, USA and WTBS that most fans are familiar with, some new entrees into the market are WPIX, Ch. 11 New York (The Eddie Einhorn Pro Wrestling USA Show 11 a. m. Saturday Eastern time), KTVT Ch. 11 Dallas (Championship Sports, 10 p.m. Saturday Central time) and a Canadian show which broadcasts AWA [American Wrestling Association] from the Winnipeg Arena. I'll try and get the call letters for that as well and time for next issue. The Satellite Program Network (SPN) has a wrestling show as well, but for some inexplicable reason, it's listed as "Franchise Showcase" or some silly title similar to that. The show is produced by Paul Boesch, former Houston wrestling promoter. Boesch shows old clips from the 50s, 60s and 70s. . . . For those who want to see what wrestling was like in different decades, it's a show you'll find most interesting even if Boesch is a terrible announcer. Also, just so I don't fall into the predicament of asking for it after the fact when nobody has a copy, if anyone has a dish or access to one

over Thanksgiving weekend, please tape the Starrcade '84 show from Greensboro [NC] for me.[44]

It is also telling that Meltzer ends his announcement about television schedules with a request for someone to tape the Starrcade, a pay-per-view championship put on by NWA that was copied by WWF in 1985 with their inaugural pay-per-view program *Wrestlemania*. These are a few examples of how fans used the *Wrestling Observer* to track and subvert the shifting terrain of televised wrestling's decentralized structure.

Televised wrestling's hybrid, decentralized structure is worth further discussion to emphasize the importance of tape trading to this community of fans. Professional wrestling has long been compared to soap operas, due to the use of melodramatic feuds and ongoing storylines that often animate a series of matches over months or years.[45] There are certainly parallels to the serialized narrative of soap operas, often emphasized by the interstitial interviews or stunts staged between wrestling matches, where rivalries and vendettas are revealed to wrestling audiences. However, if we were to compare the production and distribution of soap operas in the early 1980s with televised wrestling, it is clear the decentralized distribution of televised wrestling demanded much more work from audiences to follow pro wrestling's narratives. For instance, most soap operas on television in 1984 were distributed by national networks CBS, NBC, and ABC and aired via the same fixed-point daily schedule, with clearly listed schedules available to audiences in most media markets via *TV Guide* and local newspaper listings. In contrast, professional wrestling of the 1970s and 1980s operated like a soap whose performers consistently crossed over between different networks and programs, distribution was regionalized, main events were not broadcast or reported on, and the showrunners actively discouraged the publication of narrative summaries akin to those published in soap magazines.

Fans who understood themselves as a part of the intelligent wrestling-fan community wanted to keep up with the ongoing storyline and desired access to both studio programs and match results across US regions and other countries. To this end, fans of the 1980s had to follow the multiplicity of storylines across associations (at this time, for instance, the AWA, NWA, and WWF were distinct wrestling organizations with their own championships and stars), regions (such as Dallas, Memphis, Mid-Atlantic, etc.), and within these regions, specific tapings done for television stations in each city that aired studio matches (Winnipeg, Portland, Boston, etc.). No centralized listing of televised wrestling programs was available at this time, and wrestling programs were produced by a disparate collection of promoters who primarily looked at TV as a promotional tool and, thus, often aired one taped match cut with new interviews in multiple cities to promote a main event featuring the same wrestlers on tour across a region. The *Wrestling Observer* distinguished itself from other fanzines by creating a forum in which fans did the work of creating guides for how to find and watch wrestling programs on TV and did the work of distributing these programs through tape trading.

Meltzer relied on traded tapes to write about the wrestling industry with what came to be known as his trademark in-depth knowledge and analysis.[46] In one letter from the editor, Meltzer explains, "The time devoted to watching tapes is the backbone of the Observer and the reason I started this publication in the first place."[47] Meltzer also used the *Wrestling Observer* to trade wrestling tapes with other fans, and one of the earliest examples of this is a short column that came to be a regular featured column, Videotapes, in the *Wrestling Observer*. Meltzer would update readers on the current number of videos he had, how to get a full catalog of his tape library, and programs he specifically wanted. For example, Meltzer advises in his Videotapes column in October 1983,

> I am currently on the lookout for anyone who can trade videotapes with me from Houston, Texas, Calgary, Alberta and Alabama. I have a collection of 175 hours of highlights from throughout North America and some literally incredible action from Japan. For the nine-page list send 54¢ to cover postage to me at 1717 Midwestern Parkway #205, Wichita Falls, Texas 76302. Don't send any self-addressed stamped envelopes because the list is too extensive to fit into a regular envelope. I would also like to trade with anyone who gets Larry Matysik's St. Louis wrestling program.[48]

This column appeared regularly through issues in the 1980s, sometimes just as a component of the Editor's Notes column or with a different title, such as Videomania. Some discussions would contain longer overviews of content, such as a one-page summary of three "supertapes" Meltzer had compiled with highlights from what he had assessed as the best matches of 1983.[49] Meltzer also published readers' requests to trade with other fans, telling his subscribers in 1983, "Anyone interested in getting a copy of bouts from a certain area, a certain match or whatever let me know and I'll list it. There are probably 15–20 readers of this publication with very extensive video collections and if none of them have it—chances are it never took place."[50] It is clear Meltzer addressed the readers of his fanzine as an avid community of tape traders, a reputation fueled by the *Wrestling Observer*'s publication of an editorial board's annual ranking of professional wrestling in a variety of categories.

Meltzer first began writing up and ranking wrestling matches in a bulletin he circulated among tape-trading friends in the late 1970s, and the *Wrestling Observer* was designed with this purpose in mind, as an expansion of Meltzer's tape-trading catalog that ranked the matches listed. Meltzer would publish instructions for readers to complete, giving them a variety of categories to submit their choice for wrestler of the year, best on interviews, best tag team, most washed up, most overrated, wrestler of the year, best babyface, or best heel (pro-wrestling jargon for hero and villain), and many others (see figure 5.1). The process of ranking different categories of professional wrestling reflected Meltzer's understanding that participants in the *Wrestling Observer* were equally invested in an intelligent discussion of wrestling. Meltzer describes the process for having fans rank wrestlers when he created the *Wrestling Observer* newsletter in 1982: "This ballot is being sent to specially selected wrestling fanatics familiar with happenings in the sport on a world-wide basis."[51] Fans' desire to rank matches is an indirect result of kayfabe and demonstrated a desire to appreciate wrestling on its own terms and reward wrestlers perceived to be talented, outside of kayfabe's contrived championship belts and titles. Indeed, Meltzer advises readers completing the poll in 1984 with the following instructions: "Because of the nature of this publication I would prefer this rating be done on ability. Because wrestling results and titles won have little, if anything to do with ability, they shouldn't be considered too highly. Don't vote for the Hulk, Flair or Martel because they hold a belt, vote for them if you think they are good."[52] This passage is telling because it reveals how the *Wrestling Observer*'s annual awards gave fans the opportunity to demonstrate their in-depth knowledge of the sport and change the narrative provided by the industry and its championship titles to "retroactively rescript the master narrative," the term Noah Cohan uses to describe how sports journalist Bill Simmons draws on his knowledge of basketball history to reauthor the narrative possibilities of previous basketball games by pondering what would have happened if specific factors were different. The *Wrestling Observer*'s annual reader-awards poll gave fans the opportunity to determine their own list of the winners and losers from the previous year through a method that they felt reflected a wrestler's athletic ability and talent.

The annual *Wrestling Observer* awards is still a tradition at the current digital iteration of the publication and may be a feature of the fanzine

Figure 5.1. The cover of the 1983 *Wrestling Observer Annual Yearbook* issue featuring wrestler Michael Hayes, designed and printed in the do-it-yourself style typical to early issues of the newsletter. This annual yearbook issue is released every February and features matches, interviews, and industry highlights from the year, as well as the results of the *Wrestling Observer*'s award ratings for professional wrestlers in wide range of categories that readers voted on, including best heel, the pro-wrestling term for villain, which Hayes won that year. The *Wrestling Observer Annual Yearbook* became a de facto tape-trading guide in the 1980s and 1990s for fans who wanted to watch the category winners. (Dave Meltzer, *Wrestling Observer 1983 Annual Yearbook*, February 1984)

that it is most known for. Figure 5.1 is the cover from the 1983 annual *Wrestling Observer Yearbook*, with Michael Hayes on the cover because he was voted best heel. Fans valued annual yearbooks, and as fan Last explains, these rankings drove tape-trader interest in recordings:

> For me, even though I knew the results, because I read the *Observer*, if Dave Meltzer reports to the *Observer* that a match was five stars in Japan, everyone has to see it. Five stars, that's as good as it gets, I have to see what this is.... I mean if you're a trader, or a hardcore wrestling fan, you know, you had to see those matches that get ranked, that get talked about.... There was a famous article in his 1989 yearbook that a friend of mine who's on my network actually wrote, Jeff Bowdren called the "Greatest Matches of the 1980s," as soon as he wrote that, someone put together a five VHS set of all those hundred matches, because people had to see it.[53]

In the 1989 article referenced here, Bowdren describes how his article listing the one hundred greatest matches of the 1980s was an attempt to provide hardcore wrestling fans the recognition given to other entertainment forms at the end of a decade, such as movie critics Gene Siskel and Roger Ebert's top ten films of the 1980s. Bowdren then encourages readers to find recordings for this list: "All of these matches are available on videotape and any true wrestling fan owes it to themselves to at least try and witness them."[54] Monthly reports, annual rankings, and decade-spanning reflections made *Wrestling Observer* an arbiter of taste that provided wrestling fans with a guide to the television bootlegs they ought to obtain through tape trading and study.

In this sense, tape trading facilitated wrestling fans with the objects of study used to perform wrestling-knowledge mastery, much in the same way that tape trading provided *Starsky & Hutch* fans with the physical objects they could watch, rewatch, and freeze-frame to analyze and establish expertise in debates over the show's meaning. This is evident in the ways that wrestling fans would refer to tape viewing to legitimate their opinions on the pages of the *Wrestling Observer*. One example of this is the review in March 1985 of the Atlanta wrestling television program from a contributor named Sean Ryan. Listing his home as Anchorage, Alaska, Ryan would only have been able to access wrestling being televised in Atlanta through tape trading. However, we do not need to infer this, as Ryan made his tape viewing the title of his editorial "Atlanta Tapes Look Terrible": "I caught some of the Atlanta WWF tapes and they looked terrible. The jobber crew looked worse than anything ever brought together by the AWA."[55] Ryan then goes into analyses of specific wrestlers, demonstrating how references to tape viewing worked to establish this contributor's authority as he discusses the WWF matches being broadcast over four thousand miles away from Anchorage in Atlanta.

Given professional wrestling's use of kayfabe, rewatching tapes was even more significant as an object of study for fans looking to discern matches where professional wrestlers go off script. In pro-wrestling jargon, orchestrating a fixed match is known as a "work," and to improvise with actual wrestling skills and talents to create an unplanned outcome is referred to as a "shoot." A letter from participant Steve Munari in April 1985 discusses his use of tape replay viewing to try and ascertain whether matches were "shoots" or "works": "I just finished watching the Kazuo Yamazaki vs. Nobuhiko Takada match that you [Dave Meltzer] saw a second time. I was even more impressed than the first time. I assume you know I'm of the opinion these bouts are all true shoots and that nobody knows who will win.[56] We can see how studying tapes through replay watching was pleasurable for Munari, as he continues in his letter that he likes to "savor these rare matches" when news about Vince McMahon's takeover of national wrestling in the United States "has me down."[57] Here, then, is also an example of how wrestling fans participating in the *Wrestling Observer* made sense of themselves as connoisseurs who distinguished between what they saw as a gimmick-driven style of wrestling being promoted by the WWF and what they saw as the superior level of other wrestling organizations. Wrestling tapes became a ritual that turned watching wrestling into investigative work, and because videotape recording is a storage technology, it gave fans the means rewatch wrestling programs to scrutinize what happened. Munari's comparison of the WWF to the Japanese Universal Wrestling Federation (UWF) in this letter also points to the transnational nature of tape trading during the 1980s.[58]

The *Wrestling Observer* was a significant resource in the circulation of transnational wrestling television during the 1980s and 1990s. Wrestling fans like Meltzer, Munari, and others obtained video recordings of Japan and Mexico matches and shared them with other fans.[59] Several of the longtime wrestling fans that I spoke with noted the significance of the *Wrestling Observer* in popularizing Japanese and Mexican wrestling in the United States. Multipage stories on Japanese or Mexican wrestling were a regular feature of the *Wrestling Observer*. Figure 5.2 shows an example of the images and headline for one such three-page article with extensive information about Japanese wrestling from 1984. Fan Roy

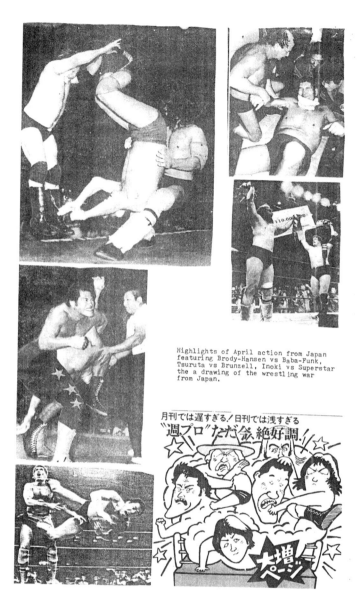

Figure 5.2. Wrestling matches in Japan, printed in the *Wrestling Observer* between regional reports from the Japanese promotions Pacific Wrestling Federation, Universal Wrestling Federation, and New Japan Wrestling Association. This layout is an example of *Wrestling Observer*'s regular engagement with international wrestling and reliance on transnational circulation of wrestling television recordings. Every issue contains reports from organizations in Japan and Canada and, intermittently, Mexico and West Germany, along with regular feature articles discussing an aspect of or changes in non-US wrestling organizations. (Dave Meltzer, "Highlights of April Action from Japan," *Wrestling Observer*, June 1984, 17)

Lucier shared with me that the *Wrestling Observer* would regularly solicit and print lists of local ethnic stores that had international tapes, letting readers know, "If you live near any of these places in the certain cities . . . these businesses sell a weekly Japanese TV show."[60] Hilderbrand notes how the video sections of ethnic grocery stores in southern California work to "provide a service to diasporic communities," making it possible for immigrants and their first- or second-generation children to access non-US media from their families' homeland.[61] Asian or Mexican grocery stores also provided wrestling fans access points to transnational wrestling television, allowing them to view firsthand and study non-US wrestling in order to participate in debates and analyses about Japanese and Mexican wrestling matches with other fans, some of which occurred in the pages of the *Wrestling Observer*.[62]

The pages of the *Wrestling Observer* became a significant forum for fans to redefine what it meant to be a wrestling fan during the 1980s when video-recording technology was becoming widely available. Dell argues that when female wrestling fans of the 1950s formed fan clubs and fan bulletins, they redefined what it meant to be a wrestling fan as a communal and explicitly female identity.[63] The industrial construct of the mark of professional wrestling's dupe loomed large in fans' distinction of themselves as more intelligent in the pages of the *Wrestling Observer* during the 1980s. This is evident in the way that contributors to the *Wrestling Observer* in the 1980s regularly distinguish between themselves and those they describe as "casual" or "average" fans that the industry imagined.[64] The *Wrestling Observer* participants criticize the promoters whose television programs were poorly staged and barely believable. One contributor complains that the producers of the AWA television matches in Minneapolis "treat the fans like complete morons."[65] This writer was not alone, as Meltzer regularly lamented the "many promoters who perceive their clientele as moronic types who accept what they are told at face value."[66] Other participants in the pages of the *Wrestling Observer* called fans they deemed uncritical as "brain-washed."[67] The subtext here is a desire to be understood in opposition to the "brain-washed morons" whom these fans believed the professional wrestling industry saw as their marks. The figure of the wrestling mark evokes the longtime association between wrestling and the feminized audience of mass culture more broadly.[68] Within broadcasting is the longstanding history of industrial logics that configure the mass audience as a feminized audience susceptible to media messages.[69] The contributors writing in the *Wrestling Observer* during the 1980s did not, to my estimation, intentionally gender themselves as masculine in opposition to feminine fans. However, given professional wrestling's historical association with female audiences and feminine desire, it is impossible to ignore the gendered cultural work implicitly accomplished by a community of mostly male fans who used fanzines and tape trading in tandem to redefine their identity as intelligent experts. In bridging the gap between regional and transnational televised wrestling, tape trading and fanzines fostered a figure of the masculine "intelligent fan" that challenged and pushed back against the industry distinction of audiences as feminized marks for the fabrication of kayfabe.

In many ways, the *Wrestling Observer*'s function as a platform to crowd-source tape-trading exchanges is like the use of other fanzines discussed in this book. Like fanzines devoted to *Starsky & Hutch*, the *Wrestling Observer* emerged as forum for tape trading because of the increased availability and adoption of videotape recording, especially the user-friendly cartridge consoles, such as the Philips VCR and the Sony Betamax. However, wrestling tape trading was distinct in its specific function within regionalized structure of professional wrestling that was dominant in the late 1970s and early 1980s. The emergence of televised wrestling home recordings in the late 1970s demonstrates how tape trading bootlegs came to specifically function as a distribution mechanism for televised wrestling beyond the region where it was broadcast, especially prior to the rise of the WWF and WCW as the behemoth national wrestling producers for television these organizations would become in the 1990s. The *Wrestling Observer* formalized and popularized tape trading in order to bridge the distributive gaps in televised wrestling distribution while also providing a forum for wrestling fans to connect and make sense of themselves as a national audience invested in professional wrestling. It is also notably a site that demonstrated a national audience for wrestling at the same time that Vince McMahon (the son) and Ted Turner began to reshape wrestling into a national form of television programming.

Much like the other case studies in this book, the *Wrestling Observer* was a significant component of a larger tape-trading distribution network for televised wrestling that included the classified sections of wrestling magazines, local supermarkets, and fan conventions. In interviews with fans who participated in wrestling tape trading during the 1980s, however, the *Wrestling Observer* is repeatedly brought up as having been a central forum for their connection with other tape traders. Tape trading facilitated fan performance of knowledge and ability to legitimate critical evaluations of wrestling. In this sense, detailing the formation of a tape-trading distribution network within 1980s wrestling-fan cultures also demonstrates how the materiality of bootlegging television recordings changed fans' relationships with wrestling and contributed to the formation of an intelligent wrestling-fan subjectivity. The figure of the masculine, intelligent, critical wrestling fan has become a staple of contemporary wrestling-fan cultures, and many of the debates within current wrestling-fan forums rely on accumulated knowledge and historical awareness of wrestling matches. VHS tapes of wrestling matches from the 1980s and 1990s are still sold on eBay or at specific collectors' websites. Indeed, tape trading now coexists with content posted on YouTube and available through subscriptions to digital platforms like the WWE channel on Peacock, which speaks to the perceived value of historical play-by-play knowledge and to the pleasure of watching and rewatching wrestling matches where the outcome is already known. In this sense, the history of tape-trading wrestling TV also illuminates the role of televised wrestling's redistribution in the historical genealogy of the current ironic self-aware metafans in contemporary wrestling-fan cultures.[70]

CONCLUSION

Bootlegging after the Airwaves

On August 27, 2018, wrestling fan Roy Lucier of southern California tweeted the photo in figure 6.1 of his pro-wrestling VHS tape collection, explaining that this was his "WWE Network and Highspots and NJPW World and everything else back in the 90's." The professional wrestling fans in his Twitter following would know that Highspots is an online retailer of wrestling merchandise, including DVDs of classic matches, and that New Japan Pro-Wrestling World (NJPW) is a subscription-based streaming service with live and on-demand Japanese wrestling matches. In 2014, the World Wrestling Entertainment (WWE) company referenced previously and formerly the WWF, launched its own stand-alone, subscription-based streaming service, WWE Network, which offers a library of WWF and WWE current and classic wrestling television, as well as content from now-defunct competitors the WWF has bought up, such as World Championship Wrestling, Mid-South Wrestling, and Mid-Atlantic Wrestling.[1] The WWE Network would later be dismantled and rolled into exclusive content available to US subscribers of Peacock streaming service, and the company has also signed licensing contracts with other transnational streaming platforms around the world.[2] Lucier's Twitter post harkens back to the history of wrestling tape trading, and the role of VHS tapes in the unofficial distribution of televised professional wrestling matches in the 1980s and 1990s, before online platforms provided access to wrestling TV. Lucier's Twitter post also, however, gets at the main difference between the circulation of broadcasting via bootlegged recordings and the availability of broadcast content on commercial streaming video on-demand platforms (SVOD): materiality and labor.

Figure 6.1. Wrestling fan Roy Lucier tweeting out a photo of his VHS collection of wrestling television recordings, joking that this was his streaming platform in the 1990s. (@roylucier, "This was my WWE Network and Highspots and NJPW World and everything else back in the 90's," Twitter, August 27, 2018, 12:23 p.m., twitter.com/roylucier/status/1034129214994169866)

Bootlegging as Embodied Distributive Labor

The work of making broadcast content available on physical objects involved a range of distributive labor. One need only look at Lucier's stack of VHS tapes in figure 6.1 to grasp the materiality of bootlegging broadcast content. Over forty tapes are in this photo alone, and much more are in his personal collection.[3] This photo is a reminder of the materiality of bootlegged broadcast content and of the invisible work involved making content distributed over the airwaves into tangible, physical objects. The specificity of this collection, from the actual programs to the handwriting and choice of duplication speed, are all physical elements of distributive labor's embodied practice, accomplished and representative of the lived experiences of Lucier's television bootlegging. I spoke with Lucier after having found him through this tweet, and he explained that at the height of his tape trading, he used four VCRs to duplicate wrestling shows that he either had recorded or obtained through trades. When he stopped collecting tapes and converted them to DVDs, he had six thousand VHS tapes in his library.[4] Other wrestling fans I spoke with similarly detailed the labor of participating in the circulation of wrestling TV. Longtime wrestling fan Brian Last explains the system he used to deal with the high volume of tape trading he did while also managing his life as a high school student:

> I would run the four VCRs. So, two VCRs would be playing, and two VCRs would be recording. And then I would go to school. And I had a deal worked out with, the teacher in the photo lab, because . . . he was illegally dubbing down there. That's where I first saw *Forrest Gump*, and it was a bootleg copy. So, he would let me set it up, and I would dub a tape there. And then up in the library, they also had a dubbing system. And they let me dub a tape there. And then when I have lunch, I would go back to the library. Get that tape because it would almost always be a two-hour tape, switch it out, put another tape in there, and dub that. So, by the time I got home, I usually have four to five tapes. Ready to go.[5]

Talking with another longtime wrestling fan, John McAdam, I shared Last's account of running multiple decks at home and school, and he confided that his system had been even more involved. At the time McAdam estimates he was doing the largest volume of tape trading, he was running ten dual-deck VCRs and selling or trading hundreds of VHS tapes a week. Like Last, McAdam's daily schedule was shaped by the demands of dubbing tapes:

> I would have all of my tapes, like ready to go, like, okay here's the master, here's the blank, here's the master, here's the blank, in a big stack. I would get all these tapes rolling, first thing in the morning, get home from work and get them rolling again, and if need be, set my alarm so I would get up at two, three in the morning.[6]

When asked how many tapes he offered in his catalog, McAdam recalled to me that the number of tapes or shows in his collection was too many to count. McAdam was known in the fandom as such a prolific collector that other wrestling fans would give him their collections if they decided to get rid of them. "I [still] have storage buckets of tapes I have not watched yet," he told me.[7] The fear today, according to McAdams, is that these tapes may disintegrate if he tries to play them back, which brings up both the ongoing labor of maintaining fragile storage mediums and reformatting, and transferring content from magnetic tape to digital files stored on hard drives, DVDs, or cloud servers. No matter which format, the work of bootlegging is labor intensive and costly, and practices include dubbing, shipping, typing up catalogs, attending conventions, sharing contact information through fanzines and magazines, or driving over ten hours to show a collection of television tapes as fans in Australia did.

In many ways, the work of bootlegging radio and television content has paralleled the technical work and expertise of the official media industries. To record, duplicate, and reformat broadcast content requires technical expertise as well as in-depth knowledge of how the industries work and of the very programs themselves. The ways in which the distinctions between bootleggers and official media workers blur are most evident when bootleggers are called upon for help. For instance, McAdam shared a story about wrestlers requesting assistance from him:

> There's a famous tag team out there, Jack and Jerry Brisco. And Jerry Brisco has worked for the WWF since 1984. And he was looking for old footage that he couldn't find of [him] and Jack, I didn't know that at first, and I get this thing in the mail from WWF headquarters, and I think, "Oh god, here we go with a cease-and-desist letter." And it's just Jerry Brisco saying, "Hey, do you have any footage of me and my brother?" I'm like, "Yeah, Jerry, I'll be happy to help you." My policy when it comes to a guy looking for his own stuff, is that it's on the house, just send me an autographed picture, saying, "John, thanks for the tapes," your autograph. So, I send Jerry this package of tapes to his home, and maybe six months later, I get a letter, it was like an 8 by 11 package that had a letter in it from WWE headquarters, and

once again I'm like, "Okay here we go." And it is a photograph of Jack and Jerry Brisco, clearly signed by the same person. It doesn't say anything personalized. Clearly, it is not even their signatures. But I'm like, "Alright, it's fine. Jerry has brought enough happiness to my life, I'll just take this."

This is one story, but it is indicative of the ways in which those in the industry, the WWF here, would come to rely on bootleggers for their archive of content and their reliability finding, dubbing, and sharing televised content, with, in this case, the company that owns the copyright to the televised content but had not bothered to make this content accessible, even within the corporation itself.

Old-time radio (OTR) fans have also blurred the line between bootlegging and official media work. Three companies—Radio Yesteryear, Metacom, and Radio Spirits—were formed by radio fans wanting to use their extensive radio collections in order to sell official sets of classic radio compilations through catalogs and bookstores.[8] These companies were all profitable and active into the 1990s, and Radio Spirits, specifically, would make arrangements with fans who had high-quality, master transcription discs to use these as source material for their commercially mass-produced tape sets. In addition to crowdsourcing members of the OTR fan community for program masters, Radio Spirits hired radio fans to author the historical booklets that accompany each box set they developed in the 1990s. For instance, Radio Spirits credited Anthony Tollin as the author of the historical booklet that accompanies the *Old-Time Radio Legends of Comedy* box set, and Elizabeth McLeod as the author of *X-Minus One: Countdown*, the historical notes that accompany the box set of the science-fiction program *X-Minus One*. Both Tollin and McLeod are fans and historians who have focused on doing deep research on classic radio because of their enthusiasm for old-time radio and their participation within the OTR fan community. Radio Spirits has also used fan labor and accumulated knowledge to produce box sets by reaching out to fans to identify the voices in programs for which the company did not have historical information.[9] To give a sense of Radio Spirits' commercial success, by 1998 it was selling classic radio compilations in four thousand stores, including Costco, Sam's Club, and Barnes and Noble, in addition to the business the company was doing via direct-to-consumer retail via catalog sales.[10] Radio collectors were not the target audience for these retail companies; the compilations they released were organized around themes, such as *Mystery Superstars* or *The Best of Jack Benny*, while OTR collectors likely had several hundred to several thousand radio-program episodes in their personal libraries and mainly sought out rare recordings not already in circulation. Nevertheless, fans' work finding, reformatting, and researching these programs not only created the community that these business leaders came out of but also these fans continued to participate in making the commercial sale of radio recordings possible up until these companies were bought out in 1998 by the conglomerate MediaBay.[11]

Bootlegging and the Production of Physical Commodities

OTR collectors' success selling professionally duplicated box sets of classic radio was part of the broader expansion in using storage technologies to commodify and commercially sell media objects during the 1980s and 1990s. The rise of videotape and DVD technologies as vehicles to distribute film as physical commodities has been well documented by media historians. This history deserves a brief summary here, as, especially with television, these technologies have translated the fan practices of bootlegging and tape trading in order to facilitate on-demand control of broadcast content into industrial practices the legacy media companies harnessed. Frederick Wasser's history of home video's rise and evolving integration into the Hollywood film industry reveals how media industries have adapted to new formats and technologies, moving from fearing the threat over nontheatrical distribution to recognizing the profitability of home video as an important windowing strategy.[12] Wasser demonstrates how the recognition of the VHS aftermarket impacted film production, as studio executives focused more and more on greenlighting projects they could predict having longer success in the global video aftermarket.[13] Joshua M. Greenberg's and Dan Herbert's histories of video-rental industries demonstrate how VHS came to be a vehicle for engaging with films as material commodities viewed in the home, and their work is a model for us to trace out how VHS culture created the preconditions for contemporary practices viewing and interacting with cinema as a flexible, on-demand leisure activity.[14]

Although films were commodified and sold as physical objects on the consumer market during the late 1970s and after, the sale of broadcast programming for aftermarkets had been previously unfeasible. This is because the sheer number of episodes produced for successful television series were ill suited to the technological limitations of VHS tape-storage space.[15] Some television series commercialized short compilations of "best-of" VHS tapes. Yet, as Derek Kompare argues, "With much higher resolution sound and image than VHS tape, random access capability, a smaller size, and, most significantly, a larger storage capacity, the DVD has rejuvenated the home video industry, and has finally enabled television to achieve what film had by the mid-1980s: a viable direct-to-consumer market for its programming."[16] As peer-to-peer file sharing arose as a form of bootlegging television that increasingly garnered the legacy industries' attention during the late 1990s, copyright owners began to use new technologies, first DVD and then digital marketplaces, such as iTunes and Amazon, to sell television episodes and seasons to viewers who wanted to control, replay, and time shift their television viewing. This is basically what the fans described in the historical sources I read for this book and what countless VCR and cassette-deck owners did during the analog era. Today, building content libraries that offer streaming-platform subscribers control and repetition is a dominant strategy within the broadcasting industries, and the profits from second-run syndication rights and aftermarkets within streaming-video services and DVD sales are points of negotiation for above-the-line talent before a legacy television production is greenlit. In an era where the practices of analog media seem to be increasingly forgotten, the histories laid out in this book remind us how the practice of bootlegging and tape trading radio and television have shaped our current media landscape. Indeed, as Adrian Johns and Ramon Lobato have documented, piracy economies do not occur in a separate sphere from legitimate commercial enterprises, but, rather, formal and informal enterprises fluctuate and operate in response to one another.[17] Fans who bootlegged radio and television demonstrated to commercial companies that there were niche markets invested in engaging with broadcast content as a tangible commodity.

Many of the radio and television tape traders I spoke with have actually held onto their personal analog-tape libraries by digitizing them. These collections are more exhaustive and customized in their preferences than any streaming service could hope to accomplish, and much of the bootlegged content they possess is not even available on a streaming platform. While the digital is often not accounted for as physical, for the purpose of this discussion we should consider digital files as physical, material objects, because they take up space as 1s and 0s on a physical hard drive. And the value of materiality, digital or analog, is choice and control. This is evident to me in my own history with bootlegging. One might surmise from this project that bootlegging happened mainly among highly engaged radio and television fan cultures; however, those are the focus for this book only because the nature of historical research has made finding other traces of home recording and sharing broadcast content difficult. I grew up in Tujunga, a small town in Sunland Valley on the outskirts of Los Angeles. Tujunga was conceived as a utopian haven for tuberculosis patients fleeing the air pollution of Los Angeles in the early twentieth century, but it would later become notorious as a site of a World War II Japanese internment camp and in the 1960s and 1970s as a Hell's Angels outpost. My parents did not know this when they bought our house in the early 1980s. They had come from London, where my father had been working as a film editor, and they settled in Tujunga because it was inexpensive and conveniently close to the Hollywood studios and the boutique sound-editing houses where my father was getting regular gigs. Tujunga's physical geography is also significant to this story, because, in the early 1980s, television signals did not consistently penetrate Sunland Valley, and terrestrial reception with a television antenna was frustratingly bad.

My mother, a shrewd woman, decided to subscribe to the local cable-television operator, King VideoCable, for a year, during which time she recorded as much television as she could on VHS tapes. Organized and systematic, my mother used almost every minute on the tape, labeled them, bought shelves to store the tapes, and stacked them there day by day. She canceled the service when she felt satisfied she had amassed a stockpile of programming sufficient to entertain our family for several years. These recordings consisted mainly of footage from the Disney Channel or Nickelodeon, as well as hours and hours of tennis matches. I spent most of my formative years rewatching these tapes and knew by heart the sequential order of my favorite *David the Gnome* episodes or fragments of programs that bookended a syndicated airing of the 1961 film *The Parent Trap* that my mother had recorded off the Disney Channel. This library was augmented by the purchase of officially released home videos of films like *My Fair Lady* or the bootlegged copies of *Snow White* and *Peter Pan* that were in the Disney vault but which my father obtained by trading his crew jacket from *Top Gun* with another editor. A transaction and sacrifice that I did not understand until I was older. The addition of film videos to our collection never compared to the bulk of the viewing library courtesy of King VideoCable. I had forgotten this portion of my family's experiences with television when I first began researching this project. However, as I looked into the histories of audience engagement with home-recording technologies to capture, store, and recirculate the content conveyed by broadcasting signals, I remembered my mother's strategy to outsmart the cable company. For that is what this work amounted to, a use of one disruptive technology (home video recording) in conjunction with another disruptive technology (cable-television systems) to circumvent the failure of broadcast reception while also mitigating cable television's somewhat prohibitive cost of approximately $14.95 a month in perpetuity (about $40 per month today accounting for inflation).[18]

The history of using home-recording technologies to record radio and television content off the airwaves is numerous, transnational, and contingent upon cultural, political, socioeconomic, and technological contexts. And, as with the broader history of media audiences and consumers, difficult to access, in contrast to the official historical traces of media companies that are available in the archives of trade journals or corporate papers. Nevertheless, I frequently find that when I discuss my research with others outside academia, they often have their own stories of bootlegging radio and television that they want to share with me. At a Santa Barbara wedding in 2019, a woman asked me about my research, and following my description, she described how her mother had recorded VHS tapes of Lifetime movies in the 1990s and shipped them to her aunt in Colombia, who would rent them out to customers in her corner store. What other histories of bootlegging exist? This project has only scratched the service, and it is my hope it will inspire further research in these mundane, everyday histories of how audiences attempted to capture the flow of radio and television content from the ephemerality of the airwaves used by stations to distribute linear broadcast schedules.

Distributive labor has traditionally been understood within the media industries as immaterial, separate from the actual work of producing radio or television, the work of making content. Official distributors are often construed within industry discourse as a sector of media workers who do not make media commodities, but, rather, they are involved in the processes that transport broadcast content from producer to viewer. However, as these histories of radio and television bootlegging make clear, to bootleg broadcast content was to make the immaterial of broadcast transmissions into the very material and physical matter of reel-to-reel tape and video cassettes.

The Future of Bootlegging in the Streaming Era

In many ways, it would be easy to look at the history of bootlegging radio and television during the second half of the twentieth century and argue that fan practices of time-shifting and binge-consuming content disarticulated from networks and schedules have won the day in the battle over defining what broadcasting content is and how it is distributed. Most content produced for network television can be found on the parent conglomerate's streaming platform. Even old television shows, such as *I Love Lucy* or *The Mary Tyler Moore Show*, are available on streaming platforms. These streaming options continue to coexist alongside the traditional over-the-air syndication of classic television on local subchannels, such as MeTV, and cable channels like TV Land. Yet, if we dig deeper into the on-demand offerings of classic radio or television, we can see that the labor of making radio and television content accessible outside linear broadcasting has transitioned from amateur bootlegger to media conglomerate, so, too, have control and choice. The materiality of bootlegged copies of taped radio and television programming made broadcast content portable, reproducible, and tangible. Bootlegging broadcasting content translated into controlling broadcast content. How does this relationship between audience and industry play out in the streaming environment of the current multichannel era?

Most contemporary radio or radiogenic sound programming is available on demand via podcasting. In her work on internet-based television, Amanda Lotz characterizes streaming television platforms as portals and outlines the main characteristics through which these portals have changed both the production and distribution of television, as well as our relationship with it: "The affordance of internet protocol technologies to deliver personally-selected content from an industrially curated library is the central difference introduced by this new distribution mechanism." Namely, we as viewers now have the ability to choose what we watch and when we watch it, a practice also commonly referred to as "time shifting."[19] However, Lotz is careful to note that this choice is determined via "industrial curation," a nod to the fact that portals, such as Netflix, use algorithms to track and recommend content held by the streaming company. And anyone who has searched for a program title previously available on a streaming portal they subscribe to, a title they perhaps had already been watching, only to find that it is no longer available, knows that industrially curated libraries change with the renegotiation and resale of content licensing and syndication.

This happened to me with the television show *Murder, She Wrote*, which I had begun to watch when it was available on Netflix, only to discover one day that it was no longer there. Several years later, I found it on Amazon Prime and watched it on that platform, before it was again removed from Amazon's streaming library shortly before Peacock launched, which is now *Murder, She Wrote*'s home, for the time being. When I first noticed the series missing from Netflix, I searched around online to find out if it was offered somewhere else (it was not) and found that my own frustration with losing my place in the series and access to this content was mirrored in the Change.org petition created by a user named Gene Thompson and titled "Bring back 'MURDER, SHE WROTE' to Netflix Streaming!!!!"[20] Thompson explained his frustration thusly,

> On the day of Angela Lansbury's birthday, October 16th, 2013, the show was removed from Netflix without warning! We, the fans, want this show back immediately. This show is legendary and one of the best shows still being syndicated on television. Please sign this petition if you think, "MURDER, SHE WROTE" should remain infinitely available to fans via Netflix! I'm going to miss coming home from work and watching Jessica solve the case.[21]

Besides myself, it is evident that a few people agreed with Thompson from comments at the bottom of the petition, and we should assume that more viewers than this probably lamented the removal of *Murder, She Wrote* from Netflix's library and later Amazon's US content library. But this a key characteristic of streaming platforms: we subscribe for content access to a library rather than paying for ownership of specific titles.

Today a viewer can also own physical copies of *Murder, She Wrote* through any number of sell-through options used by Comcast, the copyright holder, to distribute *Murder, She Wrote* episodes and seasons. We are lucky, in this respect, that we live in a world where this television show has been deemed commercially solvent enough for a conglomerate like Comcast to bother paying for the labor involved in reformatting all the analog recordings of *Murder, She Wrote* into digital files and release them via DVD set or online marketplaces like Amazon Video. We are lucky, because not all broadcasting is available like this. Television content made for streaming platforms, like *Stranger Things*, is used to differentiate streaming brands from one another and drive subscription. These original programs produced for streaming platforms will be available unless, as the introduction discusses with the case of HBO, a company decides that some content does not fit into future branding strategies or is more economically valuable as an unreleased tax write-off. Not all television is deemed worthy of reformatting or making available on a streaming platform. Try searching for episodes of AMC's talk show *The Talking Dead* from 2013, as I have, in order to teach about strategies legacy television providers use to encourage linear viewing. These episodes are only available as bootlegs, and they are not readily accessible, so that anyone who wants to find a recording, for teaching or other purposes, must connect with someone who recorded *Talking Dead* episodes on DVR and used digital tools to extract them as files.

The utopian assumption that internet television has democratized access to television could also be said to apply to podcasting, which has extricated radio from the confines of linear distribution via transmission schedules. And again, it is true that we can now choose from a host of legacy radio shows, such as National Public Radio's *Wait Wait . . . Don't Tell Me!* as well as digitally born podcasts, such as *WTF with Marc Maron*, in our pod-catching apps and listen to available episodes on our own schedules. But we should be cautious in equating the convenience of libraries, subscription based or open, with control. As with *The Talking Dead*, several years ago I was looking for an episode of the radio show and podcast *This American Life* for a research project. I was specifically looking for the episodes that I remembered having bumpers promoting *This American Life*'s first film project, *Sleepwalk with Me*. I listened to every *This American Life* show available from the month it was released and could not find the bumpers—the promos had been dynamically removed and replaced with new sponsorship spots. It was only by chance that I found an old iPod that was not internet-enabled and had those episodes still on it, as they had been originally released. I was lucky, I was able to find the content I needed and replay those first thirty seconds over and over until I transcribed them. But the moment I finished listening to the episode, the file disappeared from my iPod because I had not realized I had the preferences set to erase episodes once I listened to them.

The work of distributing radio and television to audiences that made on-demand access possible has shifted from amateur bootleggers to corporations with the rise of podcasting and television streaming portals. However, with that distributional shift, the revenue model has also shifted to prioritize a dual-revenue system, wherein television distributors make money both from advertising and subscriptions. Because, of course, broadcasting still relies on the audience commodity and flow, these structures have adapted to internet-based distributive models.

Netflix programs are rife with product placement, and their software compels us to keep watching with auto-play. In 2023 both Netflix and Disney+ rolled out a low-cost, ad-based subscription tier to their streaming platforms.[22] And, as time-shifting and access are recuperating revenue by commercial companies, broadcasting again becomes immaterial, and content continues to be used to keep our eyeballs viewing and our subscriptions renewing. It is materiality and control that distinguishes bootlegging radio and television from streaming radio and television. The practices pioneered by bootlegging broadcast content may have won out and are now the dominant mode of consuming media, a fact exemplified by the decision by the *New York Times* to cease publishing daily television schedules on August 31, 2020, in the only venue they were still being published by the newspaper, the local New York print edition.[23] Television listings have been printed in the *New York Times* since 1939, and, yet, the paper explained its decision to discontinue publishing program schedules in 2020 in terms that suggested live viewing has become outmoded: "There are now far more shows available any day, any time, on demand."[24] However, Axios in its audience research on the ways viewers consumed television in August 2022 demonstrated that when combined, linear cable (34.4 percent) and broadcast television (21.6 percent) viewing still exceed streaming (34.8 percent), a statistic that suggests the *New York Times* is not making the decision to stop publishing schedules based on a reflection of what the public actually does but, rather, upon the perception of linear television viewing as passé.[25] Whether or not streaming is the dominant viewing method, we certainly have not arrived at a utopia where all content ever is available at the touch of a button, despite streaming-platform advertisements that suggest otherwise.

In the current digital age, as before, bootlegging remains the distributive labor of obtaining content otherwise unavailable. The line between piracy and bootlegging may seem to blur further in the digital era, but the framework discussed in the introduction bears out. Bootlegging is the act of obtaining and circulating content not commercially available, while piracy circulates content commercially available in order to either make illicit money or to the avoid paying for content. For instance, when audiences work to get copies of television from other countries not distributed in their local market or when the program's distribution is staggered through windowing, that is, the delayed release of content to different transnational markets, this is bootlegging. When, for instance, scholars work to get episodes of soap operas from the 1980s or other content that has never been commercially released for research purposes, this is bootlegging. When fans of Sarah Silverman find and circulate copies of her unreleased pilot, *Susan 313*, that NBC declined to order for a series, this is bootlegging. Bootlegging is still very much a part of our broadcast ecosystem, and at its heart, it is a practice by which audiences attempt to circumvent the distributive control of media corporations. The way we access content shapes how we interpret radio and television, how we make sense of our own identity, and how we connect with other people. Today, we expect to be able to access and control our radio and television content, and this book has demonstrated this desire is not new or distinct to digital media. It has been a part of the story of broadcasting's distribution since the birth of radio, and, in all likelihood, it will be a part of the story of broadcasting's distribution after the act of broadcasting—sending out transmissions of linear schedules through the airwaves—ceases to be a mode of content distribution at all.

Notes

Introduction. Hacking Broadcast History

1. Joe Floyd to Arthur Van Dyke, cc Pat Weaver, December 7, 1951, US MSS 17AF, folder 4, box 121, National Broadcasting Company Records, Wisconsin Center for Film and Theatre Research, Wisconsin Historical Society, Madison, Wisconsin. Hereafter referred to as NBC Records.

2. John McMurria, *Republic on the Wire: Cable Television, Pluralism, and the Politics of New Technologies, 1948–1984* (New Brunswick, NJ: Rutgers University Press, 2017).

3. Stanton Osgood to Richard Pinkham and Pat Weaver, December 31, 1951, folder 4, box 121, NBC Records.

4. Dallas W. Smythe, *Dependency Road: Communications, Capitalism, Consciousness, and Canada* (Norwood, NJ: Ablex, 1981).

5. Erik Barnouw, *Tube of Plenty: The Evolution of American Television*, 2nd ed. (New York: Oxford University Press, 1990).

6. Smythe, *Dependency Road*.

7. Robert Guggenheim to Pat Weaver, October 5, 1951, folder 99, box 119; Frank Kelly to Frank Lepore, November 5, 1956, folder 1, box 200; James Nelson to Colonel Zastrow, November 15, 1956, folder 1, box 200; all NBC Records.

8. Osgood to Pinkham and Weaver.

9. Theodore Kupferman to Pete Barnum, October 17, 1951, folder 84, box 119, NBC Records.

10. Kupferman to Barnum.

11. Amanda Lotz, *Digital Media Distribution: Portals, Platforms, Pipelines*, ed. Courtney Brannon Donoghue, Paul McDonald, and Timothy Havens (New York: New York University Press, 2021), 47.

12. Ramon Lobato, *Shadow Economies of Cinema: Mapping Informal Film Distribution* (London: Bloomsbury, 2012), 2.

13. Joshua A. Braun, *This Program Is Brought to You by . . . : Distributing Television News Online* (New Haven, CT: Yale University Press, 2015), 7.

14. Lucas Hilderbrand, *Inherent Vice: Bootleg Histories of Videotape and Copyright* (Durham, NC: Duke University Press, 2009), 6.

15. Kim Bjarkman, "To Have and to Hold: The Video Collector's Relationship with an Ethereal Medium," *Television and New Media* 5, no. 3 (2004): 233.

16. Bjarkman, "To Have and to Hold," 234.

17. Braun, *This Program Is Brought to You By*, 8.

18. Ramon Lobato and Julian Thomas, *The Informal Media Economy* (Malden, MA: Polity Press, 2015), 13.

19. Hilderbrand, *Inherent Vice*, 22.

20. See Lee Marshall, *Bootlegging: Romanticism and Copyright in the Music Industry* (London: Sage, 2005) for a history of bootlegging and copyright in the music industry; see Hilderbrand, *Inherent Vice*, for an in-depth discussion of video, copyright, and bootlegging, particularly focused on film and aesthetics.

21. Alexander Russo, *Points on the Dial: Golden Age Radio beyond the Networks* (Durham, NC: Duke University Press, 2010); Derek Kompare, *Rerun Nation: How Repeats Invented American Television* (New York: Routledge, 2006).

22. Jonathan Sterne, Jeremy Morris, Michael Brendan Baker, and Ariana Moscote Freire, "The Politics of Podcasting," *Fibreculture Journal* 13 (2008), https://thirteen.fibreculturejournal.org/fcj-087-the-politics-of-podcasting/.

23. Michele Hilmes, *Radio Voices: American Broadcasting, 1922–1952* (Minneapolis, MN: University of Minnesota Press, 1997).

24. Raymond Williams, *Television: Technology and Cultural Form* (Hanover, NH: Wesleyan University Press, 1992), 80.

25. Sara Fisher, "Streaming Surpasses Cable as Top Way to Consume TV," *Axios*, August 18, 2022, https://www.axios.com/.

26. Derek Kompare, "Flow to Files: Conceiving 21st Century Media," paper given at the Media in Transition 2 Conference, Cambridge, Massachusetts, 2002, https://cmsw.mit.edu/mit2/Abstracts/DerekKompare.pdf.

27. Jane Feuer, "The Concept of Live Television: Ontology as Ideology," in *Regarding Television: Critical Approaches—An Anthology*, ed. E. Ann Kaplan (Frederick, MD: University Publications of America, 1983), 12–21.

28. Rick Altman, "Television/Sound," in *Studies in Entertainment: Critical Approaches to Mass Culture*, ed. Tania Modleski (Bloomington: Indiana University Press, 1986), 39–54.

29. Matt Stokes's 2019 documentary *Recorder: The Marion Stokes Project* tells the story of the activist, television producer, and later, recluse Marion Stokes, who with the use of her VCR recorded over eight hundred thousand hours of television between 1977 and 2012. The film ends with footage of her son donating the collection to the Internet Archive and the tapes being loaded into storage containers for transportation to the archive's holding facility.

30. See Hilmes's discussion of her use of the old-time-radio collector club, Society to Preserve and Encourage Radio Drama, Variety, and Comedy, for her

research in *Radio Voices*, ix; also see Elana Levine's discussion of using her own personal recording archive, in tandem with other fan collectors' recording libraries, for her research in *Her Stories: Daytime Soap Opera and US Television History* (Durham, NC: Duke University Press, 2020), 14.

31. Kompare, "Flow to Files."

32. Henry Jenkins, Sam Ford, and Joshua Green, *Spreadable Media: Creating Value & Meaning in a Networked Culture* (New York: New York University Press, 2013), 116.

33. Michael Curtin, Jennifer Holt, and Kevin Sanson, eds., *Distribution Revolution: Conversations about the Digital Future of Film and Television* (Berkeley: University of California Press, 2014).

34. Devin Leonard, "Nightmare on Madison Avenue," *CNN Money*, June 28, 2004, https://money.cnn.com/magazines/fortune/fortune_archive/2004/06/28/374368/index.htm; Mark Andrejevic, "The Work of Being Watched: Interactive Media and the Exploitation of Self-Disclosure," *Critical Studies in Media Communication* 19, no. 2 (2002): 230–48.

35. Rick Porter, "Streaming *Overtakes* Cable in July, Leads Platform Rankings for the First Time," *Hollywood Reporter*, August 18, 2022, https://www.hollywoodreporter.com/.

36. Susan Douglas, *Listening In: Radio and the American Imagination* (New York: Times Books, 1999), 220.

37. Smythe, *Dependency Road*.

38. Eileen Meehan, "Gendering the Commodity Audience: Critical Media Research, Feminism, and Political Economy," in *Media and Cultural Studies: Keyworks*, ed. M. G. Durham and D. M. Kellner (Oxford, UK: Blackwell), 311–21.

39. Deborah L. Jaramillo, *The Television Code: Regulating the Screen to Safeguard the Industry* (Austin: University of Texas Press, 2018), 10.

40. Igor Kopytoff, "The Cultural Biography of Things: Commoditization as Process," in *The Social Life of Things: Commodities in Cultural Perspective*, ed. A. Appadurai (Cambridge: Cambridge University Press, 1986), 64–69.

41. Kopytoff, "Cultural Biography," 68.

42. Bjarkman, "To Have and to Hold," 233.

43. John Fiske, "The Cultural Economy of Fandom," in *The Adoring Audience: Fan Culture and Popular Media*, ed. Lisa A. Lewis (New York: Routledge, 1992), 30–49.

44. Bjarkman, "To Have and to Hold," 233.

45. Barbara Klinger, *Beyond the Multiplex: Cinema, New Technologies, and the Home* (Berkeley: University of California Press), 152.

46. Charles Acland, introduction to *Residual Media*, ed. Acland (Minneapolis: University of Minnesota Press, 2006), xxi.

47. Andrew R. Chow, "How *Seinfeld* Became One of TV's Great Moneymakers," *Time Magazine*, October 1, 2021, https://time.com/6103335/seinfeld-netflix-business/.

48. Eleanor Patterson, "Maintaining Transmission: DirecTV's Work-at-Home

Technical Support, Virtual Surveillance, and the Gendered Domestication of Distributive Labor," *Television & New Media* 22, no. 6 (2021): 633.

49. Lobato, *Shadow Economies*, 13.

50. See Camile Bacon-Smith, *Enterprising Women: Television Fandom and the Creation of Popular Myth* (Philadelphia: University of Pennsylvania Press, 1991), and Henry Jenkins, *Textual Poachers: Television Fans and Participatory Culture* (New York: Routledge, 1992).

51. Abigail De Kosnik discusses fan production and digital access in "Fandom as Free Labor," in *Digital Labor: The Internet as Playground and Factory*, ed. Trebor Scholz (New York: Routledge, 2013), 98–111. De Kosnik specifically uses the term "techno volunteers" in her book *Rogue Archives: Digital Cultural Memory and Media Fandom* (Cambridge, MA: Massachusetts Institute of Technology, 2016), 51.

52. De Kosnik, "Fandom as Free Labor"; Mel Stanfill, *Exploiting Fandom: How the Media Industry Seeks to Manipulate Fans* (Iowa City: University of Iowa Press, 2019).

53. Christopher Anderson and Michael Curtin, "Writing Cultural History: The Challenge of Radio and Television," in *Media History: Theories, Methods, and Analysis*, ed. Niels Brügger and Søren Kolstrup (Aarhus, Denmark: Aarhus University Press, 2001), 23.

54. Paula Guerra and Pedro Quintela, "Fast, Furious, and Xerox: Punk, Fanzines, and DIY Cultures in a Global World," in *Punk, Fanzines and DIY Cultures in a Global World*, ed. Paula Guerra and Pedro Quintela (Cham, Switzerland: Springer International, 2019), 2.

55. Roland Barthes, "The Discourse of History," in *Comparative Criticism*, vol. 3, ed. E. S. Shaffer (Cambridge: Cambridge University Press, 1981), 18.

56. See Michel Foucault, "Nietzsche, Genealogy, History," in *The Foucault Reader*, ed. Paul Rabinow (New York: Pantheon, 1984), 76–99.

57. Marshall, *Bootlegging*, 120, original emphasis.

58. Anderson and Curtin, "Writing Cultural History," 21.

59. Anderson and Curtin, "Writing Cultural History," 21.

60. Hilmes, *Radio Voices*, xvii.

61. See Keith Jenkins, *Re-thinking History* (New York: Routledge, 2003), 32, for a discussion of the discursive work historians do constructing the past.

62. Warren Susman, *Culture as History: The Transformation of American Society in the 20th Century* (New York: Pantheon, 1985), 54.

63. Anderson and Curtin, "Writing Cultural History," 27.

64. Greta Bjornson, "Outrage at HBO Max Continues as More Animators Slam the Streamer for 'Uninformed, Money-Driven Decisions,'" *Decider*, August 19, 2022, https://decider.com/; Paige Skinner, "*Sesame Street* Fans Expressed Outrage on Social Media after HBO Max Included Episodes of the Series as Part of Its Purge," *BuzzFeed News*, August 19, 2022, https://www.buzzfeednews.com/.

65. Daniel Mitchell, @GigaBoots, "The HBO Max news has me infuriated. If this is the future of streaming platforms, destroying catalogs with no heads up for

tax write offs, people will start pirating this shit instead," Twitter Post, August 18, 2022, 2:41 a.m., https://twitter.com/GigaBoots/status/1560170073955991552.

Chapter 1. Homemade Entertainment

1. Susan Douglas, *Inventing American Broadcasting*, 1899–1922 (Baltimore, MD: Johns Hopkins University Press, 1987), xvi–xvii.

2. Douglas, *Inventing American Broadcasting*, 3.

3. Susan Zieger, *The Mediated Mind: Affect, Ephemera, and Consumerism in the Nineteenth Century* (New York: Fordham University, 2018), 2.

4. Paul Starr, *Creation of the Media: Political Origins of Modern Communications* (New York: Basic Books, 2004), 233.

5. Zieger, *Mediated Mind*, 2.

6. Corey McCall, "The Art of Life: Foucault's Reading of Baudelaire's 'The Painter of Modern Life,'" *Journal of Speculative Philosophy* 24, no. 2 (2010): 138–57.

7. Zieger, *Mediated Mind*, 130.

8. Oscar Wilde, "The Artist," in *Oscar Wilde: The Major Works*, ed. Isobel Murray (New York: Oxford University Press, 2000), 567.

9. Leo Charney and Vanessa R. Schwartz, introduction to *Cinema and the Invention of Modern Life*, ed. Charney and Schwartz (Berkeley: University of California Press, 1995), 7.

10. Kenneth MacGowan, "The Coming of Camera and Projector: Part II," *Quarterly of Film Radio and Television* 9, no. 2 (1954): 125.

11. Mary Ann Doane, *The Emergence of Cinematic Time: Modernity, Contingency, the Archive* (Cambridge, MA: Harvard University Press, 2002), 22.

12. Lisa Gitelman discusses the dominant view of newspapers via their sheer diurnal volume as ephemeral in *Always Already New: Media, History, and the Data of Culture* (Cambridge, MA: MIT Press, 2008), 27. For a more in-depth overview of the practices of scrapbooking as an attempt to manage and recirculate the ephemerality of newspapers, see Elizabeth Gruber Garvey's cultural history of scrapbooking, *Writing with Scissors: American Scrapbooks from the Civil War to Harlem Renaissance* (New York: Oxford University Press, 2013). See Lisa Gitelman, *Scripts, Grooves, and Writing Machines: Representing Technology in the Edison Era* (Stanford, CA: Stanford University Press, 1999), for an overview of the how the first phonography was the written phonetic inscription of aural language. See Jay Ruby, *Secure the Shadow: Death and Photography in America* (Cambridge, MA: Massachusetts Institute of Technology Press, 1995), for the history of Victorian postmortem photography.

13. Gruber Garvey, *Writing with Scissors*, 4, 20, original emphasis.

14. Gitelman, *Always Already New*, 39.

15. Jonathan Sterne, *The Audible Past: Cultural Origins of Sound Reproduction* (Durham, NC: Duke University Press, 2003), 202.

16. Gitelman, *Always Already New*, 61.

17. Brian Hochman, *Savage Preservation: The Ethnographic Origins of Modern Media Technology* (Minneapolis: University of Minnesota Press, 2014), xi. Also see Hochman, *Savage Preservation*, xi, for a discussion of how early ethnologists discovered the phonograph to be difficult to operate, unreliable, and prohibitively expensive.

18. Sterne, *Audible Past*, 196.

19. Gitelman, *Always Already New*, 15.

20. Sterne, *Audible Past*, 297.

21. George du Maurier, "The Telephone," *Punch's Almanack for 1878*, December 14, 1877, 2.

22. du Maurier, "Telephone Sound."

23. Emily Thompson, "Machines, Music, and the Quest for Fidelity: Marketing the Edison Phonograph in America, 1877–1925," *Music Quarterly* 79, no. 1 (1995): 131–71; Sterne, *Audible Past*.

24. See Gitelman, *Scripts, Grooves, and Writing Machines*; Sterne, *Audible Past*; and Gitelman, *Always Already New*.

25. *Edison Phonographs Catalog*, January 1, 1903, 2.

26. *Edison Phonographs*, catalog, National Phonograph Co., Orange, New Jersey, 1903, 2, private collection.

27. Ray Zone, *Stereoscopic Cinema and the Origins of 3-D Film, 1838–1952* (Lexington: University of Kentucky Press, 2014), 36.

28. Doane, *Emergence of Cinematic Time*, 22.

29. Antonia Dickson and W. K. L. Dickson, "Edison's Invention of the Kineto-Phonograph," *Century Illustrated Monthly Magazine*, June 1894, 206.

30. "Edison's Next Wonder: The Wizard Says We Will Sit in a New York Theatre and Enjoy a London Play," *Phonoscope*, May 1897, 11.

31. Gabriele Balbi, "Deconstructing 'Media Convergence': A Cultural History of the Buzzword, 1980s-2010s," in *Media Convergence and Deconvergence*, ed. Sergio Sparviero, Corinna Peil, and Gabriele Balbi (Cham, Switzerland: Palgrave Macmillan, 2017), 33. For discussions of convergence as digitalization, see Nicholas Negroponte, *Being Digital* (New York: Knopf, 1995), and Henry Jenkins, *Convergence Culture: Where Old and New Media Collide* (New York: New York University Press, 2006).

32. Ithiel de Sola Pool, *Technologies of Freedom: On Free Speech in an Electronic Age* (Cambridge, MA: Harvard University Press, 1983), 23.

33. Jenkins, *Convergence Culture*, 282.

34. David Suisman, *Selling Sounds: The Commercial Revolution in American Music* (Cambridge, MA: Harvard University Press, 2009), 146; Sterne, *Audible Past*, 189; Michele Hilmes, *Hollywood and Broadcasting: From Radio to Cable* (Urbana: University of Illinois Press, 1990), 18, 54, 144.

35. Raymond Williams, "Advertising: The Magic System," in *Problems in Materialism and Culture: Selected Essays* (London: Verso, 1980), 170–95; Susan Strasser, "The Alien Past: Consumer Culture in Historical Perspective," *Journal

of Consumer Policy 26 (2003): 375–93; John Henry Hepp IV, *The Middle-Class City: Transforming Space and Time in Philadelphia, 1876–1926* (Philadelphia: University of Pennsylvania Press, 2018).

36. Lynn Spigel, *Make Room for TV: Television and the Family Ideal in Postwar America* (Chicago: University of Chicago Press, 1992), 20.

37. Steven A. Reiss, *Touching Base: Professional Baseball and American Culture in the Progressive Era* (Urbana: University of Illinois Press), 1999.

38. Barbara Welter, "The Cult of True Womanhood: 1820–1860," *American Quarterly* 18, no. 2 (1966): 151–74.

39. Spigel, *Make Room for TV*, 15.

40. See Catherine Jurca, *White Diaspora* (Princeton, NJ: Princeton University Press, 2001), for an overview of how the home and formation of the suburbs were connected to the broader racial politics of the Progressive Era idealized colonialism and attempts to segregate and police the boundaries of white middle-class life; Dana D. Nelson, *National Manhood* (Durham, NC: Duke University Press, 1998), for an overview of how white masculinity and segregation were central to the formation of patriarchal Victorian domestic order.

41. Spigel, *Make Room for TV*, 13.

42. Sterne, *Audible Past*, 204.

43. Sterne, *Audible Past*, 204; Spigel, *Make Room for TV*, 22.

44. Klinger, *Beyond the Multiplex*, 10.

45. Williams, "Advertising."

46. National Gramophone Co., "For Evening Entertainments," advertisement, *Phonoscope*, January–February 1897, 20.

47. Suisman, *Selling Sounds*, 25.

48. "Trio to Be Tried Monday on 'Bootleg' Music Charge," *Motion Picture News*, February 15, 1930, 25; "N.Y. State Bill Hits at Bootleg Song Publisher," *Motion Picture News*, March 22, 1930, 42.

49. National Phonograph Co., "Vaudeville at Home" advertisement, *Overland Monthly*, August 1905, i.

50. National Phonograph Co., "Vaudeville at Home," original emphasis.

51. National Phonograph Co., "Opera" advertisement, *Colliers' National Weekly*, October 14, 1911, 40, original emphasis.

52. "A Corner of the Music Room in the White House," *Talking Machine World*, April 1912, cover image.

53. Kyle S. Barnett, "Furniture Music: The Phonograph as Furniture, 1900–1930," *Journal of Popular Music Studies* 18, no. 3 (2006): 301–24.

54. Burnett has discussed some of these models in his article "Furniture Music." It is also evident in the promotional materials accompanying Edison's National Phonograph Co.'s first release of disc record players in 1912, as the disc phonograph was built into a range of cabinets priced from $60 to $450 and in accordingly designed levels of decorative intricacy. See "Exhibit of New Edison Disc Phonographs and Records," *Talking Machine World*, July 15, 1912, 50–51.

55. Barnett, "Furniture Music."

56. Suisman, *Selling Sounds*, 16.

57. Lenny Lipton, *The Cinema in Flux: The Evolution of Motion Picture Technology from the Magic Lantern to the Digital Era* (New York: Springer, 2021), 155–57.

58. "Edison's Next Wonder," 11.

59. Tom Gunning, "The Cinema of Attractions: Early Cinema, Its Spectator, and the Avant-Garde," in *Early Cinema: Space Frame Narrative*, ed. Thomas Elsaesser (London: British Film Institute, 1990), 56–62.

60. Ben Singer, "Early Home Cinema and The Edison Home Projecting Kinetoscope," *Film History* 2, no. 1 (1988): 38.

61. Edison Manufacturing Co., "New 1898 Model Edison Projecting Kinetoscope," advertisement, *Phonoscope*, April 1898, 19; Lipton, *Cinema in Flux*, 157.

62. Edison Manufacturing Co., "Edison Projecting Kinetoscope" advertisement, *Phonogram*, April 1901, 234.

63. "Moving Pictures in the Parlor," *Show World*, July 20, 1907, 16.

64. Frank P. Hulette, "An Interview with Thomas A. Edison," *Moving Picture World*, July 22, 1911, 104.

65. "Two Edison Home Entertainers Will Make an Ideal Program," *Edison Phonograph Monthly*, November 1913, 6.

66. "Singer, "Early Home Cinema," 44; Anke Mebold and Charles Tepperman, "Resurrecting the Lost History of 28mm Film in North America," *Film History* 15, no. 2 (2003): 143; Coinnews Media Group LLC, "US Inflation Calculator," https://www.usinflationcalculator.com/, accessed April 10, 2023.

67. Mebold and Tepperman, "Resurrecting the Lost History," 140.

68. Alan D. Kattelle, "The Amateur Cinema League and Its Films," *Film History* 15, no. 2 (2003): 238–51.

69. Singer, "Early Home Cinema," 46.

70. Singer, "Early Home Cinema," 46.

71. Singer, "Early Home Cinema." 46.

72. "Edison Home Kinetoscope," *Motion Picture World*, June 5, 1920, 1372.

73. Mebold and Tepperman, "Resurrecting the Lost History," 141.

74. Mebold and Tepperman, "Resurrecting the Lost History," 148.

75. Mebold and Tepperman, "Resurrecting the Lost History," 149.

76. Singer, "Early Home Cinema," 48.

77. Philip M. Napoli, "Media Economics and the Study of Media Industries," in *Media Industries: History, Theory, and Method*, ed. Jennifer Holy and Alisa Perren (Oxford, UK: Wiley-Blackwell, 2009), 161–70.

78. "A Hollywood Merry-Go-Round," *Broadway and Hollywood News: Movies*, July, 1934, 7; "Information Desk," *Modern Screen*, September 1936, 66; Grace Simpson, "That Passion for Things," *Silver Screen*, July 1937.

79. "Stock Up and Advertise," *Edison Phonograph Monthly*, May 1908, 8.

80. Gitelman, *Always Already New*, 15.
81. "Edison Phonograph" advertisement, *New York Tribune*, January 29, 1911, 18.
82. Patricia Rodden Zimmermann, *Reel Families: A Social History of Amateur Film* (Bloomington: Indiana University Press, 1995), 17.
83. Merritt Crawford, "The First Thirty Years," *Movie Makers Magazine*, December 1930, 755.
84. Mebold and Tepperman, "Resurrecting the Lost History," 148.
85. Zimmerman, *Reel Families*, 14.
86. Dwight Swanson, "Inventing Amateur Film: Marion Norris Gleason, Eastman Kodak, and the Rochester Scene, 1921–1932," *Film History* 15, no. 2 (2003), 126–36.
87. Swanson, "Inventing Amateur Film," 130.
88. Zimmerman, *Reel Families*, 55.
89. See Sterne, *Audible Past*, 203, for a discussion about sound recording's potential for aural family albums during this technology's development.
90. Zimmerman, *Reel Families*, 23.
91. "Collection of Rare Records," *Edison Phonograph Monthly*, October 1907, 22.
92. Zimmerman, *Reel Families*, 8.
93. Douglas, *Inventing American Broadcasting*, 190, xxii.
94. Douglas, *Inventing American Broadcasting*, xxii, 191.
95. Douglas, *Inventing American Broadcasting*, 191.
96. George A. Blacker, "A History of Home Recording," *Audio* Magazine, April 1975, 29–34.
97. Michael Biel, *The Making and Use of Recordings in Broadcasting before 1936* (PhD diss., Northwestern University, 1977), 119.
98. Blacker, "History of Home Recording," 30–31.
99. Biel, *Making and Use of Recordings*, 331.
100. Blacker, "History of Home Recording," 32.
101. Blacker, "History of Home Recording," 29–34.
102. David L. L. Morton Jr., *Sound Recording: The Life Story of a Technology* (Baltimore, MD: Johns Hopkins University Press, 2004).
103. *Sony Corp. of America v. Universal City Studios, Inc.*, 464 U.S. 417 (1984).
104. "Magnetic Tape Recording of Television Pictures Demonstrated by RCA," *Radio Age*, January 1954, 15.
105. Blacker, "History of Home Recording," 29–34.
106. See John Briggs, "Disk Pirates Hit by Court Ruling: U.S. Appellate Bench Holds Sellers," *New York Times*, October 31, 1957, 62. I did discover a memo in the NBC Records that briefly asks questions as to what the network's policy was regarding third-party "off the air" recordings and how to deal with talent requests for copies of kinetoscope recordings. These questions appear in a longer

memo that addresses a list of policy issues, and in the files available to me, I did not find a response. See General Lyman Munson to Frank Lepore, "Special Purpose Kinescope Recording," August 25, 1950, folder 1, box 200, NBC Records.

107. Jerry Chapman, "Collecting Marches On," *Airwaves*, January 1977, 11.
108. "Radio Collector's Items," *Variety*, November 30, 1938, 35.
109. "Radio Collector's Items."
110. "Radio Collector's Items."

Chapter 2. Hello Again

1. See "Days of Radio to Be Relived," *Asbury (NJ) Park Press*, April 3, 1973, 9; Nick Piccolo, "Great Artist," *Record-Journal* (Meriden, CT), December 2, 2007, C3; Tom Coss, "Fond Memories," *Record-Journal* (Meriden, CT), May 6, 2009, M19.
2. Sal Trapani, "Convention?" *Epilogue*, zine, Spring 1971, 13.
3. Trapani, "Convention?" original emphasis.
4. Charles Seeley, *The Old Time Radio Collector's Handbook* (Kenmore, NY: Rogue, 1978), Old Time Radio Researchers OTR magazine collection, http://www.otrr.org/pg06b_magazines.htm.
5. For discussions about sound recording quality, equipment, tape format, and brand, see Thomas A. Rockey, "One Last Word to Recordists," *Radio Dial*, zine, Autumn 1971; Jack Miller, "Double Speed and Fidelity," *Hello Again*, zine, July 1972; Mel Schlank, "Tape Tips," *Hello Again*, zine, July 1972, 10; Ray Stanich, "Ray Stanich," *Hello Again*, zine, January, 1974, 4; Jerry Chapman, "Standards of Old Radio Trading," November 1976, 2, and "Equalizers," August 1977, 8, both in *Airwaves*, zine; Bruce Ruggles, "From Bruce Ruggles," *Hello Again*, zine, December 1977, 3; Gary Kramer, "Shamrock Tape: A Good Buy (If You Know What to Look For)," *Collector's Corner*, zine, April 1979, 13–16.
6. Joe Webb, "The Thrill of OTR Collecting," *Airwaves*, zine, January 1978, 8; Bob Burnham, "Why Do We Collect Old Radio?" *Collector's Corner*, zine, June 1978, 3–5.
7. de Kosnik, *Rogue Archives*, 75.
8. I am forever indebted to the OTRR members for their work making OTR fanzines from the 1960s and onward available.
9. Arjun Appadurai, introduction to *The Social Life of Things: Commodities in Cultural Perspective* (Cambridge: Cambridge University Press, 1986), 3–64.
10. Appadurai, introduction, 43.
11. Grant Bollmer, "Networks before the Internet," *Journal of Cinema & Media Studies* 59, no. 1 (2019): 142–48.
12. Peter R. Monge and Noshir S. Contractor, *Theories of Communication Networks* (London: Oxford University Press, 2003).
13. Michael Socolow, "Always in Friendly Competition: NBC & CBS and the

First Decade of National Broadcasting," in *NBC: America's Network*, ed. Michele Hilmes (Berkeley: University of California Press, 2007), 25–43.

14. Socolow, "Always in Friendly Competition."

15. Jenkins, *Textual Poachers*, 77.

16. Alessandro Jedlowski, "Small Screen Cinema: Informality and Remediation in Nollywood," *Television & New Media* 13, no. 5 (2012): 443.

17. Jerry Chapman and Joe Webb, "Our Hobby's Roots," *Airwaves*, zine, January 1977, 11.

18. Chapman and Webb, "Our Hobby's Roots." Also see "Radio Collector's Items," *Variety*, November 30, 1938, 35.

19. George Schatz, letter to the editor, *NARA News: A Journal of Old Time Radio*, zine, Winter 1982–83, 3.

20. Schatz, letter, 3.

21. Schatz, letter, 3.

22. George Jennings, "Off Mike Mutterings," *Epilogue*, zine, fall 1970, 1.

23. Morton, *Sound Recording*, 118–21.

24. Jay Hickerson, "Personal Note," *Hello Again*, zine, December, 1980, 1.

25. Charles Ingersoll, untitled editorial note, *Radio Dial*, zine, Winter 1975, 13.

26. Charles Ingersoll, *Radio Dial*, zine, autumn 1970, 4, in Old Time Radio Researchers OTR magazine collection, http://www.otrr.org/pg06b_magazines.htm.

27. One example of well-known OTR fan-hosted radio programs that began in the 1970s is Chuck Schaden, *Those Were the Days*, which aired in Chicago from 1970 to 2009, see Laura Stewart, "Thanks for Listening," *Chicago Daily Herald*, May 8, 2009, 20.

28. "Extra Special News," *Stay Tuned*, zine, October 1971, 34.

29. Jay Hickerson, "Convention," *Hello Again*, zine, November 1976, 1; David Hinckley, "Friends of Old-Time Radio Are Signing Off," *Daily News* (New York), October 18, 2011, 68.

30. Radio Enthusiasts of Puget Sound, "The REPS Showcase," https://www.repsshowcase.com/ retrieved November 4, 2022.

31. Ken Piletic, "What Is an ORCAT?" *Collector's Corner*, zine, April 1980, 18–21.

32. "OTRCAT," *Hello Again*, zine, April 1973, 6.

33. Jacqueline Lichtenberg, Sondra Marshak, and Joan Winston, *Star Trek Lives!* (New York: Bantam, 1975).

34. Eleanor Patterson, "Capturing Flow: The Growth of the Old-Time-Radio Collecting Culture in the United States during the 1970s," *JCMS: Journal of Cinema and Media Studies* 59, no. 3 (2020): 46–68.

35. Patterson, "Capturing Flow."

36. M. J. Rymsza-Pawlowska, *History Comes Alive: Public History and Popular Culture in the 1970s* (Chapel Hill: University of North Carolina Press, 2017), 1.

37. Elizabeth Guffey, *Retro: The Culture of Revival* (London: Reaktion, 2006), 12.

38. Daniel Marcus, *Happy Days and Wonder Years: The Fifties and the Sixties in Contemporary Cultural Politics* (Rutgers, NJ: Rutgers University Press, 2004), 68.

39. Marcus, *Happy Days and Wonder Years*, 69.

40. Marcus, *Happy Days and Wonder Years*, 70.

41. Eleanor Patterson, "Reconfiguring Radio Drama after Television: The Historical Significance of *Theater 5*, *Earplay*, and *CBS Radio Mystery Theater* as Post-Network Radio Drama," *Historical Journal of Film, Radio, and Television* 36, no. 4 (2016): 656.

42. Patterson, "Reconfiguring Radio Drama," 661.

43. Patterson, "Reconfiguring Radio Drama," 656.

44. Patterson, "Reconfiguring Radio Drama," 653.

45. Charles R. Acland, introduction to *Residual Media*, ed. Acland (Minneapolis: University of Minnesota Press, 2006), xix.

46. Raymond Williams, "Base and Superstructure in Marxist Cultural Theory," in *Media and Cultural Studies: Keyworks*, ed. Douglas M. Kellner and Meenakshi Gigi Durham (Oxford: Blackwell, 2005), 130–43.

47. Acland, introduction, xxi.

48. For a discussion of the ways in which *Amos 'n' Andy* representation has always been problematically racist, see Hilmes, *Radio Voices*, 75–96. Hilmes specifically discusses the erasure of black voices from radio, with the exception of white actors' minstrel performances in many radio shows, including *Amos 'n' Andy*. Melvin Patrick Ely, *The Adventures of Amos 'n' Andy: A Social History of an American Phenomenon* (New York: Free Press, 1991).

49. Kevin Hancer, "Lone Ranger Not a Racist," *Hello Again*, zine, November 1972, 5.

50. Ely, *Adventures of Amos 'n' Andy*, 9.

51. David Reznick, "Lum & Abner: An Appreciation," *Collector's Corner*, zine, June 1978, 6–7.

52. Reznick, "Lum & Abner."

53. Hilmes, *Radio Voices*, 88.

54. Reznick, "Lum & Abner."

55. Take, for example, these excerpts from two letters. Radio fan Steve Lewis commented, "I agree that times have passed them by, but the shows *are* funny to listen to today and I'm not convinced of any truly malicious intent." Letters to the editor, *Collector's Corner*, zine, July 1978, 9, original emphasis. In the same issue, one of the fanzine's editors, Joe Webb, questioned how different the performance of black comedic caricatures were from those he observed on television at the time: "I do agree that *Amos 'n' Andy* are funny today, but I still feel uneasy listening to them. Perhaps it's because I wasn't around for the original run. One question: Was Redd Foxx's series *Sanford and Son* really much different from *Amos 'n' Andy*?

If you block out the fact that *A&A* were really white men acting, the difference is small, if there is any." Letters to the editor, *Collector's Corner*, zine, July 1978, 10.

56. Gene Bradford, "Racism in Old Time Radio," *Illustrated Press*, zine, December 1980, 6.

57. David Reznick, "Racism and OTR," *Collector's Corner*, zine, Summer 1981, 4–5.

58. George Wagner, "Racism and OTR: A Reply," *Collector's Corner*, zine, Summer 1982, 4–7.

59. Wagner, "Racism and OTR," 4, 7.

60. Susan Douglas, "Letting the Boys Be Boys: Talk Radio, Male Hysteria, and Political Discourse in the 1980s," in *Radio Reader: Essays in the Cultural History of Radio*, ed. Michele Hilmes and Jason Loviglio (New York: Routledge, 2002), 485–504.

Chapter 3. Freeze-Framing Queerness

1. Letterzines are nonfiction fanzines that allow discussion and chat among groups of fans through the letters subscribers send in, which allows fan communities to engage in small, focused discussions and debates. Often pointed to as pre-internet forums, they date back as far as 1950 and are abbreviated as "lz" within fan cultures. These would be distinct from fanzines focused on publishing fan fiction, a distinction more pronounced in television fandoms than radio or wrestling fandoms, interpretive communities in which all amateur self-published fanzines are often focused on community discussions, events, and articles on topics of interest. "Letterzines," *Fanlore*, 2020, https://fanlore.org/wiki/Letterzine.

2. Cheryl Rice, *S and H*, zine, May 1980, box 67, 20, Morgan Dawn Fanzines and Fanvids Collection, University of Iowa Special Collections, Memorial Library, Iowa City, Iowa. Hereafter referred to as Dawn Fanzines Collection.

3. Francesca Coppa, "A Brief History of Media Fandom," in *New Essays: Fan Fiction and Fan Communities in the Age of the Internet*, ed. Karen Hallekson and Kristina Busse (Jefferson, NC: MacFarland, 2006), 52.

4. For the sake of transparency, I note that some fans of these buddy-cop shows were also participating in other television fan communities, such as *Star Trek*, *Blake's 7*, and *The Professionals*. I limited my research in the archive to the fanzine collections I found centered on US buddy-cop shows to consider tape trading in order to use genre as a lens to explore replay practices and their role shaping interpretation and identity formation. However, it would be inaccurate to suggest that these fans were neatly enclosed within a singular television genre or program community. The boundaries for fan participation in communities are porous and everchanging. All of this is to say, this chapter does not provide a comprehensive look at the dynamics of this fan community, but it does represent a significant investment in finding and studying the fanzines I was able to collect. I could easily

have written a book about each of the fan communities studied in this project, but my goal was to consider both the breadth and depth of tape trading broadcasting as a form of distribution prior to the digital age.

5. Joshua M. Greenberg, *From Betamax to Blockbuster: Video Stores and the Invention of Movies on Video* (Cambridge, MA: MIT Press, 2008), 171.

6. Glenn Derene, "The 10 Video Formats HD DVD Will Meet in Heaven," *Popular Mechanics*, March 20, 2008, https://www.popularmechanics.com/.

7. George Jennings, "VTR: A Glimpse of Things to Come," *Epilogue*, zine, 1970, 16–18, Old Time Radio Researchers OTR Magazine Collection, http://www.otrr.org/pg06b_magazines.htm.

8. Jennings, "VTR," 18.

9. Dana L. Friese, "Current Enterprises," *Vulcanalia*, zine, January 1967, 1.

10. Shirley Meech, "Tape Dept.," *Plak-Tow*, zine, December 13, 1967, 3.

11. "Video Room," *Wonder Stories/Denvisions: The Official Progress Report of Denvention Two*, ed. Edward Bryant and Phil Norman (Denver, CO: Denvention Two, 1981), box 223, Ming Wathne Fanzine Collection, University of Iowa Special Collections, Memorial Library, Iowa City, Iowa. Hereafter the collection is referred to as Wathne Fanzine Collection.

12. Zebracon 3 Progress Report #3, "Video Room," 3, n.d., private collection. Progress reports were planning documents sent out by fan-convention organizers as they finalized the logistics for an event. This report is undated. However, because this convention was held November 13–15, 1981, it is likely this report was created sometime in the months leading up to the event in 1981.

13. Media West Convention program, Lansing, Michigan, May 23–26, 1986, 4, box 223, Wathne Fanzine Collection.

14. Media West Convention program, 6.

15. "Diana Barbour," *Fanlore*, October 1, 2022, https://fanlore.org/wiki/Diana_Barbour.

16. Judy Maricevic, *Me and Thee 1*, zine, 1979, box 70, Debbie Hoover Fanzine Collection, University of Iowa Special Collections, Memorial Library, Iowa City, Iowa; Diana Barbour and Kendra Hunter, "Letter from the Editors," *S and H*, zine, December 1982, 1, box 67, Dawn Fanzines Collection.

17. "Con Reports," October 1979, 14–17, and June 1980, 40–41, both *S and H*, zine, box 67, Dawn Fanzines Collection.

18. *Frienz*, zine, May 1995, box 103, Organization for Transformative Works Fanzine and Fan Fiction Collection, University of Iowa Special Collections, Memorial Library, Iowa City, Iowa.

19. Morgan Dawn, "A History of Vidding," *Videlicet*, n.d., https://vidders.github.io/articles/vidding/history.html.

20. Tashery Shannon, *Rainbow Noise*, zine, February 1994, box 17, Sandy Hereld Collection of Blake's 7 Fanzines and Fan Fiction, University of Iowa Special Collections, Memorial Library, Iowa City, Iowa.

21. Morgan Dawn, in-person interview with the author, July 5, 2019.

22. Sandra Ferriday, "Calling All Miami Vicers," *Between Friends*, zine, September 1985, 44, Sandy Hereld Fanzine Collection, Texas A&M Cushing Memorial Library and Archives, College Station, Texas. Hereafter referred to as Hereld Fanzine Collection.

23. Ruth Kurz, "Paul Muni Special Con Report," *Between Friends*, zine, November–December 1985, 37, Hereld Fanzine Collection.

24. Regenia Marracino, letter, *Between Friends*, zine, November–December 1985, 17, Hereld Fanzine Collection.

25. See Jeremy G. Butler, "*Miami Vice* and the Legacy of Film Noir," *Journal of Popular Film and Television* 13, no. 3 (1985): 127–28; Andrew Ross, "Masculinity and *Miami Vice*: Selling In," *Oxford Literary Review* 8, no. 1 (1986): 143–54; John Fiske, "*Miami Vice*, Miami Pleasure," *Cultural Studies* 1, no. 1 (1987): 113–19; Bill Osgerby and Anna Gough-Yates, eds., *Action TV: Tough Guys, Smooth Operators, and Foxy Chicks* (New York: Routledge, 2001); James Lyon, *Miami Vice* (West Sussex, UK: Wiley-Blackwell, 2010); Vicenzo Bavaro, "Come and Get Your Love: Starsky & Hutch, Disidentification, and US Masculinities in the 1970s," in *Queering Masculinities in Language and Culture*, ed. Paul Baker and Giuseppe Balirano (London: Palgrave Macmillan, 2017), 65–85.

26. Signe Landon, *S and H*, zine, May 1980, 25, box 67, Dawn Fanzines Collection.

27. *Simon and Simon Investigations*, zine, May 1987, 58, box 113, Wathne Fanzine Collection.

28. Jenkins, *Textual Poachers*, 197.

29. *Frienz*, zine, February 1989, box 103, Organization for Transformative Works Fanzine and Fan Fiction Collection, University of Iowa Special Collections, Iowa City, Iowa.

30. "Smarm," *Fanlore*, n.d., https://fanlore.org/wiki/Smarm.

31. Jenkins describes fans' appropriations of media narratives for their own purposes through fan-produced texts, such as fan vids, fan art, or fan fiction, as "textual poaching." See Jenkins, *Textual Poachers*.

32. Kendra Hunter, *S and H*, zine, April 1980, 48, box 67, Dawn Fanzines Collection.

33. *Simon and Simon Investigations*, zine, September 1986, 2, box 113, Wathne Fanzine Collection.

34. Ann Gray, *Video Playtime: The Gendering of a Leisure Technology* (New York: Routledge, 1992), 17.

35. Gray, *Video Playtime*, 114.

36. Greenberg, *From Betamax to Blockbuster*, 171, 38, 34.

37. Kay Anderson, *S and H*, zine, January, 1981, 2, box 67, Dawn Fanzines Collection.

38. *Simon and Simon Investigations*, zine, March 1987, box 113, Wathne Fanzine Collection.

39. Sandra Ferriday, "Protest," *This Guy I Gotta Wait For*, zine, May, 1987,

17, box 1, Bea Schmidt Fanzine Collection, University of Iowa Special Collections, Memorial Library, Iowa City, Iowa.

40. "Frenz: Issue 10," *Frenz*, zine, May 1990, Fanlore Archive, https://fanlore.org/wiki/Frenz.

41. Dee E. Brendel, *S and H*, zine, May 1980, 20–21, box 67, Dawn Fanzines Collection.

42. "Frenz: Issue 10," *Frenz*, zine, July 1990, *Fanlore*, https://fanlore.org/wiki/Frenz.

43. *Simon and Simon Investigations*, zine, August 1987, Fanlore, n.d., https://fanlore.org/wiki/Simon_and_Simon_Investigations#Issue_8.

44. Junita Coulson, *S and H*, zine, April 1980, 20, box 67, Dawn Fanzines Collection.

45. Jenkins notes this in 1992 in *Textual Poachers*, and fans continue to create fan-authored media, placing nonexplicitly queer characters into explicit romantic partnerships, see JSA Lowe's work on slash-fan practices using characters in the contemporary Marvel Cinematic Universe in JSA Lowe, "Approaching Whiteness in Slash via Marvel Cinematic Universe's Sam Wilson," *Transformative Works & Cultures* 29 (2019), https://doi.org/10.3983/twc.2019.1695.

46. Kate McNicholas Smith, *Lesbians on Television: New Queer Visibility & the Lesbian Normal* (Chicago: Intellect Books, 2020), 93.

47. Eve Kosofsky Sedgwick, *Tendencies* (Durham, NC: Duke University Press, 1993), 8.

48. Alexander Doty, *Making Things Perfectly Queer: Interpreting Mass Culture* (Minneapolis: University of Minnesota Press, 1993).

49. Doty, *Making Things Perfectly Queer*, xi.

50. Janice Daniels, *S and H*, zine, February, 1981, 11, box 67, Dawn Fanzines Collection, original emphasis.

51. Penny Warren, *S and H*, zine, April 1981, 42, box 67, Dawn Fanzines Collection.

52. Emma Madden, "How Queer Fandom Took Control of Our TV," *GQ Magazine*, July 29, 2019, https://www.gq.com/.

53. Jason Mittell, *Complex TV: The Poetics of Contemporary Television Storytelling* (New York: New York University Press, 2015), 288.

54. Mittell, *Complex TV*.

55. Kompare, *Rerun Nation*, 203.

Chapter 4. We Had to Do It the Hard Way

1. The World Science Fiction Convention has been ongoing since 1939, with the exception of the years the United States fought in World War II. It is referred to as Worldcon, and each convention is given a localized name, thus, the 1975 convention in Melbourne was titled Aussiecon. See Camille Bacon-Smith's discussion of the World Science Fiction Convention's history in *Science Fiction Culture* (Philadelphia: University of Pennsylvania Press, 2000).

2. Gail Adams and Wendy Purcell, "An Interview with Diane Marchant," *Captain's Log*, January 1990, 33, Susan Smith-Clarke Fanzine Collection, National Library of Australia, Canberra, Australia. Hereafter referred to as Smith-Clarke Collection.

3. Twentieth Century Fox presented an advanced screening of *The Day the Earth Stood Still* at Nolacon in 1951. See "Science-Fiction Unit Cites 20th's 'Day,'" *Motion Picture Daily*, September 5, 1951, 2.

4. Allen Asherman, *The Star Trek Interview Book* (New York: Pocket Books, 1988), 11.

5. "Video Room."

6. Roberta Pearson and Marie Messenger Davies, *Star Trek and American Television* (Berkeley: University of California Press, 2014), 8.

7. See Bacon-Smith, *Enterprising Women*; Jenkins, *Textual Poachers*; Francesca Coppa, "Women, Star Trek, and the Early Development of Fannish Vidding," *Transformative Works and Cultures* 1 (2008), https://doi.org/10.3983/twc.2008.044.

8. Pearson and Davies, *Star Trek and American Television*, 7.

9. Herbert I. Schiller, *Communication and Cultural Domination* (New York: Routledge, 1976).

10. Armand Mattelart, *Transnationals and Third World: The Struggle for Culture* (South Hadley, MA: Bergin and Garvey, 1983).

11. See Arjun Appadurai, "Disjuncture and Difference in the Global Cultural Economy," *Theory, Culture & Society* 7, no. 2–3 (1990): 295–310, and John Tomlinson, *Cultural Imperialism* (London: Pinter, 1991).

12. Timothy J. Havens discusses the culture and business of selling and buying television internationally in his book *Global Television Marketplace* (London: British Film Institute, 2006).

13. Havens, *Global Television Marketplace*, 13.

14. Havens, *Global Television Marketplace*, 1.

15. Lichtenberg, Marshak, and Winston, *Star Trek Lives*.

16. Frank Walker, "Trekkies to Boldly Celebrate 25 Years," *Sydney (Australia) Morning Herald*, September 8, 1991, 18.

17. "Fans All-Out Bid for Star Trek revival," *TV Times*, Sydney, July 30, 1969, 7.

18. Susan Batho [Clarke-Smith], "The Effect of Commercialisation and Direct Intervention by the Owners of Intellectual Copyright: A Case Study: The Australian Star Trek Fan Community" (PhD diss., University of Western Sydney, Australia, 2009), 103.

19. Batho, "Effect of Commercialisation," 104.

20. Batho, "Effect of Commercialisation," 180.

21. Lichtenberg, Marshak, and Winston, *Star Trek Lives*.

22. "Club Re-Organization," *Star Trek Action Group Newsletter*, July 1974, 2.

23. Adams and Purcell, "Interview with Diane Marchant," 33; Ian McLean (Australian *Star Trek* fan since the late 1970s), phone interview with author, May 19, 2021. McLean, a Sydney resident and longtime *Star Trek* fan, was a school-

teacher for over thirty years and had firsthand knowledge of the technology present in Australian schools during the 1980s.

24. Valmai Rogers, "Correspondence," *Star Trek Action Group Newsletter*, August 1976, 9, original emphasis, Hereld Fanzine Collection.

25. Frederick V. Romano, *The Golden Age of Boxing on Radio and Television: A Blow-by-Blow History from 1921 to 1964* (New York: Simon and Schuster, 2017), 18.

26. For a discussion of political clubs meeting to listen to radio, see Alan Brinkley, *Voices of Protest: Huey Long, Father Coughlin, and the Great Depression* (New York: Vintage, 1983), 181; for reference to radio as a precursor to television in public spaces, see Anna McCarthy, *Ambient Television: Visual Culture and Public Space* (Durham, NC: Duke University Press, 2001), 45, 82, 91, 246.

27. McCarthy, *Ambient Television*, 2.

28. McCarthy, *Ambient Television*, 2.

29. Spigel, *Make Room for TV.*

30. Jonathan Gray, "Mobility through Piracy, or How Steven Seagal Got to Malawi," *Popular Communication* 2, no. 11 (2011): 99–113; Apryl Williams, "On Thursdays We Watch Scandal: Communal Viewing and Black Twitter," in *Digital Sociologies*, ed. Jessie Daniels, Karen Gregory, and Tressie McMillan Cottom (Chicago: Policy, 2017), 273–94.

31. McLean, interview. This information was confirmed by studying the television channel listings. See "Television," June 11, 1969, 12, and "Today's Television," *Sydney (Australia) Morning Herald*, December 30, 1981, 7.

32. Tom O'Regan, *Australian Television Culture* (New York: Routledge, 2020).

33. Albert Moran and Chris Keating, *The A to Z of Australian Radio and Television* (Lanham, MD: Scarecrow, 2009), 306.

34. O'Regan, *Australian Television Culture*, 3.

35. O'Regan, *Australian Television Culture*, 3.

36. McLean, interview.

37. Rogers, "Correspondence."

38. Jan McDonnell and Geoff Allshorn, "Channel 9 Melbourne TV Letter Writing Campaign," *Captain's Log*, January 1979, 1, Smith-Clarke Collection.

39. McLean, interview.

40. McLean, interview.

41. Katherine Teh, "Videos Swamp Independent Cinema," *Age* (Melbourne, Australia), January 6, 1989, 26.

42. McLean, interview.

43. Paul McDonald, "Piracy and the Shadow History of Hollywood," in *Hollywood and the Law*, ed. Paul McDonald, Emily Carman, Eric Hoyt, and Philip Drake (London: Bloomsbury, 2015), 69–102, 77.

44. See McDonald, "Piracy and the Shadow History," 77, in which he primarily discusses the piracy of film but clearly outlines the presence of these film print libraries that I first heard about from Australian *Star Trek* fan Susan Batho, in a video interview with her on January 13, 2021.

45. McDonald, "Piracy and the Shadow History," 77.

46. McLean, interview.

47. Ritz Cinema, advertisement, *Age* (Melbourne, Australia), November 26, 1976, 31.

48. See O'Regan, *Australian Television Culture*, 56, for a brief discussion of the introduction of color TV in Australia.

49. National Mutual Theatrette, advertisement, September 27, 1980, 137; Gary Linnell, "Science Fiction of the Past Has Big Following," September 29, 1983, 27; National Mutual, advertisement, January 19, 1985, 155; "Independent," March 31, 1989, 45; "The A.M.P. Cinema," April 6, 1990, 49; "Independent," February 3, 1990, 132, all in *Age* (Melbourne, Australia); and "Amusements," October 3, 1981, 52; "Revivals," December 9, 1983, 38; and "Independent," October 6, 1987, 21, both in *Sydney (Australia) Morning Herald*.

50. Rachel Shave, in-person interview with Susan Batho, Perth, Australia, 2003, transcript in appendix, Batho, "Effect of Commercialisation," 398.

51. McLean, interview.

52. McLean, interview.

53. Robert Jan, "Review: December 6th Screening of 'Trek at the National Mutual," *Captain's Log*, Austrek letterzine, February 1981, 9–10, Smith-Clarke Collection.

54. McLean, interview.

55. Arjun Appadurai, "Commodities and the Politics of Value," in *The Social Life of Things: Commodities in Cultural Perspective*, ed. A. Appadurai (Cambridge: Cambridge University Press, 1986), 3–63.

56. In an editorial in the December 1984 issue of Austrek's letterzine, club president Julie Hughes informed Austrek members that she had sat down with Bob Johnson to work out the schedule for club meetings so they coincided with marathon dates. Club meetings through the 1980s were held in the Melbourne church St. Luke's and started at 2 p.m. in order for club members to then go to Johnson's Melbourne marathons together at 6 p.m. See Julie Hughes, editorial, *Captain's Log*, December 1984, 1, Smith-Clarke Collection. This mutual arrangement continued into the 1990s.

57. Batho discusses this tension in her dissertation and how her position as both a longtime participant in Australia's *Star Trek* fan community and her research interviewing and surveying Australian *Star Trek* fans informed her reflection on the exploitative nature of Bob Johnson's reliance on fan labor to support and promote his marathons. See Batho, "Effect of Commercialisation," 62.

58. Jenkins, *Textual Poachers*, 230.

59. Gene Roddenberry collected a vast wealth of *Star Trek TOS* clips by collecting daily prints of episodes during the show's initial production and cutting them into sets of clips to sell to fans via his own *Star Trek* merchandising company, Lincoln Enterprises. Bjo Trimble, *On the Good Ship Enterprise: My 15 Years with Star Trek* (Norfolk, VA: Donning, 1983), 86. Collecting film clips composed a subset of *Star Trek* fandom in the 1970s, signified by the fact that US *Star Trek*

fan Jim Rondeau founded his fanzine *Clipper Trade Ship* originally as a place for *Star Trek* fans who collected film clips from the television series to connect with each other, as he announced his new fanzine in another *Star Trek* fanzine, *Halkan Council*, August 1975, 12.

60. Coppa, "Women, Star Trek."
61. Coppa, "Women, Star Trek."
62. Susan Batho, videophone interview with author, January 13, 2021.
63. Andrew Bauld, editorial, *Captain's Log*, February 1981, 1, Smith-Clarke Collection.
64. Fern Clarke and Jodi Williams, interview with Susan Batho, Perth, Western Australia, 2003, transcript in appendix, Batho, "Effect of Commercialisation," 428.
65. Clarke and Williams, interview, 433–34.
66. Evan Elkins, *Locked Out: Regional Restrictions in Digital Entertainment Culture* (New York: New York University Press, 2019), 52.
67. Batho, interview.
68. "Intergalactic Bizarre Bazaar 1987 Austrek Christmas Party Flyer," *Captain's Log*, December 1987, 2, Smith-Clarke Collection.
69. Clarke and Williams, interview, 441.
70. Adam Sandler, "The Merged Paramount-Viacom Duo," *Variety*, February 21, 1994, 185.
71. Batho, "Effect of Commercialisation," 368.
72. Batho, interview.
73. Batho, "Effect of Commercialisation," 120.
74. Batho, "Effect of Commercialisation," 115.
75. Batho, "Effect of Commercialisation," 120.
76. McLean, interview.
77. Batho, "Effect of Commercialisation," 130.
78. Batho, "Effect of Commercialisation," 137.
79. Batho, "Effect of Commercialisation," 207.
80. According to archival copies of the Melbourne-based *Star Trek* fan club Austrek's letterzine, the marathons were running in 1993, as the marathons are listed in the social-events calendar, *Captain's Log*, Austrek letterzine, December 1993, 3, Smith-Clarke Collection.
81. McLean, interview.
82. McLean, interview.
83. Tama Leaver, "Watching *Battlestar Galactica* in Australia and the Tyranny Of Digital Distance," *Media International Australia* 126, no. 1 (2008): 152.

Chapter 5. Enough of That Garbage

1. Dave Meltzer to Norman Kietzer, August 20, 1982, *Wrestling News* Papers, Arcadian Vanguard Corporate Archive, Mendham, New Jersey.
2. Roy Lucier, telephone interview with author, November 18, 2020; Steven Beverly, telephone interview with author, November 24, 2020; John McAdams,

telephone interview with author, December 2, 2020; Brian Last, telephone interview with author, November 24, 2020.

3. Scott Beekman, *Ringside: A History of Professional Wrestling in America* (Westport, CT: Praeger, 2006), 40.

4. Sharon Mazer, *Professional Wrestling: Sport and Spectacle* (Jackson: University Press of Mississippi, 1998), 160.

5. Mark Madden, "Going Out with Flair: I'll Miss the Game's Best Performer," *Pittsburgh (PA) Post-Gazette*, October 21, 1994, 19.

6. Chad Dell, *The Revenge of Hatpin Mary: Women, Professional Wrestling, and Fan Culture in the 1950s* (New York: Lang, 2006).

7. Henry Jenkins, "Never Trust a Snake: WWF Wrestling as Masculine Melodrama," in *Out of Bounds: Sports, Media, and the Politics of Identity*, ed. Aaron Baker and Todd Boyd (Bloomington: Indiana University Press, 1997), 50.

8. Mazer, *Professional Wrestling*, 100.

9. Cornel Sandvoss, *Fans: The Mirror of Consumption* (Malden, MA: Polity, 2005).

10. Jenkins, "Never Trust a Snake."

11. Last, interview.

12. Beekman, *Ringside*, 11, 36, 39.

13. Dell, *Revenge of Hatpin Mary*, 16.

14. Chad Dell, "Wrestling with Corporate Identity: Defining Television Programming Strategy at NBC, 1945–1950," in *Transmitting the Past: Historical and Cultural Perspectives on Broadcasting*, ed. J. Emmett Winn and Susan Brinson (Tuscaloosa: University of Alabama Press, 2005).

15. See Dell, *Revenge of Hatpin Mary*; F. Steven Beverly, "A History of Professional Wrestling as Television Programming Form: 1941–1989" (master's thesis, Auburn University, 1989).

16. Beverly, "History," 16.

17. Beverly, "History," 16.

18. Beekman, *Ringside*, 84.

19. Tim Hornbaker, *National Wrestling Alliance: The Untold Story of the Monopoly That Strangled Professional Wrestling* (Toronto, Canada: ECW, 2007), 17.

20. Hornbaker, *National Wrestling Alliance*, 17, 121.

21. Beekman, *Ringside*.

22. "TV Wrestling Helps," *Broadcasting*, December 21, 1953, 105.

23. "Wrestling Alliance Agrees Not to Hamper TV Activities," *Broadcasting*, October 22, 1956, 96.

24. "Wrestling Alliance Agrees."

25. Hornbaker, *National Wrestling Alliance*, 177–81.

26. Hornbaker, *National Wrestling Alliance*, 107.

27. Barbara Holsopple, "WIIC Cancels Studio Wrestling after 16-Year Run," July 18, 1974, 44, and Mark Madden, "Studio Wrestling," July 12, 1990, 115, both in *Pittsburgh (PA) Post-Gazette*.

28. Last, interview.

29. Beverly, interview.
30. Beekman, *Ringside*, 119.
31. Beekman, *Ringside*, 113, 120.
32. McAdams, interview.
33. Dell, *Revenge of Hatpin Mary*, 78.
34. Dell, *Revenge of Hatpin Mary*, 94.
35. Dell, *Revenge of Hatpin Mary*, 83.
36. Dave Meltzer, "Should Pro-Wrestling Be Covered in Sports Pages," *Wrestling Observer*, August 1983, 1–2.
37. Sam Ford, "The Marks Have Gone Off-Script: Rogue Actors in WWE's Stands," in *#WWE: Professional Wrestling in the Digital Age*, ed. Dru Jeffries (Bloomington: Indiana University Press, 2019), 123.
38. David Shoemaker, "How 'SummerSlam' Became the 'WrestleMania' for Die-Hard Fans," *Grantland*, July 22, 2015, https://grantland.com/the-triangle/; Nicholas Ware, "Wrestling's Not Real, It's Hyperreal: Professional Wrestling Video Games," in *Performance and Professional Wrestling*, ed. Broderick Chow, Eero Laine, and Claire Warden (London: Routledge, 2016), 49.
39. Dave Meltzer, "Titan Inks Lucrative Japan Pact; Signs Bruno," *Wrestling Observer*, September 30, 1984, 1.
40. Joe Pantozzi, "Correspondents Corner: Can Vote on a Few Things," *Wrestling Observer 1984 Yearbook*, January 1985, 16.
41. Mike Nulty, "Mr. Mike's Mondo Wrestling," *Wrestling Observer*, July 1984, 9.
42. Lee Benaka, "Before Shoot Interviews: Dave Meltzer," Weekend of Champions fan convention, Queens, New York, August 24, 1991, *Professional Wrestling Studies Association*, July 28, 2022, https://www.prowrestlingstudies.org/.
43. Walt Wolanksy, "More Praise for Dallas," *Wrestling Observer*, June 1983, 13.
44. Dave Meltzer, Editor's Notes, *Wrestling Observer*, October 22, 1984, 2.
45. Jenkins, "Never Trust a Snake," 49; Dalbir S. Sehmby, "Wrestling and Popular Culture," *CLCWeb: Comparative Literature and Culture* 4, no. 1 (2002): 6.
46. Meltzer to Kietzer.
47. Dave Meltzer, Editor's Notes, *Wrestling Observer*, September 10, 1984, 2.
48. Dave Meltzer, Videotapes, *Wrestling Observer*, October 1983, 7.
49. Dave Meltzer, Editor's Notes, *Wrestling Observer*, March 1984, 3–4.
50. Dave Meltzer, Note, *Wrestling Observer*, December 1983, 8.
51. Dave Meltzer to Jim Melby, "1982 Wrestling Observer Awards," undated (ca. November 1982), attached in the archive to a response letter, November 24, 1982, Arcadian Vanguard Corporate Archive, Mendham, New Jersey.
52. Dave Meltzer, "Awards," *Wrestling Observer*, December, 1984, 3.
53. Last, interview.
54. Jeff Bowdren, "The Greatest Matches of the 80s," *Wrestling Observer 1989 Yearbook*, January 1990, 82.

55. Sean Ryan, "Correspondents' Corner: Atlanta Tapes Look Terrible," *Wrestling Observer*, March 25, 1985, 10.

56. Steve Munari, "Correspondents' Corner: And More on Vince-a-Mania," *Wrestling Observer*, April 15, 1985, 16.

57. Munari, "Correspondents' Corner."

58. Not to be confused with the short-lived American Universal Wrestling Federation, also known as UWF, which was established when wrestling promoter Bill Watts rebranded his regional Mid-South Wrestling organization as Universal Wrestling Federation in 1986 in an attempt to take his promotion national and compete with WWF. This strategy was not successful, and UWF/Mid-South was bought by Jim Crockett Promotions in 1986.

59. Dave Meltzer mentions his contact in Japan, Koichi Yoshizawa, when he thanks him for supplying news reports, videotapes, and photos in his Editor's Notes, *Wrestling Observer*, October 1983, 2.

60. Lucier, interview.

61. Hilderbrand, *Inherent Vice*, 32.

62. Lucier, interview; Last, interview.

63. Dell, *Revenge of Hatpin Mary*, 82.

64. See Dave Meltzer, Editor's Notes, *Wrestling Observer*, June 1983, 16; George Schire, "Correspondents Corner: Mean Letters to the Titan Department," *Wrestling Observer*, September 10, 1984, 6.

65. Kevin Hancer, "Minneapolis Invasion Analyzed," *Wrestling Observer*, June 1984, 7.

66. Dave Meltzer, "Mid-South," *Wrestling Observer*, January 1984, 13.

67. Duane Mason, "Can't Understand AWA Fans," *Wrestling Observer*, April 1984, 8.

68. Andrea Huyssen, *After the Great Divide* (Basingstoke, UK: Palgrave Macmillan, 1986).

69. Hilmes, *Radio Voices*; Douglas, *Listening In*; Jennifer Wang, "The Case of the Radio-Active Housewife: Relocating Radio in the Age of Television," in *Radio Reader: Essays in the Cultural History of Radio*, ed. Michele Hilmes and Jason Liviglio (New York: Routledge, 2001), 343–66.

70. Ford, "Marks Have Gone Off-Script."

Conclusion. Bootlegging after the Airwaves

1. Marc Graser, "WWE Network to Launch in February as Streaming Service," *Variety*, January 8, 2014, https://variety.com/.

2. Todd Spangler, "NBCU's Peacock Pins WWE Network Exclusive U.S. Streaming Rights," *Variety*, January 25, 2021, https://variety.com.

3. Roy Lucier, phone interview with the author, November 18, 2020.

4. Lucier, phone interview.

5. Brian Last, phone interview with the author, November 24, 2020.

6. John McAdams, phone interview with the author, December 2, 2020.

7. McAdams, phone interview.

8. J. David Goldin, *Radio Yesteryear Presents: The Golden Age of Radio* (Sandy Hook, CT: Yesteryear, 1998); Frank Dicostanza, "Metacom Inc.'s Marketing Anything but Conventional," *Billboard*, January 6, 1996, 43; Joseph Rosenbloom, "Now Hear This," *Inc.*, October 21, 1997, 51–52.

9. Walden Hughes, phone interview with author, January 7, 2016.

10. Business editors, "Audio Book Club, Inc. Announces Strategy to Leverage Classic Radio Content on Internet Business & Technology Editors," *Business Wire*, February 1,1999, 1.

11. Business editors/high-tech writers, "Audio Book Club, Inc. Announces Acquisition of Radio Spirits, Radio Yesteryear, Video Yesteryear, and Adventures in Cassettes," *Business Wire*, December 15, 1998, 1.

12. Frederick Wasser, *Veni, Vidi, Video: The Hollywood Empire and the VCR* (Austin: University of Texas Press, 2001).

13. Wasser, *Veni, Vidi, Video*.

14. Greenberg, *From Betamax to Blockbuster*; Daniel Herbert, *Videoland: Movie Culture at the American Video Store* (Berkeley: University of California Press, 2014).

15. Kompare, *Rerun Nation*.

16. Kompare, *Rerun Nation*, 200.

17. Adrian Johns, *Piracy: The Intellectual Property Wars from Gutenberg to Gates* (Chicago: University of Chicago Press, 2010); Lobato, *Shadow Economies of Cinema*.

18. Coinnews Media Group LLC, "US Inflation Calculator," https://www.us inflationcalculator.com/, accessed April 18, 2023; David Colker, "Captive Audiences: Viewers Find They Are at Mercy of Their Community Cable Companies for Price, Services, Channels," *Los Angeles Times*, July 30, 1989, 98.

19. Amanda D. Lotz, *Portals: A Treatise on Internet-Distributed Television* (Ann Arbor: University of Michigan Library, 2017), https://quod.lib.umich.edu/m/maize/mpub9699689/.

20. Gene Thompson, "Bring Back 'Murder, She Wrote' to Netflix Streaming!!!!" undated online petition, https://www.change.org/p/netflix-bring-back-murder-she-wrote-to-netflix-streaming.

21. Thompson, "Bring Back 'Murder, She Wrote.'"

22. Nicole Sperling, "Netflix to Offer Cheaper Ad Option Beginning Nov. 3," *New York Times*, October 13, 2022, B6.

23. Alexis Benveniste, "*The New York Times* Is Ditching TV Listings after 81 Years," *CNN Business Online*, August 30, 2020, https://www.cnn.com/.

24. Benveniste, "*New York Times*."

25. Fisher, "Streaming Surpasses Cable."

Index

Note: Page numbers in *italics* denote figures and tables.

ABC network, 13, 80, 137
Acland, Charles, 12, 70–71
aesthetics of access, 4, 47, 112, 116
Altman, Rick, 7
Amalgamated Television New South Wales (ATN 7), 107
amateurism, 47–49
Amazon, 153, 157
ambient television, 106–7
American Indian Movement, 71
American Universal Wrestling Federation (UWF), 183n58
American Wrestling Association (AWA), *130*, 136–37, 141, 144
Amos 'n' Andy, 18, 54, 60–61, 71–77, 172n48, 172n55
Anderson, Christopher, 15, 17, 20
Anderson, Kay, 92
Appadurai, Arjun, 60–61, 102, 112
Arcadian Vanguard podcasts, 126
Astrex, 120. *See also Star Trek* fan clubs
AT&T, 61
Audio Home Recording Act of 1992, 11
Aussiecon, 100–101, 105, 109, 176n1. *See also* World Science Fiction Convention (Worldcon)
Australian Film Commission, 119–20
Australian *Star Trek* Club (ASTAC), 104
Australian Television and Film Securities Office, 120–21
Austrek *Star Trek* Club, 104, 111, 113–14, 179n56, 180n80; Intergalactic Bizarre Bazaar Christmas Party, *118*, 119

Balbi, Gabriele, 31
Barbour, Diana, 79, 83, 86
Barthes, Roland, 16
Batho, Susan (née Smith), 114, 116–20, 178n44, 179n57. *See also* Smith, Susan; Smith-Clarke *Star Trek* collection
Baudelaire, Charles, 25
Baycon, 83
Between Friends (fanzine), *84*, 87–88, 97
Beverly, Steven, 131
binge watching, 12, 79–80, 156
Bjarkman, Kim, 4, 10–11
blackface, 34–36, 71; sonic, 72–73, 172n48

Bradford, Gene, 73–74, 76–77
Braun, Joshua, 5
Brisco, Jack, 150–51
Brisco, Jerry, 150–51
broadcast licensing, 120–21, 147; bootlegging as resistance to, 107–8, 112–13; and resale of content, 12, 103–4, 156–57. *See also* syndication
buddy-cop television. See *Miami Vice* (NBC); *Simon & Simon* (CBS); *Starsky & Hutch* (ABC)
Burchett, Bob, 65. See also *Collector's Corner* (fanzine)
Burnham, Bob, 59, 65. See also *Collector's Corner* (fanzine)

Caldwell, John, 4
Capitol Wrestling Corp., 129
Captain's Log (letterzine), 114–15, *118*, 119, 179n56, 180n80
CBS network, 13, 69, 71, 80, 92, 137
chain broadcasting, 50, 61–62
Cincinnati Old Time Radio Convention, 68
cinema of attractions, 38–39
Clarke, Fern, 115–16
Clipper Trade Ship, The (letterzine), 113, 179n59
Cohan, Noah, 139
Collector's Corner (fanzine), 59, 65–67, *67*, 72–73, *75*, 172n55
Colman, Ronald, 63
colonialism, 32, 167n40
Colorado Radio Historical Association, 59, 65
color television, 19, 81, 108–9
Comcast, 157
commodity audience, 1, 6, 9–11, 13, 112, 158
communal viewing, 19, 104, 114–18; at Aussiecon, 100–101, 103, 105; and fan awareness of copyright law, 119–21; history of, 106–7; *Star Trek* marathons, 103, 105–6, 108–13, 121–22, 179nn56–57, 180n80
convergence, technological, 9, 23–24; and early motion pictures, 30–31, 40–41, 43; and radio bootlegging, 18, 46, 49–55
Coppa, Francesca, 80
copyright, 5, 11, 34, 54, 151, 153, 157; and NBC, 1–3, 169n109; and *Star Trek* clubs in Australia, 119–21
Curtin, Michael, 8, 15, 17, 20

Daguerre, Louis, 25
Daniels, Janice, 96
Data (letterzine), 113
Davies, Marie Messenger, 101
Dawn, Morgan, 86–87, *87*, 97
De Kosnik, Abigail, 14–15, 59–60, 164n51
Dell, Chad, 124, 127, 132, 144
Deluge Monday letter-writing campaign, 104
Desilu Productions, 103, 121
de Sola Pool, Ithiel, 31
digitization, 31, 59–60, 122, 149–50, 153
domesticity, 2, 18, 23–24, 27, 29–30, 40–43, 52–55; in advertisements, 33–38, 44–45; and media production, 44–50; and television industrial imagination, 91, 106–7; Victorian cult of, 32–33, 167n40
Doty, Alexander, 95
Douglas, Susan, 48–49
Down Under Space Kooks. See *Star Trek* Action Committee
du Maurier, George, 27–29; *Peter Ibbetson*, 25
DuMont Television Network, 126, 128

Eastman Kodak Co. devices, 42–43, 46–47
Edison, Thomas, 26–27, 29, 41; Edison Laboratories, 30–31
Edison Co. devices, 27, 32, 34–46, 53, 106, 167n54. *See also* National Phonograph Co.
Ely, Melvin Patrick, 71–72, 172n48
ephemerality, 12–13, 18, 126, 165n12; of broadcast flows, 6–7, 92, 155; and

forensic fandom, 98; and preservation culture, 24–32, 43, 44, 54–55
Epilogue (fanzine), 56–57, 59, 63–64, 81
Exhibivision, 1–2

Faddis, Connie, 96, 97
fan conventions, 82–83, 101, 113–14; and buddy-cop shows, 80, 83–88, 174n12; and old-time radio, 14, 16, 18, 56–58, 62, 64–68, 73, 77; and professional wrestling, 132, 134, 145, 150; and *Star Trek*, 100–101, 103, 105, 109–10, 113–14, 116, 119, 176n1. *See also individual conventions*
fan fiction, 14, 59, 82, 83, 86, 94, 98, 102, 121, 125, 173n1; slash, 89, 95, 97, 176n45. *See also* vidding
fan labor. *See* labor
fanzines, 14–16, 20, 150; aesthetics of, 65–66; and buddy-cop television, 79–80, 84, 86–88, 90–93, 96–98, 145, 173n4; chronology of, 59; and old-time radio, 18, 56–60, 62–73, 77, 81, 170n8, 172n55; relation to letterzines, 173n1; and *Star Trek*, 82, 102, 108–9, 113–14, 117–19, 121, 179n59, 180n80; as wrestling tape trading forums, 123–27, 132–42, 145–46. *See also* letterzines; *individual letterzine titles*
Ferriday, Sandra, 87, 92–93, 93
Feuer, Jane, 7
Fewkes, Jesse Walter, 27
film-exchange programs, 41–43
Fiske, John, 10
flow, scheduling, 3, 5–9, 13–14, 26, 62, 92, 108
Floyd, Joe, 1–2
Fong, Kandy, 113–14
Ford, Sam, 8, 133
forensic fandom, 98
Foucault, Michel, 16
Friends of Old Time Radio (FOTR), 64, 67, 67–68, 73, 77
Frienz (letterzine), 84, 84–85, 97

gender, 17, 32, 36, 77, 95–96, 107; and buddy-cop fandom, 79–80, 88–92; and home entertainment advertising, 40, 44–46; and home recording, 48, 81, 91–92; in Progressive Era radio culture, 48–49, 167n40; and wrestling fandom, 20, 124–25, 127, 133–35, 144–46
Georgia Wrestling Championship (WTCG), 131–32
Gitelman, Lisa, 29
Goldbergs, The, 76
Golden Radio Buffs convention, 56
Gray, Ann, 91
Green, Joshua, 8
Greenberg, Joshua M., 81, 91, 152
Gruber Garvey, Elizabeth, 26
Guffey, Elizabeth, 69
Gunning, Tom, 38

Halkan Council (fanzine), 179n59
ham radio, 66
Hancer, Kevin, 71–72
Havens, Tim, 102–3
Hayes, Michael, *140*, 141
HBO Max, 20–21, 157–58, 164n65
Hello Again (fanzine), 56, 59, 63–65, 71–72
Herbert, Dan, 152
Hickerson, Jay, 59, 63, 65
Hilderbrand, Lucas, 4–5, 112, 116, 144
Hilmes, Michelle, 7, 17, 71, 172n48
Hochman, Brian, 26
Holt, Jennifer, 8
Hunter, Kendra, 79, 83, 90–91, *91*

imperialism, cultural, 32, 102, 122
Indigenous cultures, 26–27, 71, 102
Industrial Revolution, 23–24, 32
Ingersoll, Charles, 64–65
Internet Archive, 7, 15, 59, 162n29

Jack Benny Show, The, 74, 76, 151
Jan, Robert, 111
Japanese Universal Wrestling Federation (UWF), 142, *143*
Jaramillo, Deborah, 10

Jedlowski, Alessandro, 62
Jenkins, Henry, 8, 31, 62, 89, 124–25, 175n31, 176n45
Jennings, George, 57, 59, 63, 81–82
Johns, Adrian, 153
Johnson, Bob, 105, 108–13, 121, 179nn56–57

kayfabe, 124–25, 127, 130, 134, 139, 142, 145
Keating, Chris, 107
Klinger, Barbara, 12, 33
Kompare, Derek, 6–8, 153
Kopytoff, Igor, 10
Kupferman, Theodore, 3

labor, 3–4, 13–15, 91, 97, 155–57, 159; and amateurism, 47–48; as embodied practice, 17, 149–50; and old-time radio fans, 60, 77, 151; and *Star Trek* fans, 101–3, 108, 113, 117–19, 122, 179n57; and wrestling fans, 20, 125–26, 147–50
Landon, Signe, 88
Last, Brian, 126, 131, 141, 149
Leaver, Tama, 122
letterzines, 173n1; chronology of, 84; and *Starsky & Hutch* fandom, 79–80, 83–93, 96–97, 99; and *Star Trek* fandom, 102, 113–14, 179n56, 180n80. *See also* fanzines; *individual fanzine titles*
Levine, Elana, 7
Lewis, Steve, 172n55
Lincoln Enterprises, 113, 179n59
Lobato, Ramon, 4–5, 14, 153
Lone Ranger, The, 60, 71–72
Lotz, Amanda, 4, 156
Lucier, Roy, 144, 147–49
Lum 'n' Abner, 72

Marchant, Diane, 100, 105
Marcus, Daniel, 69
Marracino, Regenia, 88
Marshall, Lee, 16
materiality of media, 7, 9–12, 19, 27, 146; and bootlegged print quality, 110–12; and consumer culture, 18, 34, 43, 152; and fan labor, 3–5, 13–15, 17, 147–50, 159; and social life of things, 60–61, 112; and tape trading, 26, 57, 60–61, 68, 78, 86, 99, 134, 141; value of, 153–56
Mazer, Sharon, 124–25, 134
McAdam, John, 149–51
McCarthy, Anna, 106–7
McCormack, Shayne, 104
McLean, Ian, 110–12, 122, 177n23
McMahon, Vince J., 129
McMahon, Vince K., 129, 131–32, 134–35, 142, 145
McNulty, Mike, 135
Media West Convention, 83, 85
Meech, Shirley, 82
Meltzer, Dave, 123–25, 129–30, 133–139, 142, 144, 183n59. *See also Wrestling Observer*
Metacom, 151
metafans, 133–34, 146
Me & Thee, 83
methodology of book, 15–18, 53, 58, 173n4
Miami Vice (NBC), 80, 82, 84, 87–90, 92–93, 98
Mid-Atlantic Wrestling, 130, 132, 137, 147
Mid-South Wrestling, 132, 147, 183n58. *See also* Universal Wrestling Federation (UWF)
Mitchell, Daniel (@GigaBoots), 21, 164n65
Mittell, Jason, 97–98
Mondt, Toots, 129
Moran, Albert, 107
Motion Picture World (magazine), 42
Munari, Steve, 142
Murder, She Wrote, 157
Music Publisher's Protective Association, 34
Mutual Broadcasting System, 69
Muybridge, Eadweard, 30

NARA News (fanzine), 63
National Broadcasting Company (NBC), 8, 16, 52–54, 71, 160; and chain broadcasting, 61–62; early

copyright concerns, 1–3, 169n109; and *Star Trek*, 101, 103–4; and televised wrestling, 126, 128, 137; and vertical integration, 31
National Gramophone Co., 33–34
National Library of Australia, 15, 102
National Phonograph Co., 29–30, 167n54; advertisements, 34–36, 37, 44–46. *See also* Edison Co. devices
National Public Radio, 61, 158
National Wrestling Alliance (NWA), 128
National Wrestling Association, 128
Netflix, 156–57, 159
New Japan Pro-Wrestling World (NJPW), 147, *148*
New Japan Wrestling Association, *130*, *143*
newsletters. *See* fanzines; letterzines
New York *Star Trek* Convention, 103
New York Times, 159
North American Radio Archives, 59, 65
nostalgia, 12, 48, 69; and radio collecting, 58, 65, 70, 72
NTSC (National Television System Committee) format, 103, 115–17

Old-Time Radio Collectors and Traders (ORCAT), 66
old-time radio (OTR), 14, 16, 62, 73, 162n30, 171n26; and commercial box sets, 151–52; and nostalgia, 58, 65, 70, 72; and racism debates, 18, 60–61, 71–77, 172n48, 172n55; and rogue archives, 59–60; and tape trading, 57–60, 63–70, 81–82, 102
Old Time Radio Club of Buffalo, 59, 65
Old Time Radio Collector's Handbook, The (Seeley), 58
old-time-radio researchers (OTRR), 58–59
Osgood, Stanton, 1–2

Pacific Wrestling Federation, *143*
PAL (Phase Alternating Line) format, 103, 115–16, 122

Paramount, 19, 101, 104, 110, 115, 119–21
Pathé, 31, 43, 46, 50, 53; Cinématographe de Salon Kok (Pathéscope), 41–42
patriarchy, 33, 107, 167n40
Peacock, 146, 147, 157
Pearson, Roberta, 101
Peter Ibbetson (du Maurier), 25
Phonoscope, The, 30, 38
Pittsburgh, PA, 129–30
Plak-Tow (fanzine), 82
podcasting, 123, 126, 156, 158
preservation culture, 7, 24–32, 43, 44, 53–55
Progressive Era, 18, 23–24, 29–30, 43–44, 50–55; and amateurism, 47–48; and feminized culture, 127; and home entertainment advertising, 33–40, 45–46; racial politics, 167n40; and technological convergence, 31, 41
Pro-Wrestling Illustrated, 132
Punch's Almanack, 27, *28*

queer meaning-making, 19, 80, 95–97, 124–25, 176n45

race, 17, 26, 109, 122; and home entertainment advertising, 34–36, 40, 44–45; and middle-class domesticity, 32–33, 36, 55, 167n40; and old-time radio, 18, 60–61, 71–77, 172n48, 172n55
radio. *See* ham radio; old-time radio (OTR); wireless radio
Radio Collectors of America, 64–65
Radio Dial (fanzine), 59, 64–65, 70
Radio Enthusiasts of Puget Sound, 64
Radio Historical Society of America (RHSA), 59, 63–66
Radio Spirits, 151
Radio Yesteryear, 151
Rainbow Noise (fanzine), 86
RCA, 1–2, 31, 50–53, 55
Recorder: The Marion Stokes Project, 7, 162n29
replay culture, 3, 7, 9, 12, 153–54,

Index 189

replay culture (*continued*)
173n4; and the phonograph, 30, 38, 43; and *Starsky & Hutch* fandom, 19, 79–80, 90–91, 93–99, 125, 141; and wrestling fandom, 135–36, 142, 146, *148*
Reznick, David, 72–76
Rice, Cheryl, 79–80
Roddenberry, Gene, 101, 105, 113, 119–20, 179n59
rogue archives, 59–60
Ryan, Sean, 141–42
Rymsza-Pawlowska, M. J., 69

safety film, 41, 46–47
salvage ethnography, 26–27
S and H letterzine, 79–80, 83–85, 88–89, *91*, 91–92, 96–97
Sandvoss, Cornell, 125
Sanson, Kevin, 8
Sarnoff, David, *51*, 52
Schaden, Chuck, *59*, 171n27
Schatz, George, 63
scrapbooking, 25–26, 165n12
Sedgwick, Eve Kosofsky, 95
Seeley, Charles: *The Old Time Radio Collector's Handbook*, 58
Shave, Rachel, 110
Shoemaker, David, 133
Simon & Simon (CBS), 80, *84*, 87–90, 92, 94–95, 98
Simon & Simon Investigations (letterzine), *84*, *85*, 88, 90
Smith-Clarke *Star Trek* collection, 102, *118*
Smith, Susan, 104. *See also* Batho, Susan (née Smith)
Smythe, Dallas, 1, 9–10
Society for the Preservation of Radio Drama, Variety, and Comedy (SPERDVAC), 65, 68
Society of American Vintage Radio Enthusiasts (SAVE), 64. *See also* Friends of Old Time Radio (FOTR)
Society to Preserve and Encourage Radio Drama, Variety, and Comedy, 59, 162n30

Sony Corp. of America v. Universal City Studios, Inc., 11, 51, 53, 98
South Africa's black market for U.S. media, 11, 108–9, 111
Southern Star, 120
Spelling-Goldberg Productions, 80
SPERDVAC Old Time Radio Convention, 68
Spigel, Lyn, 106–7
Stampede, 131–32
Stanfill, Mel, 14–15
Starr, Paul, 25
Starrcade, 137
Starsky & Hutch (ABC), 19, 90, 93, 98–99, 141; fan art and fiction, 86–87, *91*, 94–97; letterzines, 79–80, 83–85, 88–89, *91*, 91–92, 96–97, 101, 145; and *Star Trek* fandom, 83, 86, 89, 95, 125; Zebracon, 83–85, 174n12
Star Trek Action Committee, 104, 120
Star Trek Action Group, 105
Star Trek fandom, 68, 81–82, *118*, 177n23, 178n44, 179n59; conventions, 83, 100–101, 103, 105, 109–10, 113–114, 116, 119, 176n1; marathon screenings, 103, 105–6, 108–13, 121–22, 179nn56–57, 180n80; relation to *Starsky & Hutch* fandom, 83, 86, 89, 95, 125; and television syndication, 11, 19, 101–4, 107–9, 111–12, 120; and videotape formats, 103, 115–17, 122
Star Trek the Motion Picture, 110
Star Trek: The Next Generation (TNG), 19, 104, 107, 115–16, 119, 121
Star Trek: The Original Series (TOS), 10–11, 19, 104–5, 107–9, 114, 120, 179n59; and emergence of VTR, 81–82; at fan conventions, 83, 100–101, 103; and screening marathons, 110–12, 121
Sterne, Jonathan, 5, 29
Stokes, Marion, 7, 162n29
Stokes, Matt: *Recorder: The Marion Stokes Project*, 162n29

streaming platforms, 2, 8–9, 20–21, 147–48, 153, 156–59, 164n65
Studio Wrestling (WIIC-TV), 129
Susman, Warren, 17
syndication, 5, 7, 12, 92, 98, 136, 153–54, 156–57; and old-time radio, 69–70; and *Star Trek* in Australia, 11, 19, 101–4, 107–9, 111–12, 120

Talking Dead, The (AMC), 158
Talking Machine World (magazine), 36
tape trading, 11, 14–15, 18–20, 146–49, 152–53; and aesthetics of access, 4, 47, 112, 116; and old-time radio fans, 57–60, 63–70, 81–82, 102; and *Starsky & Hutch* fans, 79–86, 89–93, 98–99, 173n4; and *Star Trek* fans, 102, 116–17; via *Wrestling Observer*, 123–27, 132–42, 145; and wrestling territorialization, 126, 130–32, 136–38
Television Corp. New South Wales (TCN 9), 107–8
Texas A&M University Cushing Memorial Library and Archives, 15, 84
Texas Radio Historical Society, 65
textual poaching, 90, 175n31, 176n45
This Guy I Gotta Wait For (fanzine), 84–85, 87, 92–93, 93
Thomas, Julian, 5
Thompson, Gene, 157
Those Were the Days (podcast), 171n27
time shifting, 8, 12, 81, 98, 153, 156, 159
Tin Pan Alley, 33–34, 43
Tomlinson, John, 102, 177
Trammell, Niles, 8
Trapani, Sal, 56–57, 64
Trimble, Bjo, 113
Turner, Ted, 131–32, 142

United Federation of Phoenix, Arizona, 114
Universal Wrestling Federation (UWF), 183n58. *See also* Mid-South Wrestling

University of Iowa Special Collections, 15, 84, 86, 117

Viacom, 101, 119–20
Victor Talking Machine Co., 31, 36, 38, 46, 50, 52–53
vidding, 14, 80, 83, 86–87, 99, 113–14, 175n31
Vulcanalia fanzine, 82

Wagner, George, 74–77
Ware, Nicholas, 133–34
Warren, Penny, 96–97
Wasser, Frederick, 152
WEAF radio (New York), 53, 61–62
Weaver, Pat, 1–2
Webb, Joe, 59, 65, 172n55. *See also Collector's Corner* (fanzine)
Welter, Barbara, 32
Westrek, 114, 116
Wilde, Oscar: "The Artist," 25
Williams, Jodi, 114–16, 119
Williams, Raymond, 6–7, 9, 70
wireless radio, 24, 31, 44, 48–49
Wisconsin Center for Film and Theater Research, 2, 16, 53
WJZ radio (Newark), 50, 53, 61–62
Wolansky, Walt, 136
World Championship Wrestling, 130, 147
World Class, 130, 136
World Science Fiction Convention (Worldcon), 83, 100–101, 176n1
World Wide Wrestling Federation (WWWF), 20, 129–30, 130, 132
World Wrestling Entertainment (WWE), 20, 129
World Wrestling Federation (WWF), 20, 130, 132, 134–37, 141–42, 145, 147, 150–51, 183n58
Wrestlemania, 137
Wrestling Eye (magazine), 132
wrestling fandom, 18, 82, 123; and gender, 20, 124–25, 127, 133–34, 144–45; and kayfabe, 124–25, 127, 130, 134, 139, 142, 145; and knowledge, 20, 124, 132–39, 144–46;

wrestling fandom (*continued*)
and labor, 20, 125–26, 147–50; and matches in Canada, 20, 102, *130*, 130–31, 133, 136, 142–43; and matches in Japan, 20, 102, *130*, 130–31, 133, 138, 141–44, 147, 183n59; and matches in Mexico, 20, 131, 133, 142–44; and replay culture, 135–36, 142, 146, *148*; and wrestler rankings, 125, 139–41. See also *Wrestling Observer*

Wrestling Fans International Association, 132

Wrestling News magazine, 123, 133

Wrestling Observer, 15, 129–30, 138, 142–43; annual awards, 139–41; and the intelligent fan, 124–27, 132–37, 139, 144–45; origins, 123–24. See *also* Meltzer, Dave

wrestling promoters, 19–20, 133–35, 144–45, 183n58; and territorialization, 126, 128–32, 136–38

Zebracon, 83–85, 174n12
Zieger, Susan, 25
Zimmerman, Patricia Rodden, 47–48

ELEANOR PATTERSON is an assistant professor of media studies at Auburn University.

The University of Illinois Press
is a founding member of the
Association of University Presses.

───────────────────────

University of Illinois Press
1325 South Oak Street
Champaign, IL 61820-6903
www.press.uillinois.edu